ID0850902

COMPANY-WIDE TOTAL QUALITY CONTROL

COMPANY-WIDE TOTAL QUALITY CONTROL

Shigeru Mizuno

Asian Productivity Organization

Some other selected APO titles:
— Guide to Quality Control
— How to Measure Maintenance Performance
— Introduction to Quality Engineering: Designing Quality into Products and Processes
— Japan's Community-Based Industries: A Case Study of Small Industries
— The Japanese Firm in Transition
— Japanese Management: A Forward-Looking Analysis
— Japanese Management Overseas: Experiences in the United States and Thailand
— Japanese-Style Management: Its Foundations and Prospects
— Japan's Quality Control Circles
— Management by Objectives: A Japanese Experience
— Mechatronics: The Policy Ramifications
— Modern Production Management: A Japanese Experience
— 100 Management Charts
— Profitability Analysis: Japanese Approach
— Quality Control Circles at Work
— Role of General Trading Firms in Trade and Development: Some Experiences

Designed and Printed in Hong Kong by
NORDICA INTERNATIONAL LIMITED
for
Asian Productivity Organization
4-14, Akasaka 8-chome
Minato-ku, Tokyo 107, Japan

© Asian Productivity Organization, 1988
ISBN: 92-833-1099-3 (Casebound)
          92-833-1100-0 (Limpbound)

Second printing: 1989

ZENSHA SOGO HINSHITSU KANRI (in Japanese) by Shigeru Mizuno
Copyright © 1984 by Shigeru Mizuno
English translation rights arranged with JUSE Press Ltd.
through Japan Foreign-Rights Centre

Introduction

I have been involved in quality control since its very first introduction in postwar Japan, and have had the pleasure of working with a large number of Japan's leading companies as they sought to improve and standardize the quality of their goods and services. For readers coming to this field cold, it may therefore be helpful to give a little background on the history of quality control in Japan.

My initial encounter with quality control came by way of the Association of Japanese Scientists and Engineers, one of the predecessors to the Union of Japanese Scientists and Engineers (JUSE). This association was formed to raise Japanese technical levels, and one of the first things it did was to embark upon a study of the new technologies being developed overseas.

When the JUSE was formed soon after the war's end, I joined the JUSE leadership in studying wartime production methods. In 1948, with a special grant from the Economic Stabilization Board, we started our research with the electronics and specialty metals fields. Under the leadership of Toshinori Baba, then with the Ministry of Education and now professor at the University of Library and Information Science, a small group of five of us formed a quality control study group to study this new production technology that had contributed so much to helping American industry win the war. This was the start of JUSE's efforts to propagate quality control.

At the time, there was very little literature available on quality control, and the only thing we could find was a copy of an American manual on control graphs, which we borrowed from the Ministry of International Trade and Industry. Although we spent endless hours translating this book, we were still very new to the field's concepts and terminology, and I am afraid our translation may have confused as many people as it helped.

In 1949, the JUSE held its first QC Basic Course. While it drew upon the leading Japanese authorities at the time, both instructors and students were still very much groping in the dark. More than a formal course of study, it was akin to putting together a jigsaw puzzle when you do not know what the picture is supposed to be. Given the need for the instructors to prepare for each session, the course met only three days a month for six months.

It was not until March 1950 that the magazine *Hinshitsu Kanri* (Statistical Quality Control) was published. Under the able editorship of Masao Goto, the magazine carried a basic introduction to quality control, explained some of the basic tools of the trade, and attempted an overview of the literature.

As we became more active, our group grew into a QC Research Group that was able to produce a QC text for a course offered over the radio. Were we doing it again, there is much that we would do differently in that text, but the book proved very popular not only with production people but even as a university text. As of the summer of 1984, it had gone through 169 printings and sold 850,000 copies, making it somewhat of a long-run best-seller.

In 1954, I was appointed head of the Resource Utilization Research Laboratory at Tokyo Institute of Technology as part of an expansion effort by that university. Although an electrical engineer by training, I thought it would be a good idea for the institute to devote more attention to scientific measurement, control, and other technologies that are common to all fields of scientific and industrial endeavor. Quality control was clearly a priority subject, and I spent quite a bit of time developing the statistical methods that are needed for quality control.

Upon retiring from Tokyo Institute of Technology in 1970, I accepted a professorship in management engineering at the Science University of Tokyo. When I started in the quality control field, there were no formal courses of study and all of us came fresh from other fields. In fact, it was not until May 1969 that preparations even got underway to found a society devoted to the study of quality control. As chairman of the preparatory committee, I was understandably pleased to see the formal inauguration of the Japan Society for Quality Control on November 18, 1970. With fewer than 200 members at first, this was not a very big Society, but we have been fortunate in having leading industrialists as chairmen and the Society has grown both to encourage younger researchers and to spread the word. Today, there are about 2,500 members, and the Society is very active in promoting quality control studies.

Given the turbulent world situation when I was young, it was not until quite late in my life that I had the opportunity to meet extensively with overseas scholars. However, I have made up for this with a vengeance, logging a total of 32 trips and 443 days abroad between my first trip in 1963 and the time of this writing in 1984. Some of these were with the JUSE and other study missions, others were university-financed trips to attend academic conferences, and still others were on behalf of corporate clients. At the same time, I have also been active in hosting international conferences on statistics, quality control, production engineering, and the like in Japan.

The JUSE followed up its very popular basic course with a course for department heads in 1955, another for directors in 1957, and one for management personnel in 1961. I have been actively involved in all of these courses since their inception.

In the formative fifties, the emphasis was on attaining design quality, yet in the sixties the focus broadened to consider what kinds of quality should be the target and to incorporate quality control in the design and development stages. I am especially gratified by this trend because I have long argued that product quality and quality control have to start as soon as the product is conceived. For many years, this was a lonely advocacy, but it has recently become the mainstream.

In addition to giving lectures, writing textbooks, and holding symposiums on quality control, I have also had the pleasure of serving as a member of the Deming Prize Committee since its inception and seeing companies successfully institute quality control for enhanced competitiveness and improved morale.

Over the past thirty-plus years, I have advised over 300 companies on quality control and seen the field develop. The first presidential QC audit was done at Shin-Etsu Chemical in the early 1950s. Today, audits are routinely conducted on the department, division, and company-wide level, and they are proving an excellent way to involve top management in quality control and policy control. It was also Shin-Etsu that first used the QC process chart to determine what should be controlled how in the work place, and Shin-Etsu has made a major effort to clarify and delineate control standards in line and staff functions.

The idea of initial production control for quality assurance from the very start was begun by Nippon Denso, and it was also Nippon Denso that initiated the idea of distinct QC-activity steps each to be completed in turn.

Later, Toyota Motor took this one step further by devising clear statements of the items to be guaranteed at each step of the production process, explicitly delineating authority and responsibility for everyone involved, and putting all of this together in the quality assurance activities chart. This was the start of today's cross-functional management.

In the development stages, the three factors of quality, cost, and schedule are constantly creating problems for each other, and it is necessary to draw up a table of quality and cost considerations for every stage in the schedule. Integrated, this has been called QC-PERT, and I have helped a number of companies to use this methodology successfully beginning around 1963. As anyone familiar with Japanese industry will attest, Kubota's Hirakata plant was one of the best practitioners.

It is now widely known that market quality demands discovering the actual market requirements, restating them as substitute requirements, and then finding ways and means of satisfying them. Unfortunately, most companies developing new products have tended to emphasize market research to the exclusion of such steps as design quality and production technology. Quality deployment was developed to correct this deficiency. This is not that new a concept, and I was using design characteristics, control characteristics, and inspection characteristics and emphasizing the need for continuity and compatibility among them as early as 1966, but it has been ignored by a lot of companies until recently.

Traditionally, quality control has been an analytical approach trying to ferret out causes by working back from the results. This is very effective most of the time, but it is not of much use with new products or processes where there are no results to work back from yet. It was in response to this need that the design approach was developed for function deployment of the means to suit the ends. This was not especially new in itself, but it was not until Mitsubishi Heavy Industries' Kobe shipyard put it all together in a systematic whole and developed the quality chart that it became a standard part of quality control in Japan.

In advocating quality control, I have often spoken of the need to standardize technology. Most companies have technology or expertise that they have developed, but all too often it is only written down, if at all, in lists or handbooks, and there is no effort made to relate it to causes and effects. This means that the technology and expertise will not be used except by the people who developed it, since other people have no way of knowing where it is useful and what it can do. Thus I have argued that the company needs to link its expertise with its quality and show how the two are interrelated. Once this is done, the technology comes alive for a broad range of applications and improvements — in some instances even to the extent of solving problems that were thought to be unsolvable.

In writing this book, I have tried to keep the terminology to a minimum and to make it easy for anyone to understand. Consistent with this effort, I have structured it so that you can pick it up and read it in whatever order you like. If you are interested in product liability, you might want to start with Chapter 5. If you are interested in design and development, start with Chapter 11. Inevitably, this has meant that the chapters have had to be somewhat self-contained and repetitive, but I have chosen to pay that price to achieve approachability.

Proud though I am to have been a part of Japan's quality control efforts, I realize that there is still much to be done. Quality control is an unending process, and this book should be taken simply as my attempt to set down and standardize what I have learned thus far so that other people can improve upon it in the years ahead.

Shigeru Mizuno

Table of Contents

Introduction.   i

Chapter 1. Why Company-wide Total Quality Control?   1

    1.1   What is TQC?   1

    1.2   Social Changes and Product Quality   2

    1.3   The Goals of Industrial Production   3

    1.4   The Significance of Product Quality   4
         1.4.1   Industrial Product Quality
         1.4.2   Operational Quality
         1.4.3   Design Quality vs. Conformance Quality

    1.5   The Importance of Control   9
         1.5.1   The Control Circle
         1.5.2   For Effective Control
         1.5 3   The Manager's Job

    1.6   The Importance of Quality Control. 13

    1.7   Defining Quality Control 14

    1.8   Company-wide Quality Control 15
         1.8.1   Total Quality Control
         1.8 2   Company-wide Total Quality Control
         1.8.3   The T in TQC

    1.9   Corporate Administration and Quality Control 19
         1.9.1   Management, Quality, and Quality Control
         1.9.2   Management and Quality Control

Chapter 2. Management's Role in TQC **27**

    2.1   Management's Function 27
         2.1.1   Managerial Types that Obstruct TQC
         2.1.2   Promoting TQC
         2.1.3   TQC Management

    2.2   Management's Responsibility for Product Quality 31
         2.2.1   Quality Policies
         2.2.2   Priority Quality Problems
         2.2.3   Organizational Planning

    2.3   TQC as Practical Administrative Management 35
         2.3.1   Policy Management

2.3.2   Cross-functional Management
2.3.3   Control Planning

2.4   Quality Control Promotion by Middle Management 41

Chapter 3. Planning Quality Control. 45

3.1   Quality Planning 45
    3.1.1   Quality Policy
    3.1.2   Quality Deployment and Quality Analysis

3.2   Planning to Introduce Quality Control. 47
    3.2.1   Outline
    3.2.2   Planning TQC's Introduction
    3.2.3   Priority Items in Promoting TQC

3.3   Planning the QC Organization 50
    3.3.1   Issues in Planning Organization
    3.3.2   Principles of Organization Planning
    3.3.3   Organizational Standards and Regulations
    3.3.4   The Quality Control Committee
    3.3.5   The TQC Promotion Centre

3.4   Deploying Quality Control Functions 54
    3.4.1   Steps to Quality Control Functions
    3.4.2   Developing Quality Control Functions and Channels of
           Communication
    3.4.3   Control Planning

3.5   Criteria, Standards, Regulations, and Procedures 61
    3.5.1   Quality Control Paperwork
    3.5.2   Coordination Problems

Chapter 4. The Functions of Quality Assurance 67

4.1   The Significance of Quality Assurance. 67
    4.1.1   Quality Functions
    4.1.2   Defining Quality Assurance
    4.1.3   Inspection
    4.1.4   Standards for Judging Quality
    4.1.5   Repairing Defective Products
    4.1.6   The Range of Quality Assurance Activities

4.2   Important Quality Assurance Functions. 72
    4.2.1   Creating and Developing Quality Policies
    4.2.2   Establishing Quality Assurance Policies and Standards
    4.2.3   Devising and Administrating Quality Assurance Systems
    4.2.4   Assuring Design Quality
    4.2.5   Recording and Analyzing Important Quality Problems

4.2.6 Clarifying the Important Quality Assurance Functions for Production and Post-production Quality Control

4.2.7 Making Sure All Quality Assurance Activities that are Performed during Production are fully Understood

4.2.8 Carrying out Quality Inspections and Processing Complaints

4.2.9 Quality Control on Product Labelling and Instruction Manuals

4.2.10 After-sales Service

4.2.11 Product Quality Inspections and Quality Assurance System Supervision

4.2.12 Collecting, Analyzing, and Using Quality Data

4.3 The Quality Assurance System. 76

4.4 Quality Evaluation System 81

4.5 Quality Information System 81

Chapter 5. Product Liability **83**

5.1 The Consumer Costs of Defective Products. 83

5.2 Product Liability Responsibility. 84
    5.2.1 Product Liability in the United States
    5.2.2 Product Liability in Europe
    5.2.3 Product Liability in Japan

5.3 Legal Considerations in Product Liability. 87
    5.3.1 Negligence
    5.3.2 Warranties
    5.3.3 Strict Liability in Tort Law
    5.3.4 Situation in Japan

5.4 Product Liability Policy and Product Safety 90

5.5 Product Liability and TQC 91
    5.5.1 Management's Role in Product Liability
    5.5.2 Product Liability Policy and Organization
    5.5.3 Consumer Relations

5.6 Product Liability and Quality Assurance 94

Chapter 6. Policy Management and Cross-functional Management **97**

6.1 Policy Management 97
    6.1.1 Policy Management and Day-to-day Management
    6.1.2 Focal Points for Policy Management
    6.1.3 Policy Control Systems and Check Lists

6.2 Cross-functional Management 107
    6.2.1 Important Points in Cross-functional Management
    6.2.2 Promoting Cross-functional Management
    6.2.3 Cost Control

Chapter 7. Quality Control Education **111**

7.1. Importance of Quality Control Education 111

7.2 Education by Job Type 112
    7.2.1 Top Management
    7.2.2 Middle Management and Employees
    7.2.3 Quality Control Staff
    7.2.4 Line Workers
    7.2.5 Administrative and Clerical Workers
    7.2.6 Research and Development Staff

7.3 Evaluating Quality Control Eduation. 118

7.4 Setting Up a Quality Control Education Programme. 119

Chapter 8. Making Employees More Quality-Conscious **121**

8.1 Dissemination. 121

8.2 Raising Quality Consciousness 122

8.3 QC Circle Activities 123
    8.3.1 The Purposes of QC Circle Activities
    8.3.2 Points to Consider in Conducting QC Circle Activities

Chapter 9. Quality Control Activities **129**

9.1 The Quality Control System 130
    9.1.1 The System Approach and the Project Approach
    9.1.2 Quality Control Activities
    9.1.3 The Quality Control System and Quality Engineering

9 2 Quality and Cost 138
    9.2.1 Quality Design Costs
    9.2.2 Quality Manufacturing Costs
    9.2.3 Quality Costs
    9.2.4 Quality Loss Distribution

9 3 Industrial Production and Statistical Tools 142
    9.3.1 Making the Right Judgments
    9.3.2 Quality Control Steps and Statistical Tools
    9.3.3 Dispersion in Quality Characteristics
    9.3.4 Reliability

9.4 Problems in Implementing TQC and How to Solve Them 145
    9.4.1 Uninterested Top Management
    9.4.2 Middle Management's Failure to Recognize its Role in TQC
    9.4.3 Unclear TQC Targets
    9.4.4 Lack of Product Quality Policies
    9.4.5 Failure to Clarify the Scope of TQC Activities
    9.4.6 Lack of a Clear-cut Programme for Implementing TQC

9.4.7 Too Much Stress on Theory and Too Little Effort to Learn the Methodology

9.4.8 Ritualized QC Activities with Little or no Meaningful Content

9.4.9 Assuming that TQC is Limited to QC Circle Activities

9.4.10 Lack of Interest

9.4.11 Problems in TQC Headquarters

9.4.12 Incomplete Understanding of What You Want to Achieve with TQC

9.4.13 Lack of Well-defined and Uniform TQC Terminology

9.5 The Deming Application Prize 150

Chapter 10. Discovering and Analyzing Quality Control Problems 153

10.1 Methods of Analysis. 153

10.1.1 Quality Control Analysis

10.1.2 Analysis and Diagnosis Tools

10.1.3 Procedures for Analysis and Diagnosis

10.2 The Importance of Analyses in Quality Control. 157

10.2.1 Three Approaches

10.2.2 Analyzing Past Data

10.2.3 What to Do with Your Analytical Results

10.2.4 Specific vs. Common Technological Problems

10.3 Market Quality Surveys 161

10.3.1 The Purpose of Marketing Quality Surveys

10.3.2 Methods of Performing Marketing Quality Studies

10.4 Complaint Surveys. 162

10.4.1 Opening New Markets

10.4.2 Complaints

10.4.3 Tips Regarding Complaint Processing

10.4.4 Items to be Covered in Complaint Processing

10.5 Analyzing and Diagnosing Quality Problems 165

10.5.1 The Diagnosis

10.5.2 Measuring Product Quality

10.5.3 Analyzing Quality Problems

10.5.4 Regulations for Quality Analysis and Diagnosis

10.5.5 The Quality Troubleshooting Team and Analysis System

Chapter 11. Quality Control at the Design and Development Stages 171

11.1 Research and Development 171

11.1.1 Types of Research

11.1.2 Research Control Activities

11.1.3 Evaluating Research and Development Projects

11.2 Product Development and Design 174

    11.2.1 Steps in Product Development and Design

    11.2.2 The Development and Design System

11.3 Quality Policy and Development Policy 176

11.4 New Product Quality Planning 182

    11.4.1 Quality Design

    11.4.2 Quality Planning

    11.4.3 Quality Policy

    11.4.4 Basic Data for Quality Design

    11.4.5 Regulating Methods of Gathering Quality-related
        Information

11.5 Progress Control and Evaluation during Development and 187
    Design Stages

    11.5.1 Progress Control During new Product Development and
        Design

    11.5.2 Development and Design Evaluations

    11.5.3 Control Items for New Product Development and Design
        Functions

11.6 Technology Development (Specific Technology and Quality
    Control) 193

    11.6.1 Quality Deployment

    11.6.2 Quality Analysis and Process Analysis

    11.6.3 Inspiration and the QC Circle

11.7 Design Review 198

11.8 Design Change Control 200

11.9 Building a Prototype 201

11.10 Product Liability Considerations at the Development and
    Design Stage 203

Chapter 12. Quality Control in Production and Purchasing 205

12.1 Process Analysis 205

    12.1.1 The Importance of Process Analysis

    12.1.2 Effects and Their Primary Causes

    12.1.3 Latent Causes in Chemical Manufacturing Processes

    12.1.4 Selecting the Principal Causes

    12.1.5 Investigating Causes and Their Effects

    12.1.6 Deciding on Optimum Standards for Causes

    12.1.7 Process Analysis Methodology

12.2 Process Design 217

    12.2.1 Process Studies

    12.2.2 Process Capability Studies

    12.2.3 Deciding on Manufacturing Methods

12.3 Process Control. 229
    12.3.1 Control and Adjustment
    12.3.2 Selecting Control Items
    12.3.3 Process Control Standards
    12.3.4 Implementing Control
    12.3.5 Checking the Effectiveness of Your Control System

12.4 Quality Assurance in the Manufacturing Process 238
    12.4.1 Methods of Transmitting Quality
    12.4.2 Control by Process Category
    12.4.3 Interim Inspections
    12.4.4 Product Liability Prevention in the Production Process

12.5 Improving Processes. 243
    12.5.1 Making Process Improvements
    12.5.2 Implementing Process Improvements

12.6 Quality Control in the Purchasing Division 244
    12.6.1 The Purchasing Division's Role
    12.6.2 Basic Purchasing and Outsourcing Policy
    12.6.3 Selecting Suppliers
    12.6.4 Evaluating Suppliers
    12.6.5 Purchasing and Outsourcing Contracts and Quality
           Assurance Agreements
    12.6.6 Quality Control Guidance
    12.6.7 Improving Purchasing Operations

Chapter13. Quality Control in the Office **249**

13.1 Quality Control in Non-manufacturing Divisions 249
    13.1.1 Quality Control in Administrative and Clerical Divisions
    13.1.2 The Role of Non-manufacturing Divisions
    13.1.3 Problems in Implementing Quality Control in Non-
           manufacturing Divisions
    13.1.4 Introducing Quality Control in Non-manufacturing Divisions

13.2 Office Work and Quality. 251
    13.2.1 What is Office Work?
    13.2.2 Office Work Quality
    13.2.3 Two Degrees of Quality Responsibility

13.3 Control in Staff Divisions 258
    13.3.1 Control and Diagnosis
    13.3.2 Control Based on Facts
    13.3.3 Defining Your Activities
    13.3.4 Approaches to Problem Solving
    13.3.5 Controlling Quality Control

13.4 Total Quality Control Activities. 261
    13.4.1 Quality, Management, and Quality Control

13.4.2 Quality Management
13.4.3 Policy Control
13.4.4 Cross-functional Management

13.5 Quality Control and Computerization 265
13.5.1 Office Automation and Quality Control
13.5.2 Computer-aided Quality Control
13.5.3 Management Information Systems

Chapter 14. The Quality Control Audit 269

14.1 The Product Quality Audit and Quality Control Audit 269

14.2 The Need for a Quality Control Audit 270
14.2.1 The Purpose of a Quality Control Audit
14.2.2 The Effectiveness of the Quality Control Audit

14.3 Establishing a Quality Control Audit Policy 272
14.3.1 Auditing All Aspects of TQC
14.3.2 Auditing by Division and by Fuction
14.3.3 Maintaining Objectivity
14.3.4 Avoiding Rote Auditing

14.4 Quality Control Audit Targets 274

14.5 Planning a Quality Control Audit 275
14.5.1 Introducing the Quality Control Audit
14.5.2 The Quality Control Audit as a Part of TQC

14.6 Carrying Out the Quality Control Audit 276
14.6.1 Audit Data
14.6.2 Reporting on Audit Findings and Recommendations
14.6.3 The Need for Top Executive Action

14.7 Pitfalls in Conducting a Quality Control Audit 277

Chapter 15. Quality Control Past and Future 281

15.1. Early Beginnings 281

15.2 Quality Control Comes to Japan 282

15.3 Recent Trends in Quality Control 284
15.3.1 Product Quality
15.3.2 Quality Assurance
15.3.3 Practical Administration

15.4 Problems with TQC in Japan 288

15.5 Outlook for the Future 290

Index . . . .

List of Figures

1.1   The Control Circle

1.2   The Deming Circle

1.3   The Two Directions in Quality Control

2.1   The Pareto Diagram

2.2   Chronic Defects and Occasional Defects

2.3   Comparison of Chronic Defects and Occasional Defects

2.4   Relationship between Policy Management and Administration Planning

2.5   Intradivisional Management and Cross-functional Management

2.6   Table of Control Points (Sample of Job-specific Table for Technical Division)

3.1   Quality Assurance Duties of Sales Division (Partial Listing)

3.2   Part of a QC Flow Sheet

3.3   Partial Sample of Control Item Chart for Manufacturing Section Chief

3.4   TQC Promotion Plan

4.1   Quality Functions

4.2   Quality Assurance Diagram

4.3   Sample Quality Assurance Activities Chart (Partial)

6.1   The Policy Control Circle

6.2   Policy Control System

6.3   Outline of Quality Control and Cost Control Activities

9.1   The Structure of Quality Control Activities for Quality Assurance

9.2   Diagram of Quality Engineering

9.3   Organization of the QC Department

9.4   Product Competitiveness

9.5   Steps in Introducing and Promoting TQC

9.6   Deming Prize Checklist

10.1   The Control Circle

10.2   Sample Cause-and-effect Diagram for Sales

10.3   Comparison of Factors

10.4   Comparison of Product Price and Complaint Rate

11.1 Quality Control in the Development and Design Stages

11.2 Controlling Quality and Costs

11.3 Mapping Your Technology

11.4 New Product Analysis

11.5 Quality Factors

11.6 QC-PERT

11.7 Quality Table for Large Diesel Machinery (Partial)

11.8 Correlation between Functions (Quality Characteristics) and Product Structure

11.9 Quality Assessment Using Quality Table

11.10 Conversion from Quality Wanted to Substitute Characteristics

11.11 Deployment of Substitute Characteristics to Parts and Processes

11.12 Selection of Deployment Methodology

11.13 Outline of Initial Production Control System

12.1 Major Quality Control Activities for Production Process Steps

12.2 Cause-and-effect Diagram

12.3 Relations among Causes and Effects

12.4 Process Capability Charts

12.5 Distributon of Quality Characteristics (Normal Distribution)

12.6 Process Capability Assessment Standards

12.7 Relationship between Guaranteed Quality and Quality Standards

12.8 List of Control Items (Partial sample for manufacturing section)

12.9 List of Control Items (Partial sample for manufacturing division)

12.10 Communication Channels for Quality Concerns (Sample 1)

12.11 Communication Channels for Quality Concerns (Sample 2)

13.1 Staff Quality Control Functions

13.2 The Deming Circle

13.3 The Two Directions in Quality Control

1 | Why Company-wide Total Quality Control?

Japanese cars, cameras, electrical appliances, integrated circuits, and many more products are acclaimed overseas for their superior quality. While this quality is generally assumed to stem from the Japanese company's dedication to company-wide quality control, the concept of company-wide quality control is not always properly understood or implemented even in Japan.

1.1   What is TQC?

Quality control, also known simply as QC, was first implemented in the United States around 1920 as a statistical tool to improve industrial production. In its earliest days, quality control was limited to certain technical areas, and it was only later that QC gradually came to be a regular part of company-wide activities.

Every division in a corporation is responsibile for ensuring product quality. The coordination of all divisional efforts toward this end is called total quality control or TQC. This is a term coined by the American A.V. Feigenbaum (1920-), but it is by no means universally recognized. In the United States, TQC is more commonly referred to as the Feigenbaum QC system and does not have the all-encompassing meaning that it has in Japan. In Europe, total quality control is called integrated control of product quality or ICPQ.

By contrast, Japanese-style TQC is the generic term given to a broad range of quality control activities applied to all aspects of the company's operations. Although this is also called company-wide quality control or CWQC to indicate its company-wide character, this text will avoid the unfamiliar CWQC and the awkward Japanese-style TQC and refer simply to TQC throughout.

Quality control has long been applied by conventional manufacturers producing large quantities of the same kinds of product — chemical fertilizers and electrical appliances, for example. Because such manufacturers can apply improvements made in one area to all their product lines, they have found quality control to be highly effective. But with the rapid changes and diversification in consumer requirements recently, efficient mass production of just a few products is no longer any guarantee of corporate survival. Rather, manufacturers are finding that they must produce small lots of a wide variety of products – and all to ever-higher quality standards.

Originally, quality control was limited to reducing the number of defective products on the production line, but today it has been expanded into total quality control covering a multitude of other areas upstream and downstream, including design, planning, development, and marketing. Even companies in non-manufacturing industries such as construction, distribution, banking, and insurance have begun to introduce TQC into their operations.

Still, there are companies that have been applying TQC for some time and complain that they are not seeing any results. "We don't seem to be getting anywhere with TQC. We seem to have come up against a brick wall," they fume. When TQC is not showing results, there are generally very good reasons for this failure, and management would do better to search out these causes than to dismiss TQC outright. Why is TQC proving so effective in so many companies while others complain that it does nothing for them? All too often, TQC's failure is really a management failure.

Many Japanese companies have introduced and are promoting TQC without really understanding their reasons for adopting TQC or what TQC means for them. This text attempts to explain why TQC is needed, what it can do for your company, and what it will demand in return.

1.2   Social Changes and Product Quality

The current period of slower economic growth is also an era of quality. Product quality is today more important to corporate management than it has ever been before. When commodities were scarce, companies could sell almost anything. With today's market surfeits, however, increasing production is no longer the overriding goal it once was. The goal in the new era of quality is to create products that will sell. The emphasis has shifted from quantity to quality.

Likewise, it used to be up to the buyer to check a product's quality. This was the era of buyer caveat emptor. If the consumer purchased a defective product, it was his own fault. Today, products tend to be extremely complex and it is not always possible for the consumer to judge product quality. Thus the seller is responsible for its quality and is held accountable if it turns out to be defective. Caveat venditor.

Personal injury, damage, and pollution caused by defective products did not used to be important issues, but these are today crucial concerns and the manufacturer is held responsible. Consumers demand ever better-quality goods and services. Not only does a product have to satisfy exacting customers, it must also be environmentally compatible in terms of exhaust gas and other factors, should not contain toxic materials, and must meet a host of other requirements. With the increasing conservation-consciousness, the product also has to be durable. And it should be easy for the customer to use and maintain safely.

Consumer needs have diversified, and production is shifting from mass production of a few products to small-lot production of a large variety of customized products. Market internationalization has made it necessary to create products that can be used anywhere, regardless of environmental and social differences, and the global marketplace has thus been a further impetus to superior quality. As the developing countries industrialize, Japan has little· choice but to concentrate on superior high value-added products.

If safety were the only concern in quality control, companies could comfortably continue building on experience to produce the same limited product lines. But safety is not the only factor, and rapidly diversifying consumer needs mandate a constant supply of new products. Quality control has become a major concern for corporations as never before. Within this context, TQC must

1. Redirect efforts from simply increasing production to developing safe, high-quality products and supplying them to world markets, thereby achieving strong profits and enhancing the company's financial position.
2. Help workers to acquire the technical knowhow required to upgrade technology introduced from outside and promote the company's own technological research and development so as to close the technology gap and make the company a leader in product quality.
3. Strengthen the company structurally for greater adaptability to change and further progress.
4. Place a renewed emphasis on the company's social and public responsibilities to prevent pollution and guarantee safety. More than a tool for greater profitability, TQC needs to be recognized as a means of ensuring the company as a responsible member of the community.

Implementing and achieving these TQC goals will require thorough application of company-wide quality control and a willingness to break with convention in the pursuit of quality control modes that meet the changing needs of our times. Management today must be quality management.

1.3   The Goals of Industrial Production

The basic goal of industrial production is to supply consumers with the products they want, in the amounts they want them, when, and, where they want them. Consumers is used in the plural here with good reason, for their numbers are legion and meeting their needs requires not one but many products. In other words, industrial production involves the continuous and repeated manufacture of a large number of products. This is the basic difference between industrial production and one-of-a-kind craftsmanship.

Back in the stone age, the producer was at the same time the consumer, and he only had to make a given product in the quantity and quality required to satisfy his own needs. The specialization of activities which occurred over time eventually differentiated producer and consumer, at which point it became necessary for the producer to have a correct understanding of the consumer's needs in order to create products meeting those needs.

To satisfy the consumer, a product must be maximally useful. And it is to the consumer's benefit to have the product produced as economically as possible. Cost is therefore a significant factor in product quality. Industrial management is simply the task of organizing production to meet these requirements.

Industrial production is thus directed at a very well-defined goal, but are conventional measures really geared toward attaining this goal? As regards the first requirement, that of having a correct understanding of the consumer's needs, the answer is no. Traditionally, the majority of manufacturers have only been interested in meeting self-imposed targets or in simply producing for the sake of producing. Most producers have not made the kind of effort required to find out what consumers really want or need. Nor do manufacturers aim for cost-effective production, since in most cases they do not even know how to avoid generating defective products. Not understanding industrial production's true goal, the conventional manufacturer makes no effort toward attaining this goal.

1.4 The Significance of Product Quality

1.4.1 Industrial Product Quality

In speaking of product quality, we usually refer to industrial product quality, particularly the product's physical and chemical properties. This includes, for example, in the case of a machine, its dimensions, precision, and exterior finish; in the case of an electrical appliance, its insulation and electrical characteristics; and in the case of a chemical product, its purity. For all of these products, these are qualities required for their use. Here then, product quality is defined as those qualities which characterize the product's fitness for use.

Another way to put it is that product quality encompasses those characteristics which the product must possess if it is to be used in the intended manner. This is important because the consumer buys the product's usefulness rather than the product itself. In the case of an electric refrigerator, for example, the consumer is purchasing not the concept of a refrigerator but its food storage capabilities.

Whether or not a product is considered a quality product thus depends, in the final analysis, on whether or not it performs the functions for which it was intended. The characteristics and functions which are used in evaluating product quality are called quality characteristics. When the manufacturer sets its own quality characteristics and establishes its own quality standards without regard for the user's needs, these quality characteristics will not reflect true product quality. In cases where it is difficult to measure the desired quality characteristics directly, other quality characteristics are applied instead, these being called substitute characteristics. Of course, the substitute characteristics must reflect the consumer requirements to be at all meaningful.

There are other following elements of product quality besides those noted above:

1. Reasonable price

   A product need not be absolutely the best possible quality; the only require-ment is that the product fulfills the consumer requirements for its use. In addition to physical characteristics, the consumer looks for a reasonable price, which is why it is pointless to strive for product quality irrespective of price.

2. Economy

   The consumer looks for economical features such as minimal energy require-ments, minimal likelihood of breakdowns, minimal maintenance and safety costs, and broad application.

3. Durability

   The consumer expects the product to be made of durable materials and resistant to drastic change over time. Wear, loose parts, and corrosion lead to unwanted problems.

4. Safety

   A product is expected to be safe to use and to pose no danger to life or limb. Among the products that have run into problems here are automobiles (exhaust emissions) and tall buildings (altered wind patterns and broadcast reception interference). These problems lower the value of the product.

5. Ease of use

   In general, it is assumed that it should be possible to use products designed for the average consumer without any special training. The consumer expects to be able to use the product at once, continuously, and trouble-free, and assumes that there will be warning signs of possible trouble before it occurs.

6. Simplicity of manufacture

   This ties in with the product's cost. The product should be made of materials that are readily available and easy to store, and its manufacture should require a minimum number of processes and very little skill.

7. Easy disposal

   In today's densely populated society, a product that cannot be used may just be thrown away wherever one pleases. Unwanted refuse can prove at least annoying and often harmful. Disposal costs are necessarily a factor to be considered in creating any product.

A product that lacks any one of these quality elements is inferior or defective. Hence, these elements can be called negative quality factors. Their absence can doom a product, but their presence alone does not ensure that a product will survive its competition. There are still further quality elements that must be incorporated if you are to have a winning product. These are as follows:

1. Good design
   The design should be original and should appeal to consumer tastes, as with a refined design giving the impression of quality.
2. Superiority over the competition
   A product should be superior in both function and design to other products of the same genre.
3. Physical appeal
   The product should appeal to the senses (e.g., touch and taste), should be well finished, and should have presence.
4. Distinctiveness and originality
   For many products, neckties being one example, the consumer likes to know that no one else has exactly the same product.

In contrast to the negative quality factors listed earlier, these quality elements are positive quality factors. Some people call them quality appeal, an they include both functional and non-functional qualities.

Basic to all is a product's fitness for use, and it is as much a drawback for a product to be too sophisticated as it is for it to be too crude. A product that is too sophisticated is said to have excessive quality and is considered inferior. Product quality must be defined in terms of the advantages to the customer. At its very bluntist, industrial product quality is the advantage the product has for the user. No matter how good a product, the consumer will not be able to take full advantage of it if its use has not been clearly and simply explained, or if the parts needed for safe, quick, and easy maintenance are unavailable. These service requirements are another integral part of industrial product quality.

The Japan Industrial Standards (JIS) define product quality as "The totality of proper characteristics or performance which are the objects of estimation to determine whether a product or service satisfies the purpose of use or not." [1]

Data indicating product quality are derived from the product's characteristic values. Besides dimensions, precision, purity, and strength, characteristic values include cost, volume, and time factors (sometimes called efficiency qualities), as well as the number of production and assembly processes required to complete the product, production yield and costs, and delivery scheduling. Since technology shapes the product's physical properties, these properties can also be referred to as technological qualities.

Efficiency qualities, on the other hand, are defined largely by management and can therefore be referred to as management qualities. Industrial product quality incorporates both technological and management qualities, which combine to create total quality.

Assuring industrial product quality is not the job of the technical, manufacturing, or inspection divisions alone. The marketing division also plays an important role in planning product quality and providing quality assurance by

---

[1] *Japanese Industrial Standard: Glossary of Terms Used in Quality Control,* JIS Z 8101-1981. (1981). Prepared by Japanese Industrial Standards Committee, Tokyo: Japanese Standards Association. p. 2.

researching consumer needs, conveying these needs to the company's technical people, and in turn, explaining the product's proper use to the consumer. It is the accounting division's job to keep tabs on the cost of maintaining product quality. Product quality is the entire company's concern. It does not matter so much what you call it — the important thing is to *do* it.

1.4.2 Operational Quality

Product quality is by no means limited to industrial products, and the concept can be applied quite broadly. The products of a research laboratory are its research results, of a design division its designs, and of a bank its services. Quality control involves maintaining and improving these "products" whatever they are.

Product quality within a company is equivalent to the quality of operations in each division, and quality control is not limited to tangible products but includes intangible operations as well. Quality control in accounting, for example, would involve ensuring quick and accurate accounting and the maintenance and improvement of the various accounting tables and charts that the accounting division is required to produce. Airline companies, hospitals, banks, and other service-sector businesses successfully apply quality control to their operations.

Industrial product quality control remains paramount for the manufacturer, but responsible quality assurance also means the manufacturer must maintain a high quality of customer service. For most manufacturers, quality control is applied to both product quality and service quality.

Cost, volume, and time are not in and of themselves quality features, but they are efficiency qualities under the broad definition given above and come under quality control in this sense. Quality control applications and methodology can also be useful in controlling production volume, production cost, and delivery schedules. Other important areas requiring quality control are product quality planning and quality assurance.

1.4.3 Design Quality vs. Conformance Quality

The quality standards decided on before a product is made and the quality features built into a product in the manufacturing process are not necessarily the same, and they should be considered separately. Juran called the former quality of design and the latter quality of conformance.

1.4.3.1 Design Quality

Policies regarding product quality are formulated on the basis of market surveys, cost efficiency studies, and management requirements. As such, design qualities are based on thorough research into consumer needs and take into consideration how the product can be most economically produced given the plant's production technology, equipment, and control measures. The product is designed, manufactured, and sold with the quality features dictated by these policies.

Design qualities are anticipated values or targets and defined in terms of grade and class. As noted elsewhere, higher quality is not always better quality. Of two products with the same price, the higher quality product is naturally the preferred choice, but a product that is overly sophisticated in disregard of the consumer's needs has excessive quality and will be too expensive to be competitive. The available manufacturing and control technology (processing capability) must also be carefully considered in setting design quality targets. In general, the more sophisticated the design qualities the higher the production costs.

Design quality, the quality that is to be aimed for with the given technology, is also sometimes called standard quality. The opposite, whether it considers consumer needs without regard to production technology, considers only production technology without regard to consumer needs, or considers neither, is target quality – simply a production target.

Standard quality and target quality are two very different things. In the past, target quality was given preference over standard quality, and sometimes the two were confused. Product quality that is premised on higher technology levels than are available with the state of the art and that is premised on research breakthroughs is target quality, not standard quality. Target quality is a value for which you aim but not something you expect to achieve right away.

Because standard quality is defined in terms of consumer needs and manufacturing limitations, it cannot be achieved without quality control. There are people who claim that quality control is unnecessary as long as work processes are geared to established standard qualities. Yet quality control is the only way to ensure that work processes are being carried out in accordance with standard quality, and the standard qualities these people refer to are in actuality only target qualities.

Standards are all too often imposed from outside without any real standard quality being applied. This is not what the manufacturing division needs. It needs realistic standard quality. Should there be a flaw in design quality, the final product will not have the required quality even though it is made in strict accordance with original design standards. The bulk of all defective products are the result of such design flaws.

1.4.3.2 Conformance Quality

Conformance quality is the product quality that results from its being manufactured in accordance with given quality standards. It is the actual quality value as opposed to the hoped-for design quality value, and it is judged in terms of how close it comes to the design quality. A product manufactured just as it was originally designed is a good product, and one that does not measure up to the design standards is defective. This, of course, assumes that design quality is the standard quality as defined above.

Because manufacture quality must conform to design quality it is also called conformance quality. Should product quality not conform, the cause is to be found in the production process. If there is poor conformance quality because of a failure to adhere to the given work standards, there should be an inquiry into why the work standards were not followed and measures should be taken to ensure that this will not happen again. If work procedures have been followed rigorously and there is still poor quality conformance, it may be necessary to revise the work procedures themselves.

1.5   The Importance of Control

Control has many meanings, but Juran defines it most simply as "The totality of all the means by which we establish and achieve standards."[2]

Whenever we decide to do something, we begin with a plan, work according to this plan, and review the results. If the results are not as planned, we revise the work procedures or the plan depending upon which is at fault. All of this comes under the heading of control.

1.5.1   The Control Circle

Control is a continuous cycle beginning and ending with planning.

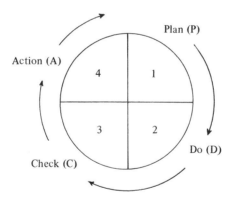

Figure 1.1 The Control Circle

The elements of the control circle are
P: establishing a plan or standard for achieving your goal
D: enacting the plan or doing
C: measuring and analyzing the results, i.e., checking
A: implementing the necessary reforms when the results are not as originally planned

---

[2]   Juran, Joseph M. (July & August, 1954). *Planning and Practices in Quality Control – Lectures on Quality Control –*, Tokyo: Union of Japanese Scientists and Engineers (JUSE). p. 2.

These four steps – plan, do, check, action (PDCA) – make up the control process. No one of these individual steps alone is control, and control is rather the linking of these steps into a continuous procedure.

1.5.2 For Effective Control

Each stop of the PDCA cycle must be gone through carefully for effective control.

1. First of all is setting up a reasonable plan for achieving your goal. This should be done with the understanding that your very first plan is unlikely to prove the most effective and will probably have to be revised later.
2. The next step is to carry out the plan.
3. This is followed by a review of what has been done. The important thing here is to clarify what results will be measured, how they will be measured, and what standards they will be compared with. These decisions to set up what are called control items are essential for effective control.
4. Finally, changes and improvements are made on the basis of the results achieved in the preceding step. Improvements should only be made within the limits of your authority (which implies that your job parameters be clearly defined). Any major changes or improvements that can only be made outside your own job, such as a major change in manufacturing procedure, should be reported to someone who is in a better position to see that this change is implemented. Likewise, failure to implement required changes that are within your authority is a failure to fulfill your own job responsibility. Effective control requires that responsibilities and authority be clearly defined, and that there be enough flexibility to change plans and standards as necessary.

Repetition of the PDCA circle leads to more effective planning and more efficient control. Juran further divides the PDCA control steps into seven sub-steps as follows: (from *QC Handbook*, third edition, 1974).

1. Choosing the control subject, i.e., selecting what is to be regulated.
2. Choosing a unit of measure.
3. Setting a standard value, i.e., specifying the quality characteristic.
4. Creating a sensing device which can measure the characteristic in terms of the unit of measure.
5. Conducting actual measurement.
6. Interpreting the difference between actual and standard.
7. Decision making and acting on the difference.[3]

Juran stresses the need at the planning stage to set standard values and clarify the methodology that will be used to detect and compare these values. The control items should be divided into steps or stages as will be explained in more detail in Sections 2.3.3 and 12.3.2.

---

[3]   Juran, Joseph M. (1974). *Quality Control Handbook*. 3rd ed., New York: McGraw-Hill. pp. 2-11.

1.5.3 The Manager's Job

1.5.3.1 Management

In Japanese, management and control are one and the same word, and management is used in business administration to refer to the making of plans based on administrative policy and the direction, instruction, supervision, and control of all operations related to implementing the plan. Management thus involves both planning and control. While quality control was originally applied only to reducing the number of defective products on the production line, it has more recently come to include planning quality as well as is often termed source control. This is a natural progression and the quality control that is being spoken of today might be better termed quality management.

1.5.3.2 Maintenance, Reform, and Development

Our work involves maintenance, reform, and development. These terms have the following meanings.
1. Maintenance: To maintain the current state of affairs, prevent change, and remain true to established standards.
2. Reform: To break with current norms, devise changes, and change standards.
3. Development: To initiate new activities or processes that break from current norms, effect changes, and set new standards.

Maintenance involves detecting deviations from the established standards, implementing measures to correct these deviations, and endeavouring to preserve standard (normal) conditions at all times. Maintenance is basic to management. Obviously, effective reforms and development cannot take place in unstable, turbulent conditions.

The lower your position within the corporate organization, the more time you must spend performing maintenance chores. However, the Western model in which rank-and-file employees only have to obey work standards decided upon and passed down from above is wrong. Effective work standards can only be devised by those doing the actual work. Furthermore, it is difficult for workers to grasp the essential points of work schedules and standards that are imposed as directives from above. This is where QC circles can prove useful in promoting improvements in work procedures and correcting inappropriate work standards.

The higher up you are in the corporate organization, the more time you will spend on development activities. Still, those at the top should remember that they have the same responsibility for maintaining standards and observing regulations as everyone else. Likewise, while management often delegates authority to make more time to concentrate on the development tasks that are their primary concern, management should never forget that they can only delegate authority and not responsibility. The ultimately responsibility remains theirs.

1.5.3.3 Planning

The planning in the PDCA circle is not something abstract that you do in your head. The first step is to identify problems, look for their causes, and devise means of rectifying them. This is planning.

In the field of health care, proper health maintenance does not mean simply going to a doctor after you have made yourself sick. Of course, someone who is sick should seek treatment, but this treating the result is not the same as preventing the causes. Proper health maintenance involves getting a thorough check-up, getting advice on nutrition and exercise, and faithfully following the doctor's regimen so you do not get sick. People who have weak stomachs, for example, should avoid foods that would upset their stomachs. Pinpointing the cause of a disease and leading a lifestyle that precludes this cause from occurring is what is meant by health maintenance.

In this context, the PDCA circle should more properly be called the CAPD circle, since the first step is that of looking for problems and identifying their causes, in other words, checking. Of course, planning is much more than simply eliminating current problems. It also involves foreseeing likely future problems that may be created by a changing environment and devising ways of staving them off before they occur. Long-term planning is looking five or even ten years ahead, defining the gap between the current situation and the desired situation, and seeking out ways to bring about the necessary changes.

Whether planning or checking, simply curing the result is not management. Real management is eliminating the causes of abnormalities and preventing their occurrence. It is thus imperative that management traces causes from the results, a process known as analysis, and this is why statistical analysis is such a powerful tool in quality control and management. Quality control is more than just a state of mind. It requires effective tools.

1.5.3.4. Action

As the above passage should have made clear, the action in the PDCA circle is action to correct causes, not effects. For example, in one plant it was found that a certain synthetic material was abnormally hard. After the problem was traced back to an incorrect combination of raw materials, the correct proportions were restored and the problem solved. This is what is meant by action.

In another example, a certain process has maximum and minimum temperatures. Adjustment, in other words control, is required to ensure that the process temperature stays within these limits. It is simple to correct deviations automatically with a rheostat or a pressure valve without ever investigating what caused the temperature abnormality in the first place. The ease of this kind of automatic control does not, however, mean that control management is unnecessary. Even though adjustments are made to keep the temperature within the acceptable limits, the cause of the problem may also cause other problems and it needs to be investigated and corrected. This is the CA of the PDCA circle.

1.6   The Importance of Quality Control

Adding the word "quality" to our earlier definition of control, we find that quality control is the totality of all the means by which we establish and achieve quality standard.[4]   As such, quality control encompasses all of the steps required in formulating and implementing quality plans.

Quality control for the production and sale of industrial products moves in a circle as shown in Figure 1.2. First the product is planned, then it is manufactured, and then it is inspected and sold. These three steps occur within the company, but there is a fourth step which takes place outside of the company involving market research to identify consumer needs, and this final step leads naturally back to the first step with planning based on the results of the market survey.

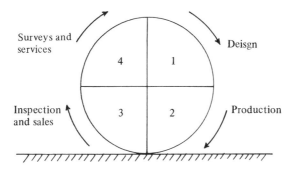

Surveys and services

Deisgn

Inspection and sales

Production

4   1

3   2

An emphasis on quality,
a sense of quality-responsibility

Figure 1.2 The Deming Circle

W.E. Deming (1900-) depicted this quality control as a wheel which turns endlessly on a foundation of quality consciousness and a sense of responsibility for product quality.

It should be noted here that detecting defective products and fixing them is not true quality control. Quality control is reforming designs, work standards, and work procedures so that there will be no defective products. Quality control is prevention.

None of what I have said thus far is particularly unusual. In fact, it should be all too obvious. In this sense, it might be said that quality control is the art of doing the obvious and doing it right.

---

4   Juran (1954), op. cit.

1.7   Defining Quality Control

Quality control was earlier defined as the totality of all the means by which we establish and achieve quality standards.[5]   In other words, quality control is planning and implementing the most economical means of manufacturing a product that will be maximally useful and satisfy the consumer's requirements.

The classic definitions of quality control are:

Deming's definition (1950)
"Statistical quality control is the application of statistical principles and techniques in all stages of production directed toward the most economic manufacture of a product that is maximally useful and has a market."[6]

Juran's definition (1954)
Quality control is the totality of all means by which we establish and achieve quality specifications, with statistical quality control that part of the means, for establishing and achieving quality specifications, which is based on the tools of statistical methods.[7]

Juran later revised this (in the third edition of the *QC Handbook* in 1974) to:
"Quality control is the regulatory process through which we measure actual quality performance, compare it with standards, and act on the difference."[8]

Japan Industrial Standards Definition (JISZ 8101)
"A system of means whereby the qualities of products or services are produced economically to meet the requirements of the purchaser. Since modern quality control adopts statistical techniques, it is sometimes especially called *tokeiteki hinshitsu kanri* ("statistical quality control", and "SQC" for short)."[9]

American National Standards Definition (ANSI ZI.7 1971)
"Quality Control: The operational techniques and the activities which sustain a quality of product or service that will satisfy given needs; also the use of such techniques and activities."[10]

Deming Prize Committee Definition
Since this text is limited to Japanese-style TQC in Japan, I will refer to SQC as simply QC. In Japan, the Deming Prize Committee defines statistical quality control in the context of company-wide quality control as:

---

[5]   Juran (1954). op. cit.
[6]   Deming, W. Edwards, (June, 1952). *Elementary Principles of the Statistical Control of Quality.* Revised 2nd ed., Tokyo: JUSE. p. 3.
[7]   Juran (1954). op. cit.
[8]   Juran (1974). op. cit.
[9]   Japanese Standards Association. (1981). op. cit. p. 3.
[10] *American National Standard, Qualtiy Systems Terminology,* Approved January 18, 1979, Revision of ASQC A3-1971 (ANSI Z1. 7-1971). Milwaukee, Wisconsin: American Society for Quality Control. p. 4.

"A system of activities to ensure the quality of products and services, in which products and services of the quality required by customers are produced and delivered economically. Quality assurance is carried out not only through the in-process or shipping inspection, but through the precise knowledge of the quality required by the customer so that new products may be planned and designed in conformity with the required quality, and manufactured in the production process in conformity with the design quality. Consequently, the responsibilities for acceptable quality, including reliability, are taken not only by those directly in charge of the product quality but by all other departments within the company as well as the management." [11]

A company's new product development, research management, raw material management, equipment installation and management, subcontracting system, and employee education and training are all scrutinized by the Deming Prize Committee.

Here I would like to stress the importance to QC of
1. Preserving product quality, and
2. Applying statistical method.

It is desirable to have the company's administrative and management divisions involved in QC, but all too often they limit their concern to reforming their own work procedures and make no attempt to implement procedures to preserve product quality, including preparing a manufacturing standards manual or initiating policies to foster the kind of workers that are essential to quality control. In applying SQC to TQC, many companies waste excessive time and energy on procedures and fail to conduct analyses of defective goods and services. TQC needs the broadest and most thorough application of SQC possible.

1.8 Company-wide Quality Control

The QC referred to in this text is the highly effective company-wide quality control that has been developed and implemented by Japanese companies — Japanese-style TQC.

1.8.1 Total Quality Control

The rapid changes that have been occurring in industry in recent years are epitomized by the following trends.
1. The consumer has become more demanding. Product safety has become increasingly important to the individual user, but there has also been a pronounced emphasis on the product's possible detrimental effects on public health and the environment. This trend is expected to continue.

---

[11] Deming Price Committee. (1986). *The Deming Prize Guide*, Tokyo: JUSE. p. 4.

2. Formerly, it was sufficient to guarantee product quality in the design, manufacture, and supply processes. But today, this product guarantee is expected to extend throughout the product's useful life. Until recently, quality control extended only as far as major changes in plant installations and work procedures. Today quality control extends even to after-sales services.

3. The cost of ensuring product quality has soared. It is today necessary not only to reduce manufacturing costs, but to reduce the cost to the consumer as well.

4. Quality control must also be applied to the unintended by-products which are created in the manufacturing process, the industrial waste that may have harmful pollution potential.

Simply inspecting products as they come off the line and removing defectives is hardly enough to keep ahead of these trends. It is necessary to prevent the occurrence of defectives so that inspections are no longer required.

Inspection does not make quality. Quality has to be built in. And in being built in, quality has to be built into the original design and emerge in the manufacturing process. This means, of course, that reforms must be made in customer services, in product documentation, and in maintenance procedures. Quality control needs to be applied at every step in industrial production and sales.

A product's quality encompasses all of its features, not just its technical qualities. This is total quality control. As defined by Feigenbaum, it includes every division and every step and is targeted at the common goal of ensuring a quality product at a reasonable price.

1.8.2 Company-wide Total Quality Control

As noted earlier, the term TQC was coined by Feigenbaum in his 1961 book by that title. According to Feigenbaum: "Total quality control is an effective system for integrating the quality-development, quality-maintenance, and quality-improvement efforts of the various groups in an organization so as to enable production and service at the most economical levels which allow for full customer satisfaction." [12]

The organization Feigenbuam refers to here does not mean creating a quality control division. Rather, it means spreading the responsibility for preserving product quality throughout all divisions and thereby carrying out quality control on a company-wide basis. As Feigenbaum says: "QC is everybody's job." [13]

QC must involve the whole company — every division and every worker at every level — and requires the integration of such formerly independent functions as raw material purchasing, work procedure analyses, work procedure management, and inspection.

---

[12] Feigenbaum, Armand V. (1961). *Total Quality Control,* New York: McGraw-Hill. P. 12.

[13] Ibid, p. 5.

All too often, especially in the United States and Europe, small groups of workers are singled out and assigned to be responsible for quality control. With the trend toward professionalism and specialization, it is understandable that companies in the United States and Europe should seek to appoint quality control specialists. Feigenbaum himself probably never thought of quality control in the very sweeping and thoroughly company-wide way it is customarily applied in Japanese corporations where everyone from corporate head to shop floor worker is involved. Yet quality control cannot possibly be really effective unless everyone is involved.

TQC has to involve everyone and all activities from corporate management to entry-level workers in everything from design to manufacturing, inspection, sales, procurement, energy management, accounting, and personnel. And even this definition should be revised as necessary to keep up with consumer concerns with product safety and pollution.

In Europe, this kind of total quality control is called integrated control of product quality (ICPQ). TQC is thus defined differently in every country depending upon its perceived importance and scope of application. At the 1969 first International Conference on Quality Control held in Japan, it was agreed that, despite the common use of TQC to mean different things in different countries, there was a need for some term to distinguish Japanese TQC. In light of TQC pervasiveness through the Japanese companies where it is practised, it was agreed to use the term CWQC (company-wide quality control) to refer to the kind of total-company, total-involvement TQC practised in Japan. I like to think that this decision was influenced by the paper I presented on "Company-wide Quality Control Activities in Japan."

Records show that quality control was first applied on a company-wide basis in Japan by Shin-Etsu Chemical, which was awarded the Deming Prize in 1953. In Shin-Etsu, a very specific, clearly defined QC policy was initiated by the company president and applied throughout the company. The first conscious application of the term TQC was made by Nippon Kayaku, a chemicals company and recipient of the 1963 Deming Prize. The TQC that has been promoted in Japan since then has grown into a purely Japanese-style TQC that goes way beyond the limitations of Feigenbaum's original concept to mobilize the entire company in the cause of quality.

1.8.3 The T in TQC

The steps in the Deming Circle shown in Figure 1.2 can be categorized into technical applications (design, manufacture, and inspection) and administrative applications (sales, market surveys, and services).

Quality control limited to the technical aspects is incomplete and still requires the participation of the people in administration and sales. The purchasing division has to look for inexpensive and good quality materials, and the personnel division must select workers and provide education and training. Every division in the corporation must participate if QC is to succeed. Neither will QC succeed without the full cooperation of the company president, top management, division and section chiefs, workshop foremen, and workers at all levels.

It is only with the participation of every division and every worker at every level that you achieve the total of TQC. Furthermore, TQC is not everyone pursuing his own quality control but everyone working together to achieve a common quality control goal. In other words, TQC is something everyone does systematically for everyone's good.

Upper and middle management's job is a lot more than simply telling workers to do their best. They must establish work standards (i.e., look for problems, discover their causes, and figure out how to prevent their recurrence), and provide the appropriate materials and equipment necessary to implement these work standards.

TQC involves clarifying problem points, diagnosing and analyzing their causes, and implementing action to rectify them. Statistical analysis is an important TQC tool, analogous to a doctor's stethoscope and thermometer, or cardiograms and encephalograms.

Because TQC begins with clarifying problems and seeking out their causes, it is a system of quality control based on factual evidence. Operating on the strength of assumptions and gut feelings leads to mistaken decisions and the application of inappropriate measures. Only after the actual facts are clarified and objective analyses are made the basis for decision-making will it be possible to implement effective measures. TQC's strength is that it uses solid tools to reach soild decisions and is not a vague, philosophical preaching.

Quality control using statistical tools is often called SQC or statisical quality control. These statistical tools are essential — so esssential that TQC might better be called TSQC. The fact that the term TQC does not include a "statistical" in it should not be taken to mean that the statistical aspects are any less important.

TQC involves everyone in the corporation and requires more than nominal participation by every division and level of worker. TQC must be a movement of every division, with every worker actively seeking to attain a common goal. This common goal is based on the principle that product quality is defined by the product's advantages for the user, and that what is to the customer's advantage will also be to the company's advantage in maximizing corporate profits and furthering the company's development.

To repeat, TQC is not everyone pursuing his own quality control activities but something everyone does in everyone's interests.

There is a tendency in company-wide TQC for the corporation to concentrate on rationalizing operations within each division without regard to resolving problems among divisions. The emphasis should be on the attainment of a common goal, which is why the word "total" is so important to this concept. Japanese style TQC is integrated quality control in which the whole company — every division at every level — is involved for the achievement of a common corporate goal, especially a product or policy goal. This is why Japanese-style TQC is better referred to as company-wide total quality control.

1.9 Corporate Administration and Quality Control

1.9.1 Management, Quality, and Quality Control

Corporate management, industrial product quality, and quality interact as shown in Figure 1.3. The areas marked A, B, and C in this figure are all integral to Japanese-style TQC.

1.9.1.1. Quality Assurance

The most important QC objective is that of assuring the quality of industrial products. This is called quality assurance of QA. QA includes, in addition to design and manufacture, making sure that product quality lives up to consumer expectations and that there are easy-to-understand, straightforward instructions explaining the product's proper use. These factors are represented by the shaded area C in Figure 1.3.

QA naturally necessitates the technology specific to the product, but control systems other than QC can also be applied effectively, including industrial engineering (IE) and operations research (OR). Nevertheless, QC plays the major role in quality assurance, and there is actually a greater degree of overlap between quality control and product quality than is shown in the shaded area C in Figure 1.3.

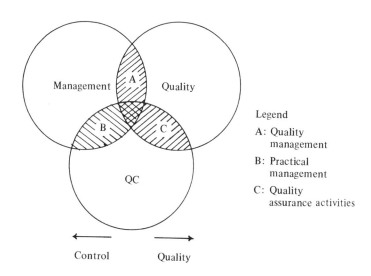

Figure 1.3 The Two Directions in Quality Control

1.9.1.2 Practical Administrative Management

In Japanese-style TQC, there are activities which directly contribute to corporate administration even though they have no direct relationship to product quality per se. The upper-left circle in Figure 1.3 represents administration and management and the shaded area B is the quality control that directly applies to administration and management. Because corporate management requires a basic concept and philosophy, IE and OR can come in handy here too. There is a good balance between the abstract quality of administration and management and the very concrete activities of quality control, and quality control can be applied in many ways to management. The shaded area B might be called practical administrative management.

As a part of TQC, many corporations place special emphasis on policy management and cross-functional management. This kind of approach has proved highly effective and is characteristic of Japanese-style TQC. Essential to product quality assurance, policy management and cross-functional management are equally useful in raising efficiency in areas with little or no direct relation to product quality.

Policy management involves clarifying management problems (both current and potential problems), devising ways of solving these problems, implementing the solutions, reviewing their results, and setting up new policies. In other words, it involves turning the PDCA circle. Policy management must be applied effectively at all corporate levels, from top to bottom. This is TQC in which everyone pursues a common goal for the common good.

Given how essential it is to corporate management, you would assume that it was being universally carried out. Such is not the case however. In too many corporations, policy management is only being partially applied. Policy management only becomes truly effective in the TQC context, and TQC methodology and techniques are effective tools for policy management.

1.9.1.3 Quality Management

The shaded area A in Figure 1.3 where the management and quality circles overlap represents quality concerns in management. This is the area so often spoken of these days as quality management.

Conventionally, management has been concerned only with profit maximization, and all management activities have been geared toward profits. There is, however, a limit to how effective this kind of management can be. In considering quality, it is often necessary to turn your thinking upside down and to realize that quality and profit are not mutually exclusive. Quality (i.e., consumer benefits) redounds to the corporation as added profits. This is the kind of management I mean when I speak of quality management.

Industrial product quality is a primary issue in corporate management. If product quality does not measure up to consumer expectations, the product will not sell; and if defective products are placed on the market, there will be complaints and costly recalls. This is why it is imperative that every effort be made to seek out the causes of inferior product quality, devise plans that will eliminate these causes, implement these plans and policies, and otherwise rotate the PDCA circle for quality policy management. This is where areas B and C overlap in Figure 1.3.

QC contributes to industrial product quality assurance, and is also effective in reducing production costs, shortening delivery times, and in other technical and administrative matters. These areas are represented in Figure 1.3 by the non-overlapping areas.

Product quality is, very simply, the quality of whatever your product is. For manufacturers, quality refers to manufactures quality. For the construction industry, this is building quality. And in such service industries as banking and retailing, it is the quality of intangible services. Every division in a corporation has its own "product." The design division produces designs, the accounting division financial statements and vouchers. Each of these "products" has a user. This is where the famous concept that "the next process is your customer" comes in. The same processes for assuring industrial product quality can be applied in creating products that meet consumer requirements in all fields. This is all part of QC.

1.9.2 Management and Quality Control

1.9.2.1 TQC and Profits

It ·is only natural that a business should· consider profits paramount. The corporation is expected to last forever, but without profits it will collapse, with drastic ripple effects for its employees and society in general. TQC would be meaningless – worthless – if it did not contribute to increasing profits.

Nevertheless, there are still a number of grossly mistaken assumptions about quality bandied about – fallacies that persist despite the example of every successful company. While I will not go into detailed explanations of why these assumptions are mistaken (by now, the reasons should be obvious), it may be useful to list them simply as a reminder.
1. A good quality product is a high-cost product.
2. It costs too much to improve product quality.
3. Quality is a concern only to the workers in manufacturing, and is no concern of management's.
4. Inspections can guarantee quality.
5. Quality is an intangible that cannot be measured, and it therefore has no relation to policy management based on attaining target values.

1.9.2.2 TQC and Increasing Sales

Quality must benefit the user. Products that have qualities that benefit the consumer will naturally be popular and sell well. While the company used to focus solely on profit maximization, this era of slower growth and more intense competition means that only quality products will sell. It is precisely at times such as the present that the corporation needs to drastically revise its thinking away from the narrow pursuit of profit and toward the pursuit of quality. This is what TQC is all about. TQC works to change management attitudes from a single-minded concern for corporate profits to a broader concern for social and consumer benefits in the realization that quality in society's best interests is also in the company's own best interests.

Lest there be any doubt, you need only look at the way Japanese manufacturers of automobiles, electrical appliances, ICs, and other industrial and consumer products have expanded their exports and greatly increased their profits by rigorously applying TQC.

1.9.2.3 TQC and Productivity

High productivity is obviously desirable, and one of the major deterrents to improving productivity is inferior product quality. With zero defects, the efforts of the people working on the production line and the energy expended in operating production equipment are 100% productive. It takes time, effort, and energy even to produce defective products — time, effort, and energy that are totally wasted. Not even inspecting for defects and repairing them before can recover or make up for this waste.

1.9.2.4 TQC and Delivery Management

Product quality also affects delivery schedules. Extra time is needed to repair defective output and to get parts and materials to replace those that have been wasted. TQC has often been applied effectively to reduce the number of steps required for production and hence to shorten delivery times.

1.9.2.5 TQC and Product Liability

Defective products have become a major social problem. Issues that were virtually ignored in the past have become major concerns as defective products cause injury and significant property loss. Manufacturers are being used by disgruntled consumers and finding themselves required to pay huge damages. I will discuss the issue of product liability in greater detail in Chapter 5. Suffice to say here that product liability is necessarily one of the company's most important concerns, and it is not unusual for huge liability judgements to bankrupt a company. The company that fails to take TQC seriously — even if it does manage to turn a short-term profit — runs a very real risk of bankruptcy.

1.9.2.6 TQC, New Product and New Technology Development, and Technology Improvement

TQC applies to much more than simply eliminating defective manufacturing processes. If the design is defective, the final product will turn out defective no matter how good the manufacturing process is. This is why TQC has gradually moved upstream from production to the design stage and to new product and technology research and development. This kind of quality control is called upstream control or source management.

No matter how superior the technology, it is severly limited if it is confined to the skill of a single worker. Technology that is only in one worker's head cannot be used by other workers and does not contribute to the company's progress. It is absolutely essential in this age of rapid technological advances to build up technological experience and make sure that everyone has access to this technology through what might be called horizontal expansion of knowhow.

Standardization and institutionalization are imperative. Texts explaining technology in a way that anyone can understand and apply are needed. These texts provide technical standards, and those that spell out work conditions and procedures are known as operating procedure manuals.

Only when technology is organized this way does it become possible to make the revisions required by changing times and to ensure that the technology is available to everyone.

TQC's statistical tools are also useful in improving technology. Happily, computers have simplified the application of these satistical tools and made TQC readily available to everyone interested in improving technology.

1.9.2.7 TQC and Improving Operations

The administrative divisions in a corporation creat "products" related to management information, including such intangible services as those offered by the sales division. Yet these "products" are seldom inspected, and defectives often go unnoticed. There are a lot more defective products in this area that fail to meet user requirements than most people realize.

Office automation (OA) has attracted considerable attention lately, but no matter how efficiently computers process data and other management information, they do nothing to improve corporate administration if the original data are wrong in the first place. Before even thinking of automating office procedures, the company should apply TQC to highlight problem areas, clarify their causes, and seek out the information required for their correction. Then and only then can OA be applied to process all of this efficiently and speedily. OA should always be firmly grounded in TQC, a fact that too many people ignore.

1.9.2.8 TQC and the Human Element

No matter how advanced computer and automation technology is, the effectiveness of this technology always depends on the people using it. This is why the human element is so important to TQC.

The Western system in which management creates standards to be blindly followed does not contribute to good quality products. Workers who reluctantly do only what they are told within their allotted time cannot produce good quality products. Good quality products are produced only when everyone is willing to put his all into his work.

Still, modern, sophisticated equipment makes it impossible for everyone in the workshop to work at his own pace and in his own way like the craftsmen of old. This is where the quality control circles come in. QC circles provide a forum for people in the workshop to exchange ideas and to stimulate each other to do better work. As of September 1984, Japan had more than 180,000 registered small-group QC circles with a total membership of over 1.5 million.

QC circles make positive efforts to seek out problem areas and to apply QC tools to resolve these problems. Today QC circles are to be found not only in manufacturing plants but in offices, banks, hotels, and other service areas as well. These QC circles play a prominent role in Japanese-style TQC, and an increasing number of Western corporations are studying the Japanese QC circles' achievements and introducing similar systems into their own operations. Obviously, a group of people cooperating closely together is more likely to achieve solid results than a single person attempting to solve a problem completely on his own.

Another part of TQC is cross-functional management whereby divisions within the corporation work together to resolve problems transcending divisional lines. All too often, people in one division are unable to solve a problem because they do not have access to all the information on all the causes. Cross-functional management helps to break down the barriers of isolation. Because TQC strives for realistic management, discussions are focused on facts and figures. As a result, it is possible to avoid irrational and emotional confrontations and to get people in different divisions talking to each other and cooperating. In every company that has instituted TQC, employees have become closer to each other. TQC teaches respect for the individual and contributes significantly to better relations among the people in the corporation.

1.9.2.9 TQC and Other Management Activities

There are many other effective control systems and technologies besides QC, including industrial engineering and operations research, and I recommend that these systems be studied and applied wherever possible. Where these systems differ from TQC is that their high degree of specialization makes it impossible for everyone in the corporation to participate in their application. The more people who understand and are skilled in these control systems the better, of course; but it is really better to leave them up to the experts than to try to train everyone in them.

Reliability engineering (RE) is another technology essential to assuring product quality and should be incorporated as a part of TQC. But in the process, care should be taken not to allow RE and other specialists to form isolated factions that fail to interact in the performance of their various functions. Every effort should be made to ensure that these specialists work closely together in solving problems critical to the corporation.

Equally to be avoided is the creation of an isolated TQC faction that fails to draw upon the expertise of engineers and other specialists already in the company. For the most effective application of TQC, statistical analysis, system design, motion study, and other special technologies and techniques, and the people most knowledgable in them, should all be made a part of the TQC programme.

TQC provides the foundation on which these control activities can be built. For example, policy management to establish and implement corporate policies is basic to corporate management, and not even the most sophisticated management techniques will be of any avail unless policy management is applied.

Companies attempting to implement policy management as part of TQC commonly run up against strong opposition from the planning and administrative divisions that would normally be responsible for policy management. The people in these divisions feel strongly that TQC's application of policy management is a flagrant infringement on their authority. While they are technically right, it is their failure to grasp policy management's essence that has made it necessary to apply policy management through TQC in the first place. Policy management is an integral part of TQC, and TQC cannot be implemented without it. Rather than putting up mindless resistance, planning and administrative divisions would do better to learn all they can from TQC policy management.

In the final analysis, TQC is a management tool, not management itself. Used properly it is a highly useful tool; but it is completely meaningless or even counterproductive when used incorrectly or not at all. It is essential that TQC be properly understood and implemented.

2 | Management's Role in TQC

Chairmen of the board, presidents, vice-presidents, managing directors, executive directors, and other directors are the administrative brain of the corporation; division and plant managers, the management corps. There is a fine distinction between the roles that top- and middle-management play within the TQC context. In fact, different TQC seminar courses are offered for top-management and for middle-management personnel in Japan. While top- and middle-management people may share many common characteristics, there can be wide divergences in their scopes of authority and responsibility depending on the size and type of corporation. Nevertheless, I will ignore the top/middle distinction here and limit myself in this text to the basic functions management needs to fulfill in implementing TQC.

2.1 Management's Function

2.1.1 Managerial Types that Obstruct TQC

At a time when nearly everyone has some familiarity with TQC, it is a shame that there are still managers who obstruct the effective implementation of TQC. The obstructive managerial types:

1. Knows nothing about TQC.
2. Knows about TQC but is totally uninterested.
3. Opposes TQC on the grounds that it is unnecessary.
4. Believes TQC is being applied when it actually is not (i.e., QC efforts are being implemented, but they are not nearly as comprehensive as they should be).

There is some hope for the first type of TQC-obstructive manager, since effective TQC may be applied once the manager learns about it. Likewise with the third type, who is generally sincerely dedicated to improving the corporation's performance and has the potential for becoming a dedicated TQC advocate once it is clear that he has misunderstood TQC. The second type not only misunderstands TQC, he is not very dedicated to his job as manager.

It is the fourth type who is the worst obstacle to effective TQC. This type of manager clings to his prejudices about TQC and does not have a firm grasp on his own corporation's performance. This type tends either to distort TQC into a spiritual movement or to limit TQC to reports and paperwork.

There is a big difference between understanding the theoretical importance of TQC and actually implementing it effectively. TQC is not effective when it has been properly implemented. Being very busy people, too many corporate executives limit themselves to a superficial understanding of TQC gleaned from popular books and introductory lectures and make no attempt to learn the nuts and bolts of its implementation. Simply agreeing with TQC principles is not going to help you succeed in putting TQC into practice.

Out of touch with floor workers and the nitty-gritty of daily operations, corporate executives often fail to develop a feel for what is really happening or the sense of crisis that things are not as they should be. As a result, they lack that sense of urgency, that awareness of TQC requirements, and that determination to meet the challenge of implementing TQC that are the essential ingredients for success. The attitude corporate executives take toward TQC will reverberate throughout the organization. Uninterested managers should not even make the pretence of participating in TQC activities. Since TQC requires all corporate employees to participate, such managers should be weeded out of the corporation at an early stage.

2.1.2 Promoting TQC
Within the corporation, managers need to do two things to promote TQC:

1. Participate in product quality assurance activities.
2. Participate in practical management TQC.

Product quality assurance activities involve identifying the consumer's quality requirements, meeting these requirements, and eliminating defective products.

Practical management TQC involves establishing clear-cut corporate policies, ensuring that everyone is familar with them, and working to achieve these policy goals. Corporate policies obviously include achieving product quality, reducing the costs of attaining this quality, and meeting production and delivery schedules, but this policy elucidation needs to clarify not only the goals but also the means to be used in achieving these goals and to otherwise rotate the PDCA circle. This is policy management.

Note that quality assurance is not the sole responsibility of the manufacturing people alone. Product designers, maintenance and safety crews, and even sales people must all be involved. The same is true of efforts to control costs and to meet production and delivery schedules as well. In TQC jargon, having people from many different divisions work together toward a common goal is known as cross-functional management. It is management's job to establish and oversee policies, to forge an organization that will be conducive to effective cross-functional management, and to otherwise to create a climate in which everyone can cooperate to the fullest.

2.1.3 TQC Management

Because TQC is something that is done, it requires some form of management, and the PDCA circle should be turning here too. I mentioned earlier that the PDCA circle is best started at C (checking) in management (See Figure 1.1), and this also holds for managing TQC.

Even though we may be doing the best we know how, no one assumes that there is no room for improvement. The same is true of the corporation. Just because it is doing well does not mean that it cannot do better. Just because it is making money does not mean it cannot make more money. Even though things may seem to be going very well now, that does not mean that there is no potential for future problems. The corporation that is satisfied with the status quo and makes no attempt to grow will soon find itself stagnating and unable to survive the competition. Not being able to see any problems is itself a problem.

Because TQC is the process of solving problems to further the growth of the corporation, it begins by identifying problem areas within your own company and pinpointing your TQC targets. Some of the common problems in implementing TQC are listed below. They are discussed in detail in Section 9.4.

1. Uninterested top management.
2. Management's failure to recognize its role in TQC.
3. Unclear TQC targets.
4. No product quality policies.
5. Failure to clarify the range of TQC activities.
6. Lack of a clear-cut programme for implementing TQC.
7. Too much emphasis on theory and too little effort to learn the methodology.
8. Ritualized QC activities with little or no meaning.
9. The mistaken assumption that QC circle activities are all you need for TQC.
10. Lack of interest.
11. Problems in the TQC headquarters.
12. Incomplete understanding of what results are expected from TQC.
13. Lack of well-defined uniform TQC terminology.

These problems are likely to occur in any company. And when they do, it is generally management's fault.

Managing TQC involves defining your goals and then setting up plans to achieve these goals. Before this can be done, it is first necessary to target the problems that need to be solved. The next step is deciding what kinds of QC activities should be implemented within each division to solve them. This involves developing and deploying QC functions — those activities required to achieve the targets. An organization plan is needed that clearly delineates the duties of each division in relation to quality control, as is a system of cross-functional management. These plans and systems require the kind of overall coordination that only management can provide, and they cannot be left to the people within each division.

In participating in TQC, management is expected to promote TQC educational activities, foster the growth of QC circles, and make a positive contribution to all types of QC-related activities.

Once TQC has been initiated, programmes need to be checked to ensure that they are effective. This is called TQC inspection or TQC audit, and it must be performed by those corporate executives who ordered TQC's implementation in the first place. Because of this, the procedure is sometimes called a presidential TQC audit, and such audits are conducted regularly, most commonly twice a year, in companies where TQC is being effectively applied. It is management's job to assist the president in his audit by drafting inspection plans and making sure that people follow through on the necessary reforms and other changes.

The results of the TQC audit should always be incorporated into the next TQC plan. This is the A or action of the PDCA circle. (Figure 1.1) With management playing a decisive role every step of the way, TQC PDCA involves:

1. Planning: Identifying the problems that need to be solved through TQC.
2. Doing: Developing QC functions.
3. Checking: Conducting TQC audits (see Chapter 14).
4. Action: Reforming the original plan according to audit results and implementing a new TQC promotion plan.

2.2 Management's Responsibility for Product Quality

It is management's job in promoting quality control to:

1. Establish and disseminate the corporation's quality policies.
2. Identify priority quality problems and see that they are solved.
3. Create an organizational plan for implementing quality control.
4. Check and revise quality assurance activities as necessary.

2.2.1 Quality Policies

While it is ultimately the consumer who determines product quality, there is really no satisfying the consumer's demand for ever-better quality. The consumer always wants the highest quality at the lowest price. As a result, in practice, product quality is determined by management's policy direction based on careful studies of production capabilities and cost effectiveness. This means that it is necessary to know the quality of your competitors' products. Cutting production costs by opting for inferior production technology in a short-term attempt to increase sales will lead to trouble very quickly.

Product quality is broadly defined and requires that a wide range of factors be taken into consideration, yet in all too many companies, quality development is left up to technicians and researchers. Product quality is a company-wide concern, and there should be a company-wide consensus on what kinds of products they are attempting to produce and what they are trying to achieve in their research and development. In actuality, however, these decisions tend to be limited to specific divisions and the products, with quality interpreted in a dozen different ways. This lack of agreement indicates a failure to fully grasp consumer requirements, as well as failure to agree on the company's equipment, production, and worker capabilities.

All of these factors are management concerns, a point I will discuss further in Chapter 11. The people in product development need to know what kind of product they are to create, its quality requirements, and the direction and limitations of the corporation's quality policies. And as I will reiterate at greater length in Chapter 5, it is crucial that management set forth clear directions concerning product safety and pollution hazards.

2.2.2 Priority Quality Problems

Designating priority quality problems and getting people working on them is an important part of management's job. In TQC, this is done by preparing a list of critical problem areas. What would happen, for example, if all of a product's quality characteristics were to prove defective? The cost of correcting these defects would be phenomenal. But neither defects nor the cost of correcting them are distributed evenly throughout all of a product's quality characteristics, a fact that facilitates implementing TQC.

Determining the distribution and frequency of defects is an important TQC process, and frequency distribution charts indicating the type of defect and its costs are convenient tools here. In Figure 2.1, the types of defects are listed

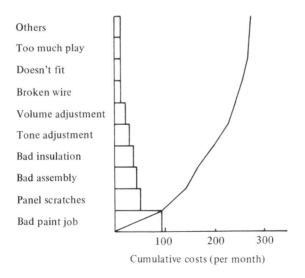

Figure 2.1 The Pareto Diagram

along the vertical axis and the cumulative cost of each defect is indicated on the horizontal axis. This particular figure shows the defects found in a certain electrical appliance. As you can see, defective paint jobs, scratched panels, defective assembly, and defective insulation (the first four defects listed) accounted for 80% of the total cost of repairs, while the six other defects combined were only 20%.

This kind of figure is called a Pareto diagram after Vilfredo Pareto (1848-1923), an Italian social economist who invented the diagram to show the distribution of wealth in a society.

2.2.2.1 Chronic and Occasional Defects

Defects can be categorized into chronically occurring defects and occasional defects that only occur sporadically. These two categories relate to each other as shown in Figure 2.2.

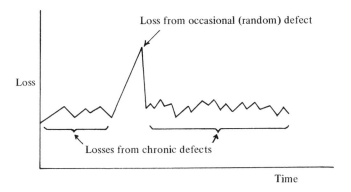

Figure 2.2 Chronic Defects and Occasional Defects

By their very nature occasional defects tend to stand out and are quickly corrected, but chronic defects are very often overlooked. With a control chart, it is relatively simple to identify problems, seek out their causes, and take some kind of corrective action. (The control chart is a statistical tool that indicates changes in product quality with control limit lines demarcating the boundaries between normal and defective products. Quality lines that exceed these boundaries are warning signals that action should be taken.)

Like a chronic ailment that the body gets used to and begins to accept as normal, chronic defects are difficult to identify. Occasional defects, on the other hand, are localized, like an aching tooth or an upset stomach, and are easy to detect and cure. Yet over time, the cost incurred from chronic defects will be greater than the temporary loss engendered by occasional defects. It is also common for occasional defects to derive from chronic defects. Thus there should be no less a priority on detecting and rectifying chronic defects.

Figure 2.3 compares the different characteristics of occasional and chronic defects. As can be seen, chronic defects are traceable to a broad range of possible causes extending to many different divisions, which is all the more reason that everyone needs to cooperate to eliminate them. No one person or division can do the job alone, and it is clearly management's job to seek out and identify the chronic defects so that they can be corrected.

	Occasional Defects	Chronic Defects
Data	Can be analyzed with narrow range of data	Need wide range of data
Analysis	Simple causes	Complex causes
Correction	Can be localized	Must involve wide range of measures
Analyst	Person responsible for that job	QC Headquarters staff
Corrector	Person responsible for that job	Management-level

Figure 2.3 Comparison of Chronic Defects and Occasional Defects

2.2.2.2 Management- and Worker-caused Defects

Defects can be caused by management or by floor workers. Failure to provide the required guidance and standards is a management-caused defect, whereas failure to adhere to standards is, like mistakes on the production line, a worker-caused defect. In tracing worker-caused defects, it is not uncommon to find that they actually arise from incorrect standards and other management-caused defects. Of course, in many instances only the shop floor workers have the requisite knowhow needed to create certain standards, and it is to be hoped that workers will take the initiative in revising and improving standards as necessary. This is what QC circle activities are about, yet this is not the same thing as disregarding agreed-upon standards.

When a QC circle succeeds in making improvements in its work area, it frees management to concentrate on bigger problems. In fact, the degree to which they encourage management to concentrate on bigger problems in the broader perspective is one measure of the effectiveness of QC circle activities.

2.2.3 Organizational Planning

Feigenbaum states that organizing TQC does not mean setting up a quality control section or division but means

1. creating a communications network for quality information and
2. assigning people to quality control activities.

Quality information includes both information that comes from outside of the company (e.g., consumer feedback) and information that comes from inside the company (e.g., information on processing capabilities conveyed from the manufacturing division to the design division). All too often, this quality information is insufficient or completely lacking. The organization of a communications network for prompt and accurate transmission of vital quality-related information and data is basic to quality assurance. Simply establishing a quality control division to collect all this information is meaningless unless measures are also taken to ensure that the information is conveyed to each division and that each division has clearly defined control responsibilities and acts on the information.

Management must therefore be responsible for clarifying quality responsibilities (quality functions) and control responsibilities (quality control functions), both of which are discussed in detail in Chapter 3, on a divisional level.

If the marketing division is not TQC-conscious, for example, management may want to send sales personnel to outside TQC seminars and workshops. Yet even this is no guarantee that the division will immediately implement TQC. How can you expect the sales people to implement TQC if TQC is not included anywhere in the marketing division's duties? It is management's responsibility to define the marketing division's duties in regard to quality control activities. The same is true for all administrative activities.

TQC is everyone's responsibility. As Feigenbaum has said, because TQC is everybody's job, it is nobody in particular's job. Yet the fact that it is nobody's job does not mean that everyone can ignore it. Rather, he means that there is no one who specializes solely in TQC. It is wrong to think of TQC as a specialist's job. Yet in the United States, QC is considered the responsibility of professional quality control experts, and the kind of TQC envisioned by Feigenbaum is virtually nonexistent.

Some companies established quality control divisions right at the start as they began to implement TQC. As a result, other divisions assumed that QC was the new division's job and failed to become quality-conscious. While some-one obviously needs to be appointed to coordinate and promote TQC's implementation and to take care of the organizational and other clerical jobs related to QC, this office should be assigned to a vice president, managing director, or someone else from top management. Because the TQC centre's job is not to actually carry out TQC itself but to encourage all of the company's divisions to be quality-conscious, the person in charge of the TQC promotion centre must be a reliable person known and trusted throughout the company. He must have a thorough understanding of TQC, be dedicated to its promotion, and understand the various divisional problems. Rather than issue orders and notices, this person needs to be a gentle but persuasive force for the promotion of TQC.

You can tell a lot about a company's understanding of and commitment to TQC from the people it selects to staff the TQC centre. A company that staffs the TQC centre with people near retirement age that it is anxious to get rid of is obviously not going to succeed at TQC. Nor is it enough for the president to appoint a vice president or managing director to head the TQC centre and then just sit back and listen to their progress reports. The president has a responsibility to conduct TQC audits and to be the first to require reforms.

2.3   TQC as Practical Administrative Management

2.3.1   Policy Management

Management's job in promoting quality control within the context of practical administrative management is policy management — establishing policies and checking regularly to make sure that these policies are being implemented. It is thus necessary to clearly define corporate policies and to set up management plans. Policies can be categorized into

1.   administrative policies,
2.   work policies, and
3.   management policies

or into

1.   long-term policies (long-term management plans) and
2.   short-term (business-year) policies.

In terms of quality control, it is necessary to have both a product quality policy and a quality control policy.

Administrative policies directed at achieving sales and profit targets are important, of course, but they are not sufficient in and of themselves for TQC. Because TQC involves pinpointing priority issues and problems and is a process of improving the overall corporate structure, it requires its own specific policies, policies which are directed at quality control.

As noted earlier, the first goal of quality control is to ensure that purchasing the product is to the consumer's advantage. Corporate profits are a by-product of achieving this goal. It is thus important that the corporation have a clearly defined policy placing the priority on the product's advantages for the consumer. Such a quality policy must contain the following elements.

1.   General policy: guidelines for the direction and nature of activities.
2.   Targets: the goals that are to be attained.
3.   Methods: the methodology that will be employed to achieve the specified targets and the implementation plan for applying this methodology.

Target control involves establishing divisional target objectives and carrying out the activities required for their attainment. Setting target objectives is an important procedure, but if there is no clear-cut methodology and if all the exhortation workers get is to "go to it!" there is no way to determine whether the chosen methodology was actually effective and might be applied to attaining future targets or whether it should be revised. This will be true regardless of whether the final targets are met or not.

A target is a result, and the methodology or means the cause leading to that result. A company may plan for long-term growth, for example, but it cannot achieve long-term growth unless it achieves year-to-year growth in its business-year policy management. Only after you have implemented the means required for the attainment of targets on a daily, weekly, monthly, or yearly basis can you claim to be implementing TQC policy management. This is why analysis – seeking out the causes of any given result – is so important in TQC.

It is meaningless to establish impossible goals and demand that they be achieved. For example, it will be impossible to expect the sales force to double sales at a time when sales are chronically slow. And if you do set impossible goals, people will recognize that they are unrealistic, ignore them, and then regretfully report at the end of the year that they were unable to achieve the target. Repeating this pattern year in and year out is not what policy management is all about.

Establishing goals that are too easily attained is equally meaningless. Policy management goals should be neither too high nor too low. Effective policy management involves seeking out appropriate methodologies, discussing their implementation among workers at all levels, and finally making a shared commitment to achieving realistic goals.

To summarize, any policy must meet the following requirements.
1. It must be based on a thorough analysis of the current actual conditions and the target goals.
2. It should place the priority on product quality and be directed at improving the overall corporate structure and culture.
3. It should be presented in clear and simple language.
4. It should specify concrete goals and clearly define the target.
5. It should specify priority issues and problems.
6. It should define the methodologies to be employed.
7. It should take the form of a mutual commitment among all levels in the corporation, and should not be imposed from above or be a compromise.
8. It should be more concrete and specific the lower down it goes on the corporate ladder.
9. It should have definite time limits, goals, and clearly defined scopes of applicability.
10. It should incorporate methods of transmitting throughout the corporation all the new knowledge acquired in the process of its attainment and of checking its results.

The programmes to be enacted in achieving a policy goal are comprised of the planning, doing, checking, and action elements of the control circle. They should clearly state who should do what when, and should take a form that can be easily compared to actual results later.

Figure 2.4 illustrates the relationship between policy management and administrative planning. Policy management is generally an important part of administration in most corporations, but in many instances it is not being implemented to best effect. Priorities in policy management are:

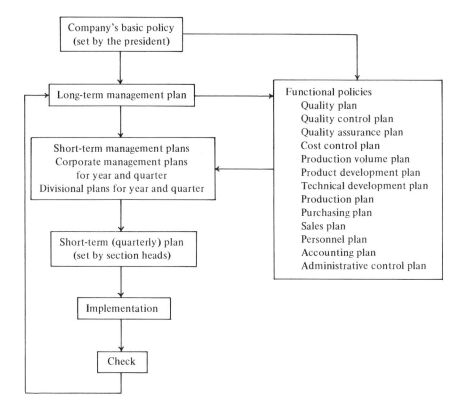

Figure 2.4 Relationship between Policy Management and Administration Planning

1. Setting goals.
2. Deciding priorities and means.
3. Assigning personnel to specific tasks.
4. Providing necessary funding.
5. Drawing up a control plan.
6. Drawing up a total quality control plan.

These items are discussed in greater detail in Chapter 6.

While management's job in policy management should be clear by now, it does not hurt to elaborate. Management's job is:

1. To articulate the corporation's present circumstances and possible future problems, to draw up business-year and long-term administrative plans to resolve these problems, and to clarify these plants to everyone in the corporate structure.
2. To investigate the best ways to transmit the corporation's policy goals and set them in motion, and to issue the necessary instructions for their implementation.

3. To keep track of the progress being made in implementing policies, to diagnose the effectiveness of what is being done, and to apply the lessons learned in setting new policies.
4. To check whether or not goals have been attained, and to issue new instructions as necessary where problems remain.
5. To prepare and regularly update a policy manual that incorporates an in-depth analysis and an evaluation of policy management to date, and to appoint someone to head a policy management division handling the clerical functions required for top management policy audits (with the understanding that this TQC office or headquarters must work closely with the corporation's planning and supervisory divisions).

2.3.2 Cross-functional Management

Quality control involves activities within and among divisions. The former might be called vertical activities and the latter horizontal activities. Because cross-functional management is the overseeing of horizontal interdivisional activities, it might be thought of as a company-wide activity to achieve specific goals. Another name for the same thing is management by objective. In trying to stimulate total company-wide involvement in quality control, it is not enough to have each division implement quality control in its own activities. Very often, in fact, it is impossible to attain established goals when the effort is restricted to divisional activities and no effort is made to resolve interdivisional problems. Not only should every division work to solve its own problems, all divisions should cooperate closely to achieve TQC.

Cross-functional management within the TQC context naturally involves activities to ensure quality control (Q), but also extends to managing costs (C) and production schedule (D). It is common to tackle each of these areas separately, but QCD should be treated as a single unit requiring total quality control for optimum results.

It is possible to go even further in assuring QCD by implementing product planning control (new product development control), technology development control, sales control (orders control), and other aspects of cross-functional management. In services, for example, these other aspects would include personnel control and clerical work control.

The interaction of intradivisional control activities (divisional management) with cross-functional management is depicted in Figure 2.5. Intradivisional control activities can be managed by the division head, but interdivisional activities require agreement on issues among all divisions. This interdivisional coordination is achieved through a system that can be illustrated by a chart in which the PDCA steps are represented along the vertical axis and the consumer, top management, and divisions along the horizontal axis. This kind of chart, however, will not indicate which division should do what jobs. It is therefore also necessary to make up a chart showing the different quality assurance items and the work required for each item. Merely drawing up these charts, of course, is meaningless unless they are acted upon and PDCA is implemented to make improvements in light of the results obtained.

Cross-functional management requires cross-functional policies. For example, in quality assurance, it is necessary to clarify assurance standards (e.g., deciding on the product's useful life). All too often, policy management is restricted to vertical control activities within a division and there is virtually no interdivisional cross-functional management. Control activities within a single division are easy to define and implement; but it is more important that cross-functional management activities be defined and implemented, even though this is more complex and requires greater effort.

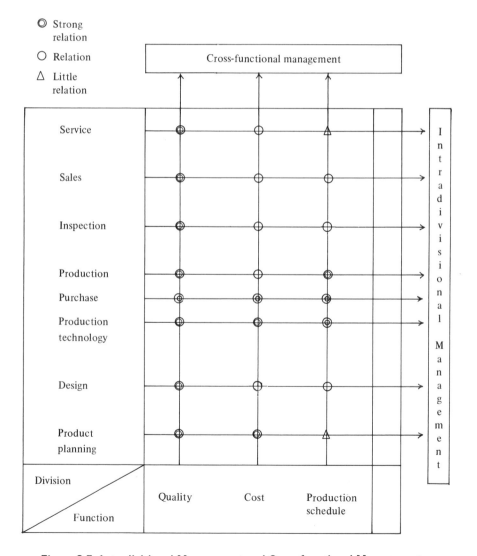

Figure 2.5 Intradivisional Management and Cross-functional Management

With cross-functional management, as with TQC, it is necessary to appoint people to be responsible for its execution. Unfortunately, even when a cross-functional management committee is established, it often restricts itself to drafting organizational charts and lists of activities and little else. At one company where every director headed a division, it was found that this system tended to encourage division heads to rely on their directors to make and clear important decisions. As a result, the company changed its organizational structure so that directors were responsible for different functions (e.g., quality assurance or personnel management) instead of divisions. This had the beneficial effects of making division heads more aware of their responsibilities and promoting cross-functional management.

Top management's role within the context of cross-functional management is:

1. To define cross-functional policies and oversee their implementation. This is done concurrently with the plotting of long-term management plans and business-year policies, and is incorporated into individual division policies. At this level, top management has the same responsibilities as listed under policy management.

2. To assign directors to supervise different functions which they oversee from a corporate perspective rather than a divisional perspective. Directors are free to advise divisional heads on any issue as they deem necessary.

3. To establish a cross-functional management committee for planning, checking results, and instituting reforms. This committee should be formalized as a top-level group, not an informal gathering, and the committee chairman should be the cross-functional management director.

4. To periodically review the results of cross-functional management. At the early stages, TQC analyses and audits are conducted on a divisional level, but such audits should be performed on a cross-functional management basis as soon as possible to highlight interdivisional activities, problems, and solutions. It is also important to keep track of how close the company has come to achieving its cross-functional policies. In other words, it is necessary to check whether the corporation is applying all of its resources toward TQC.

2.3.3 Control Planning

When you are following the PDCA circle for control, you must be very specific as to how the CA, control and action, processes are to be carried out. This has already been touched upon in Section 1.5.2, but elaboration is in order here. Managing daily operations is called daily control, although this is often called policy control when it entails managing new processes that are incorporated into the business-year policy. Once some experience has been built up with these new processes they are shifted back to daily control. The same is true for cross-functional management.

It is always important to clarify which of the 5-Ws and 1-H (who, what, where, when, why, and how) will be the control standards in any specific case.

These are called control items and the chart listing them is called a control item chart. Control items within each job type are called job-specific control items. In addition to defining the control items peculiar to your job, you should decide which control items you will use to check on whether your subordinates have understood your directives correctly and are carrying them out effectively. This is something that should be thoroughly discussed with both superiors and subordinates for thorough and effective control.

Too often, employees do not know what is expected of them or what they should be reporting on because top management has failed to specify its control items. It is also common for top management to issue directives without having thought them through thoroughly, which can cause confusion and makes it impossible to act in a real emergency. Top management should leave daily operations to the people who are doing the work and concentrate on meeting unexpected situations and other kinds of emergencies. There have been numerous and rapid changes in the domestic and international business environments in recent years, and the unexpected is rapidly becoming the norm. One mistake could doom the company forever. This is all the more reason that control standards should be made explicit. Figure 2.6 is a sample list of control items for a director in charge of technical control.

2.4 Quality Control Promotion by Middle Management

Division heads and section chiefs should work to promote quality control within the corporation in a number of ways:

1. Elaborate on policies outlined by top management and set up concrete programmes for their implementation.
2. Follow their own programmes and have the people under them follow these programmes to achieve the stated goal.
3. Evaluate results and work out new plans (policy management).
4. Analyze and evaluate product quality, the processes for quality assurance, and the plans for implementing these processes, decide on priorities, and assign problems to workers to be solved.
5. Collect information and data on product quality inside and outside of the corporation, analyze these data, and prepare data that will determine standard qualities. Deciding on design quality is the job of upper management.
6. Encourage QC circle activities and analyze, standardize, and institutionalize QC circle innovations.
7. Set standards for all operations related to assuring product quality (including cost and delivery criteria) such as overall quality standards, technical standards, work standards, and control standards. Revise these standards as necessary.
8. Work to carry out cross-functional management effectively as dictated in top management policy decision.

Job Function	Control points			Control items	Priority	Control documents		Frequency	Control method	
	Quality	Schedule	Cost			Document	Author		When	What
Technology Improvement	(Improving necessary technology)			Comparison with planned level of technical acquisition	A	Table of planned vs actual technology acquisition	Head of technical control division	Once a month	When exceed parameters	Hold technical conferences, determine causes, and take necessary actions
				Comparison with other companies' technical levels	A	Table comparing own and competition's technology	Head of technical control division	Once every two months	When other companies get technical lead	

Note: The term control points is used here to mean the items that are controlled.

Figure 2.6 Table of Control Points (Sample of Job-specific Table for Technical Division)

To go into more dtail on some of these items:

Concerning (1), there are times when other jobs must be done in addition to the daily routine. Yet how can you do any policy jobs if the daily routine takes all of your time? It is therefore imperative that tasks that you do not have to do daily be eliminated from your daily routine and that all daily routines be standardized to open up time for other jobs when required. This is where it becomes necessary to know who is supposed to do what and how.

On (4) and (6), every effort should be made to incorporate QC circles into TQC. It is indeed gratifying to know that QC circle reports are becoming a regular occurrence in many companies, since this shows how QC circles have proliferated and how successful they have been. Yet if you listen carefully to these reports, you will find that the QC circles are often being called upon to correct inadequacies elsewhere in the company. For example, there are times when a QC circle will report on improvements it made in production equipment, and yet no one considers it odd that the QC circle has had to do something that should have been done by the production technology division.

Efforts by workers on the job to make improvements in processes which they deal with every day are to be applauded. Still, a company should not be too quick to point with pride to improvements made by its QC circles when the only reason the QC circle tackled the problem was that the division responsible for this area was negligent in the first place. It is not uncommon to hear reports like this, and while I applaud the QC circles for their efforts, at the same time I am disappointed by their failure to understand what they should really be doing.

It is useful to have division heads and section chiefs rate the QC circles on their reports and commend them for their achievements, but it is wrong for them to only be looking at the results and not providing any guidance for the circles. Granted that the QC circles operate on their own initiative, it is still incumbent on the division head or section chief to suggest important problems relating to corporate policies and to give the QC circle advice and guidance as it works to find solutions.

Regarding item (5) above, this is an important point for quality control, as already noted, and the fact that this is a responsibility of the division head or section chief is indicative of the vital role these management people should play in quality control.

As for item (7), the concern here is management-caused defects and worker-caused defects. It is management's primary obligation to prepare standards and to make sure workers understand and apply these standards. In fact, worker participation is needed to revise and improve standards. There are many causes of defects that only can be detected at the shop level, but workers must not be allowed to get so absorbed in improving operating procedures that they forget to follow the current procedures and maintain standards. As Juran has pointed out, when small improvements can be left to shop floor workers and their QC circle activities, management is freed to concentrate on its real job – that of ensuring the company's future, including product quality design, new product development, and the institutionalization of success. While QC circles are necessarily judged on their problem-solving records, they should more properly be judged by how much they have done to free management for planning and other future-oriented activities.

On item (8), institutionalization as it is generally understood (i.e., institutionalization for a single operation or job) can usually be left to lower-level people within the company. Top management's institutionalization concerns should be with interdivisional issues, e.g., institutionalization of interdivisional management functions relating to product quality assurance and new product development. This important point is still not well-enough understood. Because it involves resolving problems occurring among different divisions, this institutionalization might also be called system-establishment. Establishing a system is the process of institutionalizing operations both within and among divisions, and this, above all else, is the most important quality control job of division heads and section chiefs.

It is heartening to see how many companies are making an honest effort to better define job-specific control items within their organizations, but they still need to take this one stop further and clarify interdivisional control items and control policies related to quality control (i.e., establish management standards).

It is essential that the division heads and section chiefs serve as important supports for top management in priority quality problem solving, policy management, cross-functional management, and management planning.

3 Planning Quality Control

Managing quality control means following through on the four steps of the PDCA circle — planning, doing, checking, and acting. Management cannot expect to make any progress in quality control simply by ordering that it be implemented. Just as design is the first step to building in quality, so is planning the first step to effective quality control. There can be no implementation when there is no plan to implement.

Management must therefore creat a well-defined progamme for quality control and make sure that all employees understand the programme. As Juran has pointed out, most quality control programmes fail because management has failed to creat a clearly understood programme for quality control. Just as companies need long-term financial and market planning, they also need long-term quality control planning.

3.1 Quality Planning

The term quality planning tends to conjur up images of market research and other kinds of marketing-related product planning. While these are, of course, needed, the emphasis in planning quality control should be on the process for developing the desired quality and establishing a management system to see this process through. This management system is a cradle-to-grave system covering all processes from a product's birth to its final disposal, and it must be planned out ahead of time.

A product's quality should be defined in terms of a total system rather than just as individual features. The product can be classified as mechanical, electrical, or chemical, but these categories generally overlap and interact in a complex system, and it is this total system that should be the target of quality control.

The automobile, for example, has serious quality problems with its exhaust gases, and it is thus not just a mechanical product but also a chemical product.

A system can be a group of interacting, interrelated, or interdependent elements forming a collective entity or a functionally related group of elements. Likewise, product quality is made up of many quality elements functionally related to serve the product's intended purpose (see Section 11.4.2). The important elements in planning quality are establishing and developing quality policies to improve product quality.

3.1.1 Quality Policy

Quality has many meanings and can be widely applied, which is why it should be a company-wide concern. Everyone involved in the quality control process should have the same understanding of the target quality and how it is being developed. Yet in many corporations, it is left to a single technician or researcher to decide on the type of quality that will be developed.

Individual divisions tend to have their own widely divergent approaches to and interpretations of quality — a lack of cohesion most often resulting from a failure to analyze the market's quality requirements and from a lack of consensus on the company's production, processing, and personnel capabilities. Succeeding in product development demands planning that draws on the company's strengths and gets around its weaknesses. It is thus helpful here to draw up a chart of the company's resources, and to conduct a thorough analysis of all relevant factors, both long- and short-term.

The importance of market research is often stressed, but it is seldom pointed out how important it is that the company analyze its own capabilities and objectives. A careful analysis of the company itself is prerequisite to making decisions on the degree of quality a new product should aim at, how this quality is to be developed, and what quality and development policies should be devised to guide and define the product's quality development.

As noted in the preceding chapter, it is management's job to provide the necessary policy guidance. And this guidance must permeate throughout the corporate structure so that everyone shares the same perspective.

3.1.2 Quality Deployment and Quality Analysis

Quality deployment is a way of obtaining the quality characteristics required in a new product by studying customer requirements, defining the necessary quality characteristics, and thereby arriving at the most appropriate product design. It is a highly effective means of establishing quality policy by defining customer requirements, clarifying sales points, and selecting the appropriate substitute characteristics for quality designing. Although this is discussed in greater detail in Section 11.6.1, it is important to say a few words about it here as well.

Through quality deployment, it is possible to define the relationships among a product's quality elements, among use characteristics (the finished product's quality characteristics) and the quality characteristics of each individual part (parts deployment) and among the assurance items for each step in the quality assurance process (step deployment). These quality characteristics and their interrelationships can be quantified and analyzed using such analytical tools as experimental planning and regressive analysis in a process called quality analysis. This approach is becoming increasingly popular in matching process and analyses of manufacturing elements and their characteristics to design quality.

Quality deployment and quality analysis are especially effective in restructuring, up-grading, and applying specific technologies. There is a tendency to regard quality design as a specific technology problem unrelated to quality control, but in actual fact, quality control helps to assure quality design by contributing to advances in specific technologies.

3.2   Planning to Introduce Quality Control

3.2.1   Outline

3.2.1.1 Purpose
Quality control requires management, and the four steps of the PDCA circle — planning, doing, checking, and acting — should be applied.

In planning quality control, the first step is to clarify why you are introducing quality control. A company may institute TQC in a general revamping of all its operations, but it is often not clear what specific operations and policies should be improved and revised. There must be a clear understanding of the reason for introducing quality control into the corporation.

3.2.1.2 Priorities
The next step is to establish priorities. Even though you would expect a company embarking upon a major reform effort to set priorities, this is all too often overlooked. More likely than not, the only guidance provided is a sweeping, "promote quality control!" As a result, this quality control does not have the desired impact even if it is applied throughout the corporation.

Suppose, in the ideal case, you have a company that has managed to grow without making any major mistakes along the way and it turns out stable-quality products with no major defects. This is good, but there is no guarantee that this happy state of affairs will continue indefinitely. When the corporation considers its future prospects, it will inevitably discover something in its current mode of operations and practices that has the potential for developing into a major problem. This is the priority, and its discovery and designation is another reason why quality control involves long-term planning.

3.2.1.3 Aspects
Planning quality control operations should cover:

1. Quality policy, quality control policy, and management of these policies (policy management).

2. Organization.
3. Education and training.
4. Dissemination and motivation.
5. Collecting and analyzing data on priority quality issues.
6. Collecting and applying quality information.
7. Developing quality control functions, functional quality control (quality assurance, cost control, producitivity control, etc.).
8. New product and new technology development.
9. Standardization.
10. Organizing and implementing control systems (control tools and daily control items).
11. QC circle activities.
12. QC audits (inspection) and audit results.
13. Future planning.

Each of these items should be included in the corporation's plans for the year, specifying when it will be introduced, how long a period will be allowed for it to be assimilated, when it will be expanded, and when the particular plan in question will be completely institutionalized. It should be clear which plans will be introduced in what year, what the targets are, what has been achieved so far, and what problems remain to be tackled. Yet before any of these steps can be taken and TQC fully adopted, the corporation has to have a firm understanding of the issues and problems it hopes to solve and must know specifically what it wants to achieve by implementing TQC.

Simply listing the quality control items that you hope to institute between January and December of a given year does not give you a viable programme. The programme will only prove effective when you repeatedly follow the PDCA circle, beginning with checking and going through action, planning, and doing, to analyze the corporation's current situation and spotlight areas requiring reform.

The sample table at the end of this chapter shows the steps in planning, introducing, and promoting TQC; and a suggested checklist for introducing and promoting TQC is given at the end of Chapter 14.

3.2.2 Planning TQC's Introduction

It is important to introduce quality control correctly, because the way the concept is introduced affects its effectiveness and success. Time after time, quality control has been delayed, rendered ineffectual, or even fostered anti-quality control sentiment because it was not introduced correctly in the first place. These first steps are crucial, and if you fall down here you will have to spend all your time getting back on your feet and will not have any time for quality control. It is very difficult to recover from mistakes at this stage.

The fact that only the success stories are publicized makes it all the more difficult to know how to introduce quality control into the company. You do not get to see the mistakes other people made, and the fact that these pitfalls are unposted makes it all the easier for you to fall into them as well.

Plans for introducing QC should be drawn up exactly the same way as plans for its application. This plan, mapping out how quality control is to be implemented, is generally in two stages:

1. Dissemination, education, and training.
2. Implementation and organization.

Implementation follows introduction but the two are not easy to keep distinct. There is no specific point at which you can say you have finished introducing QC and are now going to implement it. I have thus chosen to consider dissemination, education, and organization as aspects of introducing TQC.

Planning how to introduce quality control is the first step in planning how to promote TQC, and it includes the following items.

1. Education planning

   This means planning in-house workshops to explain the concept of quality control and the tools for its implementation to all employees, at every level within the corporation from shop floor workers to top management, in both offices and plants. Employees should also be sent to outside QC workshops and training sessions, and an effort should be made to take advantage of TWI (Training Within Industry) and MTP manpower training programmes as well.

   The level and degree of education should be tailored to different job types and duties and the appropriate textbooks should be acquired. It is also necessary to estimate the amount of time, number of personnel, and costs of instituting this educational programme.

2. Organization planning

   You also need to plan how to organize your company's quality control activities, including allocating staff, selecting the people who will supervise QC-related activities within each division and section, and establishing a cooperative quality control supervisory committee with representatives from all divisions and all levels in the company. This plan should also cover how these various people and organizatons are supposed to function.

3. Management implementation planning

   This entails preparing and establishing various standards, organizations, control and management tools, compiling books of standards and guidebooks, and making sure everyone has these materials readily at hand.

4. Analysis planning

   Analysis planning is planning and preparing analysis systems for each quality control process, establishing standards, analyzing workshop data, planning new tests and experiments, and analyzing their results, and planning and analyzing sampling inspection procedures.

5. Other control planning

   The main areas here are the measurement instrumentation and preventive safety measures.

6. Clerical procedures planning

   Quality control can help to improve many clerical jobs. QC's statistical tools can be applied to costs, labour management, safety, market research, and many other areas to good effect. Here too, work standards should be established and a system of reporting, budgeting, and accounting introduced.

It is not unusual for company employees both in the office and in the factory to begin studying quality control on their own initiative, and some quality control programmes have been successfully introduced as a result of growing enthusiam within the company. Still, numerous problems are likely to remain, and it is impossible to overemphasize the importance of planning the quality control programme *before* it is introduced. Each item to be introduced should be plotted on a graph that clearly shows the time that it is expected to take from initial introduction to final institutionalization, specifying each of the CPDA steps (checking the current situation, planning, doing, checking again, and revising), and estimating how long each step will take to complete.

3.2.3 Priority Items in Promoting TQC

Because your priorities will largely govern what you do when, they need to be carefully thought out in relations to your company's particular situation. Some of the prime possibilities, and the ones that led the list drawn up at the First Symposium on Quality Control in Hakone, Japan, 1965, are given below for your reference.

1. Establishing and clarifying policies, goals, and plans.
2. Encouraging awareness of the need for management and quality control.
3. Instituting educational programmes and following through with workshops, materials, etc.
4. Implementing quality control and quality inspection procedures.
5. Creating a plan for quality control and specifying control items.
6. Clarifying top management policy.
7. Systematizing the quality assurance system and revising it as necessary.
8. Standardizing quality control processes.
9. Setting evaluation criteria.
10. Assigning responsibilities and specifying authority.
11. Organizing the channels for information exchange.
12. Getting everyone to participate.
13. Developing quality control methods.

The important points in TQC are getting everyone to participate, long-term implementation, and improving profitability (by working for the customer's benefit, the company assures its own profits), and the first step is to ensure that everyone in the corporation, from top to bottom, understands this.

3.3 Planning the QC Organization

Organization is crucial in planning how to promote TQC.

3.3.1 Issues in Planning Organization

1. As Feigenbaum has pointed out, organizing quality control does not mean

just establishing a quality control division or section. Rather, it means:
  (1) creating an information network to disseminate data and other quality control information to everyone concerned, and
  (2) instituting a system which will get all divisions and all people at all levels in the corporation participating in quality control.

2. An organization that encourages divisional rivalry is detrimental to quality control and beneficial to no one.

3. An organization should be structured around its people, not the other way around. Check to make sure that you are not simply working to meet the needs of the organization instead of using the organization to meet your own needs.

4. Committees are one way to ensure that all divisions and all workers participate in quality control, but they are by no means the only way. A committee can debate and consider, but it cannot implement, and there is always the danger that the committee will become just another place to pass the buck.

5. Have responsibilities and duties been sufficiently defined? This should be done concretely with specifics in writing, not just verbally.

6. Have cross-communication channels been set up within the corporate organization so that all divisions and all employees are working together on quality control? Is there horizontal as well as vertical contact among the people taking care of quality control operations?

7. Have clear procedures been outlined for changing the organizational structure when necessary?

Companies are generally slow to introduce quality control into their clerical, marketing, and management activities, primarily because of the way their organizations are structured. Even when a company does introduce quality control into its administrative operations, it seldom specifies quality control responsibilities. No wonder quality control does not seem to get very far in the clerical, marketing, and management areas. There is no point in insisting on quality control unless you also specify exactly who is responsible for doing what. Management's first job is to assign specific quality control jobs to specific people in these divisions.

The organization should be structured for a speicific purpose. If you want to pinpoint where profits are being generated, for example, you might organize the company by product. Much planning goes into organizing the company, but the new organization is seldom reviewed to see how well it is functioning or to gather information in preparation for the next reorganization. Here, too, the PDCA circle is useful in planning reorganization, and this is why it is important to outline the procedures for restructuring as necessary.

3.3.2 Principles of Organization Planning

Organizing means much more than dividing a company's operations into specialties and divisions. The purpose of organizing is to define authority and responsibility to best implement management policy and achieve management goals. Thus the organization must satisfy the following requirements.

1. There must be clear lines of authority and responsibility from top to bottom. Here, authority and responsibility refer to the extent to which a person can make demands on others within the corporation.
2. Each person within the corporate organization needs to report to his immediate superior, and not to a committee of people. At the same time, everyone should know exactly who he reports to and who reports to him.
3. Top and middle management authority and responsibilities should be clearly spelled out in writing.
4. Responsibilities should always be accompanied by the authority to do the job.
5. The number of management levels in the corporate structure should be kept to a minimum.
6. It is management's job to work to incorporate new and unusual developments into quality control standards.
7. Production line and clerical staff functions should be clearly differentiated, and both groups of people urged to participate equally in quality control.
8. There is a limit to how broadly any single manager can manage.
9. The organization should be elastic enough to adapt quickly to changing conditions.
10. Rules and regulations should be kept as simple as possible. Among other things, this means the minimum number of management levels and the minimum number of committees.

Some companies have several intermediary ranks between division head and section chief, such as assistant division head, deputy division head, and acting division head. If the assistant division head is responsible for some part of the division head's work, his responsibilities and extent of authority should be specified in writing. This way, everyone else in the division will know exactly what they should be reporting to him. If, on the other hand, the assistant division head does not have de facto authority in certain areas but only works under the division head, this fact should be made explicit so that the other people in the division can report directly to the division head and follow his instructions. This is a very important way to avoid confusion over the lines of command and scopes of authority.

3.3.3 Organizational Standards and Regulations

Organizing quality control obviously has to entail establishing work regulations and decision-making criteria. The quality control section does not actually implement quality control. Rather its job is to provide support by outlining operational plans. Each division needs to know the extent of its responsibility for designing quality, diagnosing and analyzing critical quality problems, assuring quality, preventing defectives, developing new products, and so forth.

3.3.4 The Quality Control Committee

The quality control committee should be just that, and its responsibilities and functions should be spelled out in detail. The committee's charter should cover its goals, functions, structure, and procedures for calling a meeting. This committee should have a chairman, vice-chairman, and secretariat, and the chairman should be a person relatively high up in the corporate structure, such as a vice-president or plant manager.

The quality control committee can deliberate, but it is up to individual division heads to carry out its decisions. Accordingly, the committee should specify how measures are to be carried out and how their results will be checked later. Otherwise, it will be totally ineffective.

It is recommended that sub-committees be set up within the quality control committee for quality standards, work standards, new products, and other specific issues and problems. The new products sub-committee, for example, would consider whether a new product idea is feasible in terms of the work and technology it would involve, including looking into the product's design and structure, estimated manufacturing costs, and whether or not the planned production volume would justify the proposed allocation of resources.

The technical sub-committee should look into technical problems and possibilities for innovation, as well as seeking out the organizational obstructions to smooth production and investigating new measurement tools and manufacturing equipment.

The quality control committee's primary responsibility is to seek out critical quality problems. It should be especially concerned with major chronic problems rather than small occasional problems. In carrying out this responsibility, it is the committee's job to interpret quality problems in terms of cost and estimate the loss to the corporation in financial terms. Next, the committee must calculate the cost of solving the quality problems and report its findings to the quality control division or section. Obviously, the committee has to include people from product design, marketing and customer service, production planning, purchasing, inspection, and quality control if it is going to function effectively.

3.3.5 The TQC Promotion Centre
The TQC promotion centre performs the following functions.
1. It drafts proposals for the promotion of TQC. To do this, the people in the TQC promotion centre must have a firm grasp on how TQC is being successfully or not-so-successfully implemented in other companies, what their own company's problems are, where their company stands in terms of quality in comparison to the competition, how many if any defective and inoperative products there are in its product line, how frequent customer complaints are, and what problems exist among divisions and in the company's relations with its customers, suppliers, and sub-contractors.
2. It drafts proposals for quality and quality control policies.
3. It keeps tabs on current issues and problems in the company's policy and functional management systems.
4. It lists critical quality problems and checks to see that action is taken to solve them.

5. It sets up plans for QC education, QC workshops and other QC dissemination activities conducted by experts from both inside and outside the company.
6. It drafts diagnostic checklists for top management and division head QC audits, and functions as the secretariat when such audits are being made.
7. It keeps track of TQC results.

In doing all this, the TQC promotion centre should keep in mind that it is supposed to be acting as a support to QC activities and not issuing instructions. Looking for divisional flaws and criticizing will only serve to antagonize people. The TQC promotion centre should be somewhere anyone can go for advice and meaningful guidance.

Assigning QC jobs and establishing an information network for the exchange of quality information are top management responsibilities, but it is the TQC promotion centre's job to draft the necessary plans for top management.

Accordingly, the people at the TQC promotion centre must

1. know about TQC and be capable of solving their own problems,
2. be able to help divisions solve their problems,
3. be trusted by everyone in the corporation at every level and be impartial and fair, and
4. be aware that their role is a support role and that they should not be overly concerned with getting credit for everything they do.

Given these requirements, it should be clear that people who are already well-established within the corporate structure and who have a good record of achievement should be selected to staff the TQC promotion centre.

3.4 Deploying Quality Control Functions

3.4.1 Steps to Quality Control Functions

The quality control functions referred to here are the various things that quality control should do and the functions it should fulfill. In planning how to promote quality control within your own company, you must start out by defining the specifics of these quality control activities.

Quality control has traditionally been most emphasized on the manufacturing line, but this is no longer sufficient. The imperative today is not only to meet customer requirements but to ensure that your product benefits society at large. Quality control on the production line may be strictly enforced for an automobile, for example, but this does not solve the problem of such design defects as exhaust pollution. Poor design is just as likely to generate defective output as inadequate manufacturing quality control is; which is why quality assurance is crucial from the beginning.

Product quality can slip at the packing and shipment stages as well. And no matter how superior a product may be, its quality will readily deteriorate in the face of improper use and maintenance. Disposal is also becoming a major quality control problem today.

Quality control is something that needs to be applied at every step of the way, from product planning to final disposal. Everyone is responsible, from manufacturing and design divisions to the retail stores and repair shops outside of the company. Quality control is very much a company-wide activity that extends beyond the corporate structure.

The steps from a product's birth to disposal are:
1. Planning
2. Designing
3. Test production
4. Manufacturing
5. Supplying
6. Using
7. Maintenance and repair
8. Disposal (collection and recycling)

These basic steps can be further broken down into numerous intermediary stages. For example, the pre-manufacturing stage includes design, installation of production equipment, and the ordering and purchasing of needed parts.

In implementing quality control, it is necessary to know what operations are involved at each step. This means deciding on the quality functions required at each step and making sure that these functions are carried through. And in order to know each function's purpose and who should be doing it, it is necessary to define the 5-Ws and 1-H (who, what, where, when, why, and how).

3.4.2 Developing Quality Control Functions and Channels of Communication

Function deployment is a useful tool for developing quality control functions and clarifying quality control jobs, and it provides a framework in which the goals can be used to determine the methods. In contrast to the analytical approach, which involves studying results to unveil their causes, function deployment can be called the design approach.

The analytical approach is highly effective in seeking out the causes for defective products and correcting them. Obviously, the statistical method is one of the best tools for analysis. Yet when the motive is to develop a completely new product or a completely new operation, not just to improve upon something that already exists, the analytical approach is not enough. A design approach is required, and Figure 3.1 is an example of a function deployment chart for appropriate quality assurance activities within a sales division.

Every one of the 5-Ws and 1-H must be answered to carry out function deployment correctly and effectively.
1. Why: Why is this function required?
2. What: What is this function intended to achieve?
3. Where: Where should this function take place (at what step in the overall process)?
4. When: When should this function be implemented?
5. Who: Whose responsibility is it?
6. How: How will it be carried out?

The sales division is frequently criticized for not taking quality control activities very seriously, but this lack of enthusiasm is understandable when

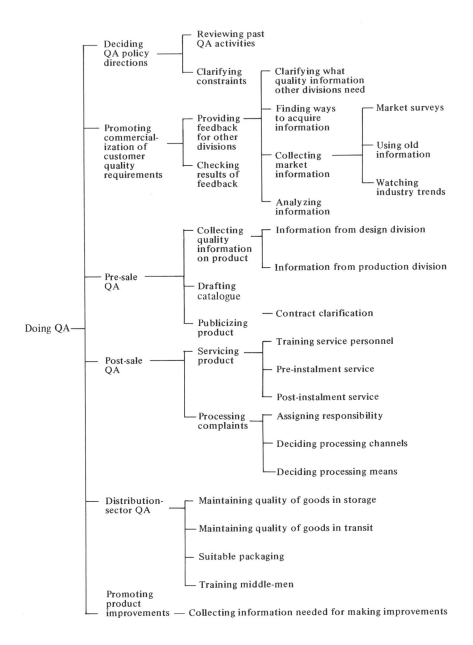

Figure 3.1 Quality Assurance Duties of Sales Division (Partial Listing)

you think that all too often quality control is not included in the sales division's duties. How can people be expected to understand and cooperate in the absence of specific guidelines? Part of the process of clarifying quality functions is to clarify who is supposed to do what and when.

This is done in two steps: first deciding on the quality functions and then deciding on quality control procedures for these functions. Even though there is a difference between the quality functions and the activities to control these quality functions, it is sometimes impossible to differentiate clearly between them, and the term quality control functions as used in this text refers to the combination of the two.

The 5-Ws and 1-H can also be applied to control activities: what control items, who is in charge, where and when controls should be applied, why controls are required, and how these controls will be applied. Deciding on the control items involves not only specifying the functions requiring quality control but also listing all subordinate functions. In this sense, deciding on control items is one and the same as setting control standards, and texts and handbooks containing such listings are control standard books.

Quality control functions that must be performed daily are called daily control items. Many control functions also are required by company policy and can hence be called policy control items.

3.4.3 Control Planning

The importance of establishing control standards is widely recognized today and is a major focus of TQC activities, particularly in clarifying the control responsibilities for different divisions and job types.

Control items come under the following broad categories.

1. Job functions: What job functions should be checked and how should they be checked to enable you to perform your duties most efficiently? (daily control items)
2. Work processes: What procedures in your work process should be checked and how? This can be applied to clerical processes equally as well as to manufacturing processes. (daily control items)
3. Systems: Which functions should be checked? For example, how can you ensure that customer complaint processing is being carried out and quality control standards are being applied efficiently and effectively? (functional management control items)
4. New projects: The higher the management level, the more important quality control for new projects and undertakings should be. (policy control items)

All of these categories can be combined under job-specific control items. These would be control items to check that the people at each level within the company's organization are fulfilling the quality control requirements peculiar to their particular job position. Is the chief of the accounting section, for example, delegating control items to the people working under him as effectively as he can to ensure that they get done with maximum efficiency?

Control items for work processes can be charted in a QC process chart (see Figure 3.2). This same QC process chart can then be referred to in preparing control item charts for individual job positions. These are sometimes called control system charts (see Figure 3.3).

There is no established terminology for control items and they are sometimes called check points. Still the most commonly accepted definitions of these terms are:

Check point: Something that is checked (e.g., production cost).

Control item: The specific item(s) that can be changed (e.g., the material costs and yield ratios that determine production costs).

Some control process charts call the when and where the check points and the what the control item. Elsewhere, control activities assigned to subordinates are called control items and those items that the person making the assignments is personally responsible for are called check points. In still other companies, a distinction is made between check points for control items that are checked against results and inspection items that are checked against causes.

Whatever terminology you decide on, there are a number of points to be especially careful of in drawing up your control item chart:

1. Simply initialing an item on the list is not quality control checking. Quality control means adhering to the established standards in performing your job. Naturally this means everyone must know his reponsibilities and limits of authority, but that is not in itself quality control. Neither are texts and other information sources in and of themselves control resources. Control means checking to see that work is being performed according to agreed-upon standards and taking action when reforms are required.

2. Policy decisions and important problems should also be taken up as quality control items.

3. It is important to establish priorities so that you will know where quality control should be applied when you do not have time to do everything.

4. It should be quite clear who is responsible for what aspects of quality control and what the limits of their authority are.

5. Records should be kept of all actions taken. Reviewing actions taken to see whether they were effective or not helps in deciding whether or not and how they should be made the new standards. Records also help when it comes time to assign this work to someone else.

6. Control items are checked against causes. The causes themselves are checked against inspection items. Standards decided on at the planning stage are also sometimes called direct check items. All of these are important.

7. Quality evaluations are also control items and should be included in quality reports for management.

In doing all of this, do not forget that some kind of quality control is necessary for the very process of following through on each of these steps. In other words, the channels of communication for quality control need to be institutionalized and managed properly. The fact that it is seldom possible to have enough time

Name of process	Process chart	Control items			Sampling means	Measurement means	Data representation	Control means	
		Quality	Amount	Cost				Who	How
		Moisture content	Weight: kg	Electrical power	Random from each lot $n = 5$ $\sigma_S =$	Infrared drying $\sigma_M =$	$\bar{x} - R$ Control chart	Section leader	See Process Control Standard #

Figure 3.2 Part of a QC Flow Sheet

Note: Entries shown here are simply examples, and it is important to draw this up your own way to clarify who does what, where, how, when, and why (the 5-Ws and 1-H).

Job Function	Control point	Control item	Priority	Control documents		Fre-quency	Control policy	
				Document	Author		When	What
Raw material quality assurance	Prevent contami-nation	Error rate on checking material quality	A	Table of control error rates	Head of materials section	Once a week	When exceed parameters	Review checking means
Product quality stabilization	Reduce initial defect rate	Processing time	A	Trouble-shooting table	Head of first production section	Every other week	Whenever more than one day over limit	Hold conference to ensure measures being taken

Figure 3.3 Partial Sample of Control Item Chart for Manufacturing Section Chief

for new product development is all the more reason that each step needs to be properly carried out in a smooth progression. Each step should be completed before moving on to the next step, and this means it is necessary to establish evaluation standards enabling you to decide whether or not the time is right to move on to the next stage.

Another important procedure is to draw up an organization chart showing what each division is doing in quality control. This kind of chart facilitates communication and information exchange among divisions, another reason that control items need to be clarified so that everyone can understand them. Some of the main functions and activities that should be shown in this organization chart are listed below.

standardization	quality design	materials control
quality assurance	demand projection	production planning
inventory control	product research	equipment control
yield control	equipment planning	outsourcing control
personnel control	complaint processing	
cost control	new product development	

Simply drawing up an organization chart of these functions is obviously not enough. It should also be made clear what each division is expected to achieve. For example, a list of quality assurance activities for production and marketing might specify

1. items requiring quality assurance,
2   work required to assure quality,
3. people responsible for quality assurance, and
4. data required for quality assurance control.

Only after each of these has been clarified will it be possible to carry out quality assurance activities.

The kind of quality assurance activity I have outlined here is known as the systems approach. It is common to find quality control activities and duties listed up without any indication of how they interrelate. No matter how much a company may try to apply such a list, it is likely to be disappointed in the results. A chart like that shown in Figure 3.1, on the other hand, takes the functional approach, making it clear what should be done to achieve a given aim. Because people will understand exactly why they are doing something, they will also know whether they have achieved the goal. It is useless to simply list things to be done without explaining their purposes. Furthermore, functional development will ensure that you do not overlook important steps in the process. It is impossible to overemphasize the importance of taking a systematic approach for implementing quality control activities.

3.5   Criteria, Standards, Regulations, and Procedures

3.5.1 Quality Control Paperwork

In implementing quality control it is necessary to establish an organization, set the necessary criteria and standards, and conduct quality control activities paying close attention to these criteria and standards. It is important that the given criteria and standards be closely adhered to. Haphazard application is not going to lead to effective quality control. Quality control is a democratic process in which everyone follows the same rules and principles.

Applying these criteria and standards will require a variety of different documents (control tools). In general, these include reports, memos, requests, inquiries, requests for permits, certifications, notices, applications, replies, and records. Naturally, the form and content of these documents will vary depending on what they are for.

Regulations, for example, should

1. Clarify responsibilities and limits of authority.
2. Define the extent of applicability.
3. Not increase paperwork.
4. Not slow things down.
5. Not be open to different interpretations.
6. Be easy to understand (flowcharts and diagrams are helpful).
7. Clearly state what each document is, its purpose, who should fill it out, and who it should be sent to.
8. Specify a trial period during which problems can be detected and regulations revised.
9. Always be revisable.
10. Specify emergency standards and regulations to be applied in exceptional cases.

Very often the number of documents becomes excessive and they are not filed correctly, such that it becomes difficult to find the right form when it is needed. The care that is to be taken in filing all documents is thus another important facet of quality control.

Regulations should be minimal and easy to understand. Regulations become complicated when people refuse to delegate. As a general rule, it is better to delegate than to insist that top management decide on every single item. In the process, of course, decision-making standards are needed to ensure that decisions are made objectively and that the same decision would be made no matter who made it. In most companies, top management has the final say on everything and decisions are based very much on subjective views. This is a very dangerous situation.

It is also common to find everything left to committee. The only quality control regulations some companies have are those relating to the organization of quality control. There will be some issues, including interdivisional questions, that may have to be handled in committee, but it should not be necessary to get a committee decision on every single quality control item. With accepted standards and regulations, quality control can be conducted smoothly on a daily basis without frequent recourse to committee deliberation. (Although writing all of these regulations down may seem to result in a lot of regulations, it is not the generation of new regulations but the systematic structuring of regulations that already exist informally. And writing them down will often highlight the opportunities for consolidation and fewer regulations.)

A list of standards and criteria, regulations and procedures, and records and reports follows. The names I have chosen are simply the most commonly used and may easily vary from company to company. The list is meant simply as a reference.

1. Criteria and standards: material criteria, semi-finished product criteria, product criteria, equipment criteria, measurement equipment and device criteria, tool criteria, blueprint and diagram criteria, quality standards, design standards, inspection standards, work instructions, technical standards, process control standards, and work standards.
2. Regulations and procedures: organization regulations, quality committee regulations, quality control committee regulations, technical committee regulations, new product committee regulations, research management procedures, technical management procedures, inspection procedures, material procedures, control chart handling procedures, daily scheduling procedures, process procedures, measurement procedures, equipment and machinery control procedures, quality data procedures, criteria and standards control procedures, regulations control procedures, quality analysis procedures, plant testing procedures, process control procedures, outsourcing procedures, defect handling procedures, complaint handling procedures, and tool procedures.
3. Records and reports: control checklist, cause and effect table, analysis checklist, quality control process chart, report on criteria and standards revisions, report on control chart revision, emergency bulletin, request for investigation of abnormality, report on emergencies and abnormalities, analysis plan, request for non-standard processing, report on reactivation after non-standard processing, process abnormalities checklist, request for revison of standards, report on non-standard processing results, complaints form, complaints cause and processing chart, complaints investigation form, complaints decision form, complaints cause and processing report, and monthly complaints processing report.

Not all of these documents are always required. The company must decide which are applicable to its type of business and organization, and should keep its documents as simple as possible. The important thing is that these documents function in a systematic and integrated manner and that they are easy for any and all to understand.

3.5.2 Coordination Problems

1. Standards have to be applied if they are to mean anything. Simply having the standards written down somewhere is not enough. Are all stages of quality control being carried out according to the agreed-upon standards?

Are standards being applied to quality design, work procedures, sampling, measurement, judging abnormal values, and seeking out and correcting abnormalities? Have purchasing, storage, inventory, and supply, production design decisions, inspection, defect handling, product shipment, and marketing all been institutionalized? Everything within and outside of the company — all plans, designs, production, supply, and services — needs to be standardized. Work procedures are not the only things that need to be standardized in setting quality control standards.

2. Standards must meet the following conditions:
    (1) They must apply to specific activities.
    (2) They should leave no room for discretion.
    (3) There should be no leeway for different interpretations.
    (4) They should realistically apply to actual conditions.
    (5) They should cover emergency situations and defective products.
    (6) They should include provisions for abnormal situations.
    (7) They should be written down.
3. By definition, standards are expected to be rational and objective. This means they must be based on careful statistical analyses, not only on experience and subjective assumptions.
4. Are directives issued on a daily basis consistent with company standards? Your standards may not apply to everything and every possible situation. When directives have to be issued, they must not contradict the standards.
5. What provisions have been made for exceptional cases, emergencies, and changes? Regular, daily operations can probably be carried out without standards. It is when something unusual comes up that guidance is needed. Establishing standards for unexpected and emergency situations should be an ongoing process.
6. How do your standards relate to the company organization? Standards must specify what actions are to be taken by which division and at what level of authority. Standards set the limits to responsibility and authority.
7. Regulations should be simple enough for anyone to understand. It is thus better that they be presented in the form of a chart or diagram rather than as a long list.
8. Everyone in the company should know the standards and regulations.
9. Are your standards and regulations being managed effectively? Standards and regulations are never perfect, and will need to be revised over time and as circumstances change. They must be regularly checked and changed as needed.
10. What are the procedures for revising standards and regulations? Are they being changed according to procedures?
11. Has a well-defined system been established for deciding on quality standards for new products? How quickly can this system be put into motion?
12. Regulations and guide manuals for policy management and functional management should also be created.
13. Studies should be done to see if standards and regulations are proving effective.

Schedule / Key activities	Introduction (1st year)	Promotion (2nd year)	Consolidation (3rd year)	Planning for future
1. Start-up organization	Vow to introduce QC Establish TQC headquarters Appoint director for TQC Appoint TQC committee	Vow to aim for Deming Award		Audit by Deming Award Committee
2. Policy control	Analyze current situation Clarify responses in annual and long-term plans			
3. Operational improvements	Review current situation Organize control items	(omitted)	(omitted)	(omitted)
4. Standardization	Review company regulations Review work standards			Organize systematic handling of quality information Use computers

5. Priority quality issues
6. Functional control
  6.1. Quality control
  6.2. Cost control
  6.3. Schedule control
	Record and draft possible solutions
	Get firm grasp on current problems
	Draft flow sheets and activity charts
	(omitted)			

7. Education and dissemination 8. QC circle activities 9. QC activities 10. QC audit	Hold in-house TQC convention Take part in TQC convention President's audit			
Impact	Provides good understanding of current situation Ensures everyone thinking in same directions			
Problems remaining	Analysis of causes of major complaints Solving problems in introducing new products			

Figure 3.4 TQC Promotion Plan

4 The Functions of Quality Assurance

4.1 The Significance of Quality Assurance

4.1.1 Quality Functions

Everything we do that relates to quality is central to quality control, yet our efforts should be directed to prevention rather than correction. Figure 4.1 shows the fundamental quality functions.

Quality is not assured through inspection alone. Instead, it requires rational design and the correct implementation of quality control procedures and operations (preventive functions). Quality assurance is investigating to make sure that quality inspection and quality control operations are being carried out correctly and checking design, manufacturing, and marketing divisions to see whether they are all working to maintain the targeted quality level. Finally, quality assurance requires that the findings of these investigations be reported to management.

There is a long tradition of inspecting for defects, but it was not until recently that companies became aware of the need for preventing defects and that true quality control came into existence. Even today, many companies are still insufficiently aware of quality assurance, and this is all too often one of the last aspects of quality control to be applied. However, growing recognition of the importance of quality assurance has led to expanded research on how quality assurance should be organized and implemented, and it is now more widely applied than in the past.

When the objective is to confirm the product's quality, inspections, quality control supervision, and verification of the quality of products that have already been sold (part of product quality supervision) all become important. And since inspections and quality control activities are carried out at the command of top management, reporting back to top management on these activities and the results are also important parts of quality assurance.

Inspection procedures should be designed to confirm that the product is meeting the consumer's use requirements. If your inspections do not do this, the procedures should be revised to check:

1. Customer requirements: those features the consumer requires to use the product.
2. Inspection features: those features the manufacturer guarantees through inspection.
3. Control features: those features that come under process control.
4. Design features: those features incorporated into the product by its designer.

These features are generally stipulated separately, but the fact is that they are closely interrelated and these interrelationships should be made clear so that quality assurance will achieve what it is intended to achieve — top quality products.

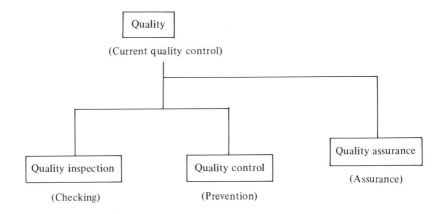

Figure 4.1 Quality Functions

4.1.2 Defining Quality Assurance

First, let us define quality assurance. This may seem unnecessary, since the generally accepted definition of quality assurance is to guarantee product quality, but what, exactly, does guaranteeing product quality entail?

Since the earliest days of mass production, products have been inspected to see if they are accpetable, and inspection has a long history. Gradually there emerged a growing awareness that inspection alone is not enough and that there is a need for preventive quality control. Yet it is only in the last 50 years or so that inspection in the sense of quality control has been practised. More recently, there has developed a need to confirm that quality control and quality inspection are being carried out properly and effectively, and it is the process of verification that is known today as quality assurance.

In the Japanese language, the word *hosho* which is used to mean assurance has homonyms meaning security and compensation. These words are often used interchangeably, even though their meanings are very different. The first *hosho,* meaning assurance, implies confirmation or making sure of something, and this is the term generally used for product guarantees and warranties. Thus the term *hinshitsu hosho* in Japanese has broader application than the English equivalent of quality assurance.

Hosho	security (in the sense of protect)
Hosho	compensation (in the sense of redeem)
Hosho	guarantee (in the sense of contract or promise) assurance (in the sense of verify)

Also in Japan, quality assurance is applied at every step from a product's conception to the day it finally becomes obsolete; from product planning and designing to the making of a prototype, preparing for manufacture, manufacturing, supplying, using, providing maintenance and repairs, and disposing of (collecting and recycling) the product when it has outlived its usefulness. It may therefore be more meaningful to say that quality assurance includes the full range of quality activities. Naturally, these quality activities need to be carried out on a company-wide basis.

Within each step of quality assurance, it is necessary to conduct a quality evaluation to find out whether or not you are ready to move on to the next step. It is also necessary to collect, analyze, and apply quality data and information from both inside and outside of the company.

The following are some of the accepted definitions for quality assurance (the first two of which are in the sense of guaranteeing and the last two of which are in the sense of assuring).

Quality Assurance Guidebook Definition
Quality assurance is the act of ensuring that the product is of such a quality that the consumer can purchase it worry-free and use it for a long time in worry-free satisfaction. [1]

JIS Definition (JISZ8101-1981)
"The systematic activities carried out by a producer to guaranty that the quality required by the consumer is fully satisfied." [2]

---

[1] Asaka, Tetsukazu; and Ishikawa, Kaoru, eds. (1974). *Hinshitsu Hosho Gaido Buku* [Quality Assurance Guidebook], Tokyo: JUSE. p. 3. (in Japanese).

[2] *Japanese Industrial Standard: Glossary of Terms Used in Quality Control,* JIS Z 8101-1981. (1981). Prepared by Japanese Industrial Standards Committee. Tokyo: JUSE. p. 4.

ANSI Definition (ANSI-ZI-7-1971)

"All those planned or systematic actions necessary to provide adequate confidence that a product or service will satisfy given needs."[3]

Juran Definition

"Quality assurance is the activity of providing, to all concerned, the evidence needed to establish confidence that the quality function is being performed adequately."[4]

4.1.3 Inspection

The inspection is just one, not the sole, quality assurance activity.

JIS Definition of Inspection (JISZ8101-1981)

"To judge whether individual article is non-defective or defective by comparing the test result of some sort of means with a quality criterion, otherwise to judge whether each lot is acceptable or not by comparing with an acceptability criterion."[5]

If every single product is tested and found to satisfy the appropriate quality standards, and if every single defective product can be repaired to make it meet these quality standards, then the consumer is certain to get a good quality product. But in actuality, it is highly questionable whether

1. it is possible to perform infallible tests,
2. the quality standards are always appropriate and meaningful,
3. judgments are always correct, and
4. defective products can be effectively reworked.

Even if you could guarantee that there are no problems on any of these points, it costs money to conduct inspections and rework defective products. As is clear from the axiom that "quality must be built into the product," if the causes of defects can be eliminated in the design and manufacturing stage, inspections can be rendered unnecessary and it becomes possible to supply the consumer with quality products at reasonable cost. The purpose of inspection is to eliminate the need for inspection. This is what is meant by preventive functions that will prevent the occurrence of defective products, and this is why quality control has become so important.

4.1.4 Standards for Judging Quality

There are instances in which customer complaints still come in even though

---

[3] *American National Standard, Quality Systems Terminology.* Approved January 18, 1979, Revision of ASQC A3 − 1971 (ANSI Z1 − 1971), Milwaukee, Wisconsin: American Society for Quality Control. p. 3.

[4] Juran, Joseph M. (1974). *Quality Control Handbook.* 3rd ed., New York: McGraw-Hill. pp. 2-23.

[5] JUSE (1981). op. cit. p. 57.

the inspections are being performed faultlessly. Obviously the inspection items and the standards against which product quality is being judged are either inadequate or inappropriate. Some manufacturers decide on what they will look for in an inspection in complete disregard of the actual quality features (use features) that the consumer requires of the product. In such cases, a comparison of the complaints and the items designated for inspection will soon show that the inspection items are inadequate or inappropriate.

It is also common to find inspection standards that have no relationship to the conditions under which the product is likely to be used. For example, a certain product may get very hot when it is used and yet the manufacturer does not bother to inspect it under high-temperature conditions. This is clearly another case of inspection error.

4.1.5   Repairing Defective Products

All inspection does is separate the defective products from the acceptable products prior to shipment. As quality assurance, it is limited to that particular moment in the product's life cycle. The discovery of one defective product in a lot suggests that all the products in that lot are also potentially defective. A product may be perfectly acceptable when it undergoes inspection, but because it contains the potential defect, you never know when it will break down. As I will point out later in my discussion of product liability, even if a product passes inspection, it may prove defective in use and may thus eventually lead to trouble with the customer and even a suit for damages.

Even when a defective product is repaired before shipment, this repair seldom goes beyond a superficial correction of a single part. In general it is impossible to fully repair a defective product. Defects discovered in such "repaired" products have often led to product liability disputes.

4.1.6   The Range of Quality Assurance Activities

Quality assurance covers everything from product planning to application, maintenance and repair, and disposal. Quality assurance activities, therefore, must clearly define what is to be done at each stage to guarantee quality throughout the product's life cycle (in other words, define the quality functions), effectively implement these functions, and review what has been done so that all quality control functions can be revised as necessary.

Quality assurance covers not only quality control activities within divisions but also among divisions (cross-functional management).

It is also important to make it very clear how all of these activities and functions will be supervised and managed, including product design, quality transmission, and quality measures. I will go into these items in greater detail later. Here it is sufficient to list those items required to assure quality.

1. Designing quality: deciding on the quality required for new products and

new product types, and establishing, revising, and eliminating criteria.
2. Purchasing and storing materials: materials control inventory control.
3. Standardization.
4. Analyzing and controlling manufacturing processes.
5. Inspection and processing of defective products.
6. Complaint processing quality supervision, and quality inspection.
7. Equipment and installation management: constructing and installing equipment, preventive safety measures, measurement procedures.
8. Personnel management: placement, education, and training.
9. Management of outsourcing and subcontracting.
10. Technology development: new product development, research management, and technology management.
11. Diagnosis and supervision: auditing quality control activities and supervising quality control operations.

In the past, quality assurance consisted primarily of procedures designed to verify product quality prior to shipment. Today, however, quality assurance has changed from seeing that a product has been made according to specifications to checking on how the product is being made and how it is used and serviced after it has been sold. Quality assurance must now also extend to ensuring the product's reliability since, except for those few products that are intentionally designed to be disposable, products are also required to be durable.

Defective products have become a major social problem over the past couple of decades, and quality assurance that does not take the company's liability for product quality into account is meaningless today. I will discuss product liability in the next chapter.

4.2 Important Quality Assurance Functions

Once this is realized, it soon becomes clear that the main important quality assurance functions are:

1. Creating and developing a quality control policy.
2. Establishing a quality assurance policy and quality assurance standards.
3. Devising and implementing a quality assurance system.
4. Spelling out the quality assurance procedures for each stage of quality control.
5. Quality evaluations for each stage.
6. Assuring design quality.
7. Recording important quality problems and analyzing them.
8. Clarifying the important quality assurance functions for production and post-production quality control.
9. Making sure all quality assurance activities that are performed during production are fully understood.
10. Carrying out quality inspections and processing complaints.
11. Conducting quality control on product labeling and instruction manuals.
12. Product quality inspections and quality assurance system supervision.

13. Collecting, analyzing, and using quality data.

These functions will be further discussed in Chapters 11 and 12, but it is well worth devoting the remainder of this section to describing some of the major functions.

4.2.1 Creating and Developing Quality Policies

A company must consider consumer requirements and whether or not it has the technological and manufacturing capabilities to meet these requirements before it goes on to make design quality, production, supply, or other new product decisions. And once these decisions have been made they should be conveyed in clear, detailed language to all employees concerned. Traditionally, these kinds of decisions have been left up to just one or a few designers and technicians, but such decisions concern the whole company and top management, more than anyone else, should be responsible for making them.

4.2.2 Establishing Quality Assurance Policies and Standards

In one European country, Japanese automakers have gained a reputation for making repairs even faster than domestic automakers, most probably because the manufacturer of the Japanese car considers this kind of maintenance and repair service an integral part of its quality assurance policy. Top management's policies are always important.

Yet absolute quality, admirable though it is as a general policy, may prove prohibitively expensive as a manufacturing proposition. Thus the decision, for example, on whether a washing machine should be built to last for 10 years or 15 years must be a conscious management policy decision based on careful study of the relevant factors, and it is not a decision to be left up to the product designers.

Likewise, deciding on what kind of maintenance and repair services to offer and how to provide the necessary quality assurance are also decisions that should be made at the management level.

4.2.3 Devising and Administrating Quality Assurance Systems

Some system is required if effective quality assurance is to be achieved and the functions outlined above fulfilled. At the same time it is important to devise an effective way of administrating this system so that quality can be guaranteed for every process and every type of product at every stage.

4.2.4 Assuring Design Quality

At the design stage, technology is applied with the goal of meeting the established quality assurance standards. Quality design should strive to conform to these quality assurance standards, and it is important here to develop substitute technical characteristics to measure how closely the product meets consumer requirements and to clarify the relationship of parts quality to finished product quality (quality development and quality analysis). Recently there has been considerable emphasis on the need to conduct design reviews at the design stage.

Design reviews were already a part of the quality evaluation conducted at each quality control step, but it has not always been clear how, exactly, such reviews should be made. Design reviews are also important from the perspective of assuring product safety, and there is a need to specify and implement effective procedures for carrying out this important function. Once design quality has been decided upon, it is important to remember to confirm that the company's production system is capable of producing this quality within the manufacturing process. I emphasize this because companies that implement QC with only an imperfect understanding of it tend to ignore their own manufacturing limitations when they design new products. We are talking here not about the production capacity but about the level of quality that can be achieved with the company's manufacturing system.

4.2.5   Recording and Analyzing Important Quality Problems

Product defects that may prove dangerous to the user and chronic defects that may not be noticeable but could lead to major losses for the company are extremely important quality problems requiring immediate attention. These kinds of problems should be recorded as soon as they come up, and every effort should be made to ensure that they are solved as quickly as possible.

4.2.6   Clarifying the Important Quality Assurance Functions for Production and Post-production Quality Control

An important function at the manufacturing stage is analyzing and correcting problems that showed up in trial production and in preceding production processes. Routine QC activities, particularly inspection, provide this kind of quality assurance in daily production. There are companies that conduct check-point inspections, in addition to their routine QC activities, for important assurance items. Assuring production capability is vital to assuring product quality, an issue I will discuss in greater detail in Chapter 12.

There are numerous opportunities for things to go wrong in the packaging, storing, shipping, selling, and assembling processes. Accordingly, it is necessary to establish standards for each and every step within these processes. Standards should also be checked to make sure that they are meaningful for the product in question. This kind of pre-checking is an important quality assurance step, and one that should not be overlooked.

4.2.7   Making Sure All Quality Assurance Activities that are Performed during Production are Fully Understood

Virtually every company today promotes quality control in manufacturing, from materials delivery to product shipment, but there are often disparities among the quality levels designated for each manufacturing process and among the actual QC implementation capabilities. There is thus no guarantee that the intended level of quality control is being performed at every single stage of production.

At some factories, a quality assurance circle headed by the plant manager may check on quality controls for each process, shore up areas where quality control is weak, correct abnormalities, and otherwise keep tabs on quality control activities for all manufacturing processes to ensure that manufacturing quality will be maintained throughout every line. This is also part of effective quality assurance.

4.2.8 Carrying out Quality Inspections and Processing Complaints

Complaints about quality (including latent complaints that may never be voiced) indicate that quality assurance is inadequate. The manufacturer should constantly be conducting research to find out whether consumers have found its products satisfactory and, if not, where the dissatisfaction exists. This research should be accompanied by efforts to immediately correct any quality problems that may be discovered. Should the product prove clearly defective, the manufacturer should recall it and otherwise do everything in its power to rectify the situation.

4.2.9 Quality Control on Product Labelling and Instruction Manuals

A product may meet all quality requirements but prove unsatisfactory in the market because improper labelling or unclear instruction manuals lead to improper use. Making certain that the quality standards for labels and all explanatory materials are just as high as those for the product itself is thus an important part of quality assurance. This is especially significant in product liability cases.

4.2.10 After-sales Service

No matter how good a product is, it will eventually deteriorate with use. Breakdowns will be more likely the more often it is used and the older it gets. Ensuring that the company is set up to provide after-sales inspections, maintenance, and repair service is also a part of quality assurance. Shortcomings here can be extremely serious, as in the case of a customer who died as a result of improper repairs to a microelectric oven.

4.2.11 Product Quality Inspections and Quality Assurance System Supervision

I have described just a few of the functions that are vital to quality assurance. Recognizing the necessity of these functions, providing systems for carrying them out, and implementing them will, for the most part, guarantee that the consumer gets the quality he is looking for.

Even when a product has passed inspection prior to shipment, there is still the possibility that it may be transformed into a defective product by the time it reaches the consumer. It is thus necessary to find out whether the customer has received the product in good shape. If he has not, each of the functions outlined above should be checked to see where the proper quality assurance system failed. Once the problem point is located, action needs to be taken to ensure that the same mistake does not recur. This is the process of conducting a product quality audit.

It is also necessary to check whether the whole quality assurance system is appropriate and whether it is being implemented properly. This is done by conducting a quality system audit which not only entails getting a firm grasp on quality assurance as a whole but extends to judging the appropriateness of all of a company's quality control activities.

4.2.12 Collecting, Analyzing, and Using Quality Data

The consumer's quality requirements are constantly changing with the introduction of new technologies and the diversification and upgrading of life styles and living standards. While the basic principle of quality assurance remains the same, the actual quality assurance activities will necessarily change. What is right for quality assurance today may not be right tomorrow.

Not only consumer requirements but materials, production equipment and facilities, and work processes can all be expected to change and improve. Likewise, the way the consumer uses the product may change at any time. Obviously, design quality must change accordingly.

Quality needs to be constantly improved, but it is just as necessary to make sure that quality never deteriorates. How often have I heard complaints about a product that proved totally unusable because it had not been shipped or stored properly. Its quality had been allowed to deteriorate through mere carelessness.

To keep quality assurance activities consistent with changing quality requirements, it is imperative that you collect up-to-date and correct quality information and data and make changes based on careful analyses of these data. With the advances in computer technologies, computers have helped to speed up quality data acquisition and application, and computer-aided quality control (CAQC) is attracting considerable attention these days.

A system must be devised for the efficient and effective collection, analyses, and application of quality data. This is described in more detail in Section 4.5.

4.3   The Quality Assurance System

It is most important that quality control be performed at every stage in the product's life, from its first conception to the end of its life cycle, in line with this basic concept of quality assurance functions if the ultimate goal of quality assurance is to be achieved. Several factors must be considered here.

I have already discussed what has to be done to ensure product quality and how it should be administered in Section 3.4, and will describe the quality assurance procedures for each stage in a product's life in Chapters 11 and 12.

Quality assurance is an interdivisional concern. In complaint processing, for example, the marketing division receives the complaint, the inspection division checks on the product's inspection results and its manufacturing processes, and the design division checks for design quality problems and makes revisions where necessary so that the problem does not recur. This kind of interdivisional activity and its administration comes under cross-functional management. Quality assurance is one aspect of cross-functional management. For a discussion of the significance of cross-functional management and top management's role, refer back to Section 2.3.2.

Within a single division, the division head can make sure that everyone participates in any given activity, but in interdivisional or cross-functional activities, there must be prior agreement on what is to be done, how, when, and by whom. In other words, a system is required.

One of the marketing division's responsibilities is to convey the market requirements immediately and accurately to the design division. Yet many marketing divisions are not even aware that they should be doing this sort of thing. Even when the head of the design division asks for customer feedback, he does not have the authority to command the marketing division head, his equal, to get the kind of information he so badly needs. As a result, getting information on customer quality requirements and conveying this information to other divisions should be formally incorporated into the marketing division's duties as a part of its quality assurance activities. It should also be specified how this information is to be conveyed from the marketing division to the design division. If this is done, the result is an interdivisional system for quality assurance. Of course, effective means of managing this system must also be devised.

Normally, a quality assurance system diagram will show the customer, top management, and individual divisions on the horizontal axis and each section of the PDCA circle on the vertical axis. This kind of diagram, however, still does not show what has to be done. For this, you need a chart of quality assurance activities.

Figure 4.2 is an example of a quality assurance diagram and Figure 4.3 shows a quality assurance activities chart.

In setting up a quality assurance system make certain that:

1. The route for information feedback is clearly outlined.
2. Development steps are listed on the vertical axis and the relevant activities for each step on the horizontal axis. It should be clear who or which division is responsible for each activity.
3. Procedures and tools (devices and documentation) and operation rules (criteria and standards) are specified.
4. The items to be evaluated and how they are to be evaluated before going on to the next step in the quality assurance process are specified.
5. The system is revised periodically as everyone becomes more experienced in its application.

A function policy is required for effective cross-functional management. For example, as already discussed, it is necessary to specify the important points and assurance standards (such as how long the product's effective life should be) for each product for quality assurance. Too often, policy management has been limited to top-down management within the confines of a single division and without the kind of interdivisional cooperation that cross-functional management is actually all about. Along with this, it is also important in quality assurance to

Company-wide Total Quality Control

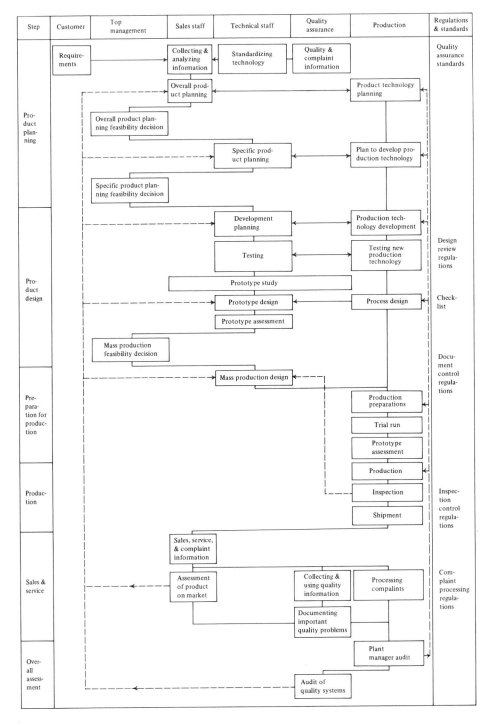

Step	Customer	Top management	Sales staff	Technical staff	Quality assurance	Production	Regulations & standards
Product planning	Requirements	Overall product planning feasibility decision / Specific product planning feasibility decision	Collecting & analyzing information / Overall product planning / Specific product planning	Standardizing technology	Quality & complaint information	Product technology planning / Plan to develop production technology	Quality assurance standards
Product design		Mass production feasibility decision	Development planning / Testing / Prototype study / Prototype design / Prototype assessment			Production technology development / Testing new production technology / Process design	Design review regulations / Checklist
Preparation for production			Mass production design			Production preparations / Trial run / Prototype assessment	Document control regulations
Production						Production / Inspection / Shipment	Inspection control regulations
Sales & service		Assessment of product on market	Sales, service, & complaint information	Collecting & using quality information / Documenting important quality problems		Processing compalints	Complaint processing regulations
Overall assessment				Audit of quality systems		Plant manager audit	

Figure 4.2 Quality Assurance Diagram

| Step | | Assurance activity | Implementation measures | Person responsible | Relevant regulations | Notes |
Large	Small					
Pre-par-ation for pro-duc-tion	Evalua-tions	Assess production quality in terms of target quality and target cost	Assess suitability of production quality	Plant manager		
		Decide on feasibility of full-scale production	Decide on pro-duction quality feasibility	Plant manager		
Pro-duc-tion	Indi-vidual pro-cesses	Decide on feasibility of full-scale production	Assess production prototype and ensure feedback on standard parts	Head of division concerned		
		Ensure stable quality for materials and parts purchased from outside suppliers	Training to enable main suppliers to maintain quality	Head of purchasing		
			Receiving inspec-tions at appropriate quality levels	Head of quality assurance		
		Maintain stable product quality	1. Control processes with work stand-ards, QC process charts, control charts, etc. 2. Train workers 3. Analyze processes and enter improve-ments on work standard charts 4. Maintain process capability 5. Treat deviations and prevent recurrence 6. Conduct priority control of crucial parts and processes	Head of production		
			1. Analyze and solve priority quality problems 2. Do measure-ment controls 3. Maintain quality despite changes in design, process, and suppliers	Head of quality assurance		
			Plant and equip-ment controls	Production technology chief		
	In-spec-tion	Assess suitability of finished product quality	1. Inspect character-istics, functions, and finish 2. Train inspectors 3. Separate out defectives	Head of production		

Figure 4.3 Sample Quality Assurance Activities Chart (Partial)

designate who is responsible for what. If necessary a quality assurance committee can be established.

This quality assurance committee would:

1. Prepare drafts of quality assurance diagrams and activity charts.
2. Investigate current quality assurance activities and revise the system as needed.
3. Establish criteria and standards for quality assurance.
4. Perform product quality inspections and administer the quality assurance system.

It is impossible to show everything in a single quality assurance diagram. Work flow and management methods will vary for a new product, a simple model change, and for different product types, and it may be possible to skip some steps in simple model changes. Cross-functional management should thus be flexible enough to change its quality assurance diagrams and activity charts to suit them to each situation, but the reasons for allowing certain steps to be skipped should always be made clear.

Carrying out quality assurance effectively means making sure that there is adequate feedback on the results of such activity and that plans and procedures are revised in line with this feedback. Yet when you listen to reports on quality assurance programmes, all you are likely to hear is a description of a particular quality assurance system with no explanation of whether the system is working effectively or how it has been revised. It is impossible to judge a quality assurance system unless you know where there have been problems and how they have been resolved. In other words, the PDCA circle needs to be applied.

It is also important to realize that feedback can come through several channels. Where such feedback comes from and where it goes to should be clearly shown on the quality assurance diagram. Checking a quality assurance diagram against actual operations, you are likely to find that things are not being carried out the way the diagram says they should be — or you are just as likely to find that no clear channels have been established for passing on feedback from its source to the people who can do something about it. This is quality assurance in name only and, not being practised, it will naturally be ineffective and very likely allow defective products to get through.

Cross-functional management in quality control includes quality assurance activities (Q), cost control (C), and production or delivery volume control (D). Each of these consists of operations that are carried out in a step-by-step process. Problems arise when these are managed separately without allowing for their interrelationship — without a comprehensive control system. Costs cannot be reduced except in close conjunction with quality assurance.

The quality assurance diagram is a pictorial presentation of work procedures and their sequence. At each step there should be a quality evaluation system (including inspection) and a quality information system to disseminate quality data and knowhow.

You only get a really effective quality assurance system when you have

1. a quality assurance work procedure system,
2. a quality evaluation system, and
3. a quality information system.

4.4   Quality Evaluation System

Quality evaluations are made for two reasons: to check whether it is possible to go on to the next step and to find out what revisions have to made at the present quality level. As with quality assurance operations, quality evaluations must be administered and the evaluation system changed whenever it may seem necessary.

Quality evaluations are done for:

1. Product planning.
2. Newly developed products.
3. Test results on newly developed products.
4. Prototypes.
5. Test mass production results.
6. The final decision to mass produce.
7. Product inspection.
8. Commercial quality and consumer responses.
9. System supervision.

Items (2) through (4) are carried out as a part of design review.

Quality evaluations are made using check lists, and care should be taken that use characteristics (also known as functional characteristics) and their substitute characteristics have been clearly defined in the process of quality development before they are applied as evaluation criteria.

4.5   Quality Information System

The following kinds of information are required for quality assurance:

Information for quality planning (including quality design).

Information on usefulness, use characteristics, production capability, and complaints.

Information on product liability and safety.

Information on product reliability — time (e.g., mean time before failure), lifespan (e.g., downtime), and application probabilities (e.g., the likelihood of user mistakes).

Quality information also includes any kind of information useful to practical administrative management or policy management. Since good quality is in the consumer's interest, any kind of information that will clarify the burden that poor quality imposes on the consumer is important to effective quality management. This kind of information comes under user quality costs (see Chapter 9).

Yet quality information is by no means limited to quality characteristics. All cost, volume, and delivery (CVD) information is quality information.

Of course, quality information has to be applied to mean anything, but before it can be applied it needs to be processed (categorized, put into a systematic format, analyzed, and evaluated), stored, and disseminated. It should also be kept in mind that you are not collecting and processing information simply for the sake of collecting and processing information. Your purpose is to get that information to the people who can use it, and this means you need to know who needs what kind of information.

A quality assurance diagram should be drawn up to help construct an effective quality information gathering and dissemination system. This diagram should show exactly how what information is to be transmitted among divisions and should indicate feedback channels. Among the various kinds of quality information charts are:

1. A chart showing who is responsible for information application at each step in the quality assurance system. How information is to be gathered, transmitted, and analyzed should be spelled out at each step, and it should be made clear who is responsible for making decisions using this information.
2. A chart showing the sources of information and how quality information is being applied. The kinds of information and their sources include

   Quality information on parts and materials from outside the company: supplied by affiliated companies and suppliers.

   Quality information on parts and materials from inside the company: acquired in the design stage and obtained at the time parts and materials are delivered.

   Quality information on markets: acquired upon delivery and during production processes and gathered from retail outlets and sales offices.
3. A chart showing quality information channels for normal and emergency situations.

Which of these charts will prove most useful will depend on the degree to which your company uses quality information. In addition to these charts, standards and regulations need to be established and the tools for transmitting and using quality information need to be specified.

By applying the quality information system this way, you will be better able to pinpoint problems and correct them at their source. The system is an excellent way to supervise quality activities. Just do not forget that the system itself must also be supervised.

5 Product Liability

5.1 The Consumer Costs of Defective Products

While it is important that the product meets its intended usage requirements, meaning that it be an effective product, it is also axiomatic that no product, no matter how useful and convenient, is any good if it endangers its intended user. Despite this, the newspapers are filled with stories every day of consumers injured or endangered by ordinary consumer products, and this is rapidly becoming a major social problem. Even when the person has had expert training and extensive experience in using the product, product defects can easily take a major toll in lives and property, as in the case of a pilot attempting to fly a flawed airplane, and there is no reason to expect the ordinary consumer to do any better with defective products in the home. Those few corners that the manufacturer cuts can be the ones that kill his customers.

Some of the factors contributing to the rise in product liability cases are:

1. With the scarcity of expert help, products that were once used only by trained experts are now increasingly used by novices in the home.
2. With the increasing sophistication of the market and the fierce competition among companies, new products and new models are coming onto the market with instruction manuals that the ordinary consumer can just barely understand, and most people cannot possibly hope to understand all the technical quality and maintenance details.
3. Market competition among companies is leading some companies to emphasize appearance rather than functional quality.
4. There are many products such as pharmaceuticals that, while highly efficacious if taken properly, can be dangerous or even deadly if abused.
5. The shift to mass production and cost-cutting may mean the products are put on the market even though they are marginally defective.

6. With the flood of new products being produced, it is impossible for the regulatory agencies to monitor quality adequately.

This problem of product quality is especially important with products used by the general public, such as ordinary home consumer goods, rides and other machinery at amusement parks, and even the vending machines at train stations and other public places. These products, referred to as consumer products, are the focus of governmental safety and liability efforts.

In the United States, this movement found expression in the passage of the Consumer Product Safety Act of 1972, and the establishment of the Consumer Product Safety Commission to formulate safety regulations under the provisions of this law. In line with these efforts, the National Electronic Injury Surveillance System has been established in Washington to monitor reports of consumer injuries and to set priorities for consumer safety regulatory work. This NEISS has installed computer terminals in 119 emergency wards nationwide and is now able to update injury statistics daily. At present, the NEISS receives approximately 400,000 injury reports a year, and it is estimated that there are about 9 million consumer injuries annually. In especially important cases, the government conducts interviews and other fact-finding activities, and the Consumer Product Safety Commission issues monthly reports on injuries to children and other important injury categories.

While there is no institutional compilation of data on consumer injuries in Japan, some inkling of the situation can be obtained from data on record at the Japan Consumer Information Center and the local consumer centres. More and more consumers are taking their problems and complaints to these centres every year, and it is estimated that approximately half of the 150,000 complaints filed every year have to do with quality functions, safety, and health. In 1968, the Basic Law for Consumer Protection went into force, and this was soon followed by the Consumer Product Safety Law in 1973. Shortly thereafter, the Product Safety Association was founded and went to work drawing up safety standards and creating a readily identifiable mark that manufacturers could attach to products to show that they had passed safety inspection.

Companies are also becoming increasingly aware of the need for enhanced product safety, but the situation in Japan still lags somewhat behind that in some countries where companies designate product safety managers and require their approval for all design and production plans.

5.2 Product Liability Responsibility

Product liability refers to the fact that the manufacturer may be required to provide indemnification for property damage, commercial losses, or personal injury resulting from product defects. As such, it has also been called manufacturer liability or product responsibility.

Although the social and legal climate regarding product liability varies widely from country to country and from year to year, it is worth reviewing some of the salient developments to date. Generally, the tendency is toward broader interpretation of the manufacturer's responsibility and larger liability claims.

5.2.1 Product Liability in the United States

American product liability law and practices are probably among the strictest anywhere in the world, and it is thus useful to look first at the United States. Among the more conspicuous features:

1. There has been a sharp increase in the number of product liability suits, and there are now scores of thousands of cases per year. In fiscal 1985, for example, there were 13,554 product liability suits filed — a 370% increase over the past decade.
2. At the same time, there has been a sharp increase in settlement value. Even in tort law, punitive damages have been levied in the case of particularly gross offenses. Class actions are also on the increase, meaning that a single injured party can bring a case on behalf of all victims and the manufacturer who loses a class action is forced to pay similar damages to all parties to the suit. Punitive damages are being assessed in an increasing number of cases and in even-larger amounts. Fiscal 1985's average award of $1,850,452 was a 270% increase over the average for fiscal 1984, and there were over 400 cases in fiscal 1984 with judgements in excess of $1,000,000 dollars (vs only 24 ten years ago).
3. While the manufacturers are defendants in most of these product liability suits, there is a tendency to sue everyone involved, including retail outlets.
4. The scope of product liability suits is broadening from design and production defects to include packaging, labelling, and even manuals or other product information.
5. Although it used to be possible for manufacturers to escape liability for unavoidable design and production problems by labelling the product clearly, clear labelling, while still obviously required, no longer offers any immunity. Design problems are increasingly at issue, and it is not uncommon for design people to be asked to testify in court.
6. Product liability insurance has become almost prohibitively expensive, and many smaller companies are now forced to self-insure or to go without product liability insurance.
7. Manufacturers are now being held responsible for the product's safety not only under normal usage but in all conceivable usage situations.
8. Whereas product liability suits used to be restricted to consumer products, industrial products now account for over half of all suits. Injuries suffered in the course of one's work, of course, are covered by workmen's compensation, but, in view of the generally low ceiling on workmen's compensation settlements, more and more workers are rejecting that route and turning instead to product liability suits.
9. There is no generally recognized limit on the warranty period for product laibility suits, and some manufacturers have been sued over products that

they made more than 20 years previously. However, there is a growing awareness of this problem and many states have moved to legislate a limit on liability (usually ten years or so).

10. However, despite this spate of suits and the widening definition of product liability, the courts do sometimes decide that the risk was unavoidable or unknowable given the state of the art at the time. Likewise, courts take the risk: benefit ratio into account in deciding awards, and companies have been found blameless when the benefits derived from the product's manufacture far outweigh the risks entailed in its use.

11. Even if the product is manufactured, packaged, and sold in accordance with government regulations, the company can still be held liable for injury or other damages.

As may be seen, companies are held strictly accountable for product liability in the United States, and there have been a number of companies that have gone bankrupt in the face of widespread or particularly expensive claims. Because it is generally thought that manufacturers should build safety into their products even if it does mean they have to charge a little extra to compensate for these product liability prevention costs, manufacturers are expected to be able to compensate consumers for damages. However, this process can backfire on the consumer if the safety standards are so high that they result in prohibitively expensive products.

There are thus moves in the United States to correct the excesses of product liability litigation, and the product liability crisis has attracted considerable attention in recent years. In April 1976, President Ford signed an executive order creating a federal task force of people from 10 different executive agencies to study product liability, and this task force's recommendations, submitted in November 1977, then became the basis for the Uniform Product Liability Law. This Law represented an attempt to formulate uniform federal product liability standards (replacing the patchwork of sometimes-contradictory state regulations), to enable corporations to take out product liability insurance, to ensure that victims are able to get appropriate compensation, to encourage companies to place a higher priority on product safety, and to streamline the judical process.

However, the product liability crisis continues unabated, with sharp increases in the numbers of cases and the amounts of awards. In October 1985, a working group of officials from the 10 executive agencies was convened to study the situation. This group's report, issued in March 1986, then became the basis for the Product Liability Reform Bill of 1986 submitted in April 1986 to correct abuses in eight areas.

5.2.2 Product Liability in Europe

There are fewer product liability cases and the settlements are less expensive in Europe than in the United States. Whereas the product liability problem goes well beyond the purely legal aspects to also encompass product liability insurance, workmen's compensation, the judicial system, the tax system, and product safety technology in the United States, it is largely limited to the legal effort to coordinate and unify the different countries' laws and regulations in Europe.

Seeking to ensure greater legal uniformity among the Community's 12 members, the EC Commission drew up a directive on product liability law that was then formally adopted by the Council of Ministers on July 25, 1985. This directive provides no-fault liability for all products (excepting raw agricultural products and livestock) and sets liability limits for the different classes of damages. It is expected that the EC member countries will bring their domestic legislation into line with this directive within three years.

In January 1977, the 21-nation Council of Europe announced its draft of a product liability protocol. Under the draft as it currently stands, it is to come into force if ratified by three member states, and parties to the protocol are expected to bring their domestic laws and regulations into line with the protocol within six months of ratification.

5.2.3 Product Liability in Japan

While there have not been that many product liability cases in Japan, those there have been have entailed very large sums of money. The first major product liability case was in 1955, when there were 12,000 poisonings and 131 fatalities when the stabilizer in baby formula produced by the Morinaga Company was found to be arsenic-contaminated. Other major cases were the thalidomide cases that emerged around 1960 and the 1968 group actions brought against Kanemi Soko for its manufacture of mercury-contaminated edible oil. In the late 1960s, there was increasing recognition of the need for some legal framework for consumer protection, and the Basic Law for Consumer Protection was enacted in 1968.

Although there is not a very large body of case law on product liability in Japan, Japanese manufacturers have good reason to tread very carefully in this field, both because of the increasing number of cases in Japan and because export products are subject to the laws and regulations of the countries where they are used. Product liability protection is thus an urgently important part of product quality. Although many companies have tended to try to keep their product liability claims in the closet and to pretend that this is not a serious area of concern, product liability is clearly one of the most important areas of product quality today.

5.3 Legal Considerations in Product Liability

While legal scholars are better positioned to debate the technicalities of product liability law, it is nonetheless imperative that people responsible for product quality and quality control have some awareness of the field. Drawing upon the American experience, this field may generally be divided into the three areas of negligence, warranties, and strict liability in tort law.

5.3.1 Negligence

Under the rules of negligence, the company is liable in the following situations.

1. *Defects in manufacture or workmanship*

   Although it is difficult for the customer to prove cause when the final product is not what was intended due to defects in manufacture or workmanship, it frequently happens that new products are judged defective and the manufacturer held negligent simply by virtue of the problem's arising.

2. *Design defects*

   Every new product is fraught with the danger of defects. As a result, the courts must decide whether the benefits of the product's availability outweigh the risks that it creates (the risk: benefit ratio). Under this criterion, a product is often deemed defective if it is more dangerous than consumers are led to believe. However, pharmaceuticals manufacturers and others may be excused from liability in the case of side-effects and other dangers that they could not foresee or know about, assuming, of course, that the manufacturer has made every effort to learn about such dangers and exercised all due care to avoid them.

3. *Defective labelling*

   The issue of defective labelling arises when the manufacturer or retailer fails to warn the consumer adequately of the dangers that may be encountered in using the product and how to minimize these risks. It is clear that the manufacturer has a responsibility to provide full information about the product and instructions for its safe and proper use. A toaster, for example, should be clearly labelled lest a consumer get burned putting his hand on top of the toaster while it is in operation, and the manufacturer is even expected to include warnings against the more common ways that the product might be misused.

Should manufacturer negligence be proved, the manufacturer is obviously held liable for damages, regardless of whether they arise from faulty manufacture or workmanship, faulty design, or faulty labelling. In seeking damages, however, the plaintiff generally has to prove the following points.

1. That actual injury was suffered.
2. That the injury was caused by the defendant, either willfully or through negligence.
3. That the plaintiff's civil rights were violated as a result.

As may be seen, the manufacturer cannot be held liable for negligence unless the chain of causation between the negligence and the injury can be proved, and this is generally a very difficult proposition to prove. At the same time, it is very difficult for the lay consumer to prove design and manufacturing negligence in the face of contrary testimony by the manufacturer's experts, and this has long been a major impediment to consumer protection.

What is meant here by labelling negligence is the failure of the manufacturer to provide adequate labelling warning the consumer of possible dangers and advising on ways to use the product with minimum risk. When these warnings and instructions are clearly printed on the label, the manufacturer cannot be held responsible for the consumer's failure to read or heed the label. Likewise, the manufacturer is not held liable when contributory negligence (the unsafe misuse of a normally safe product) or the voluntary assumption of risk (using a product that the user knows is defective or unsafe) can be proved.

5.3.2 Warranties

This is the area of explicit or implied contract guarantees that the manufacturer gives to the consumer, and the manufacturer is obviously held liable when the product violates the terms of the warranties. There are two main types of warranties:

1. *Express warranties*

   These are the warranties expressly stated in the instructions for use, catalogues, labels, advertising, or other media, and the manufacturer is clearly liable for their non-performance.

2. *Implied warranties*

   These implied warranties come into play when the product fails to function as it should or is unsuited for the market, regardless of any disclaimers that may or may not be proffered. Examples here would include broken glass in foodstuffs and pharmaceuticals with severe side-effects. Both of these cases are clearly unsuited for the market, the one as a foodsuff and the other as a pharmaceutical, and their discovery would be a violation of implied warranties. Even if the product is flawless, the manufacturer may be held liable if the manufacturer falsely implies that it is suited for a different use from the one it was originally intended for.

5.3.3 Strict Liability in Tort Law

Under strict liability in tort law, a manufacturer may be held liable even when it is impossible to prove causal negligence or breach of warranty. In such cases, the plaintiff must prove:

1. That the seller sold a defective product.
2. That the defective product was the cause of the injury.
3. That there was actual injury.

Even though it may be extremely difficult to prove that the product was defective, the very fact that the incident took place may be taken as prima facie evidence of the defect, as in the case of carbonated beverage bottles that exploded, in which case the mere fact of their exploding is evidence that the bottles were defective. As a result, the law has increasingly tended to favour the plaintiffs and to place a greater burden or proof on the defendants. Because this area does not require the existence of any express or implied warranties, it is possible for the manufacturer to be held liable for injuries suffered by a third party.

Both the EC Commission directive and the Council of Europe protocol have adopted the concept of no-fault liability.

5.3.4   Situation in Japan

In Japan, manufacturers may be held liable for illegal acts (under Articles 709 and 717 of the Civil Code) and contract liability (under Articles 570, 415, and 416 of the Civil Code). However, the tendency in recent years has been to make it easier for consumers to bring product liability suits by easing the rules of evidence for product defects, the casual relation between the defect and the injury, and manufacturer negligence.

In April 1975, a special consumer relief study committee within the Economic Welfare Council's consumer policy division issued a report summarizing two years of study on this issue. In this report, the committee recommended that shortcomings in Japanese product liability law be rectified not with a major overhaul of the Civil Code but rather with the enactment of a new product liability law. Under this proposed new law, the manufacturer would be required to prove non-negligence in cases where it was particularly difficult for the consumer to prove that the manufacturer had acted negligently or illegally, with the expectation that the manufacturer would be held liable unless he was to prove his innocence.

5.4   Product Liability Policy and Product Safety

Product liability policy may be broadly divided into defences against product liability suits and preventive measures against the production of defective products. While the defences are primarily legal, product liability prevention is sub-divisible into engineering and other "hard" measures to employ the best available product safety technology and educational and other "soft" measures to ensure that the product is stored and used safely.

Product liability prevention is not strictly limited to product quality but is a far broader concern embracing legal considerations and the entire range of manufacturer-consumer relations. At the same time, while quality assurance has traditionally focused on preventing recurrence, product liability prevention is concerned with preventing even that first occurrence.

Given this context, the question naturally arises as to what degree of product liability prevention is needed at the corporate level and what standards apply here. Drawing upon my long involvement in this field, including service as chairman of the first Japanese product liability study mission (August 1973), I can only conclude that there are no absolute standards and that the company has to do everything within its power for product liability prevention. At best, there are only rough guidelines on product safety such as those embodied in the safety and durability standards set by the different states in the United States.

Painful though product liability claims may be for the company, the commercial losses, sometimes amounting to over ten times the indemnification, are even more important. Among the various forms of commercial loss are loss of sales, profit deterioration, higher insurance premiums, excessive administrative costs, lost labour, losses arising from failure to meet export inspection standards, lost opportunities from failure to expand markets or increase market share, the costs of recalls, and more.

These costs can ruin a company, and it behooves every company to make every reasonable effort to ensure maximum product safety. Indeed, it would not be remiss to place the highest priority on product safety – including not only upgrading hard technologies but also making improvements in administration and other "soft" areas – even if that means the sacrifice of some immediate economic gain.

5.5   Product Liability and TQC

Never before has it been so important that the company build quality into its products. We are, as it were, on the brink of a new era in product quality, especially since the problems of product liability are not restricted to the manufacturing process alone but extend to planning, design, prototype production, research, and every other area all the way through to sales, maintenance, and final disposal. It is, for the product, a cradle-to-grave concept. While the economic need for company-wide quality control and TQC have long been emphasized, it is impossible for the company to be socially responsible in this new era of product quality unless it makes a total company-wide commitment to build quality and safety into all of its processes and products.

5.5.1   Management's Role in Product Liability

Management therefore needs to ask itself:

1. Do we have a product quality policy defining what kinds of products we want to produce?
2. Do we have a long-term plan for product quality control?
3. Are we getting regular reports on product quality and issuing the appropriate instructions in light of these reports?
4. Are we providing the necessary information and instructions on product safety and pollution prevention to everyone throughout the company?
5. Are we checking not only production processes but even design and other processes to see that the consumer's interests are being served?
6. Are we taking product liability prevention measures? Do we have policies for inspecting products and processes, for foolproofing things, and for ensuring that all safety measures work properly? Are we ready to do recalls promptly if an important defect is discovered? Are we ready to submit material quality reports, and other documentation as evidence if need be?
7. Are we set up to control any problems that may reasonably be anticipated in light of past defects or accidents?
8. Are we fully defect-cost-conscious and aware not only of the repair, disposal, and other costs to the company of defective quality but also of the injury,

maintenance, pollution, and other costs to our customers? Do we have plans to reduce these costs and are they being effectively implemented?

9. Do we have people charged with collecting and analyzing quality data?
10. Are we aware of the corporation's responsibilities to society and are we acting to fulfill these responsibilities (including our responsibility to produce durable and non-polluting products even though consumers may prefer the convenience of disposables)?
11. Are we working not simply to protect ourselves against product liability suits but to develop the new products and new technologies needed to make society better?
12. Does everyone in the company, from the chairman of the board to the lowest labour, take pride in the active effort being made to produce safe, quality products?

5.5.2 Product Liability Policy and Organization

It is imperative that top management stress the importance of product safety and product liability prevention in their quality policies, that they make this emphasis known to all employees, and that they monitor the company's performance to see that these policies are carried out. In the United States, it is not uncommon for top management personnel to be called to testify in product liability cases and to be questioned closely about this. As a result, there is often a director responsible for product liability prevention and a product liability prevention committee within management councils.

It is obviously essential that the product liability prevention committee be able to draw upon people from all divisions throughout the company, including design, production, quality control, servicing, and legal affairs, and the committee itself should be headed by someone from top management reporting directly to the president. Among the main responsibilities of the product liability prevention committee are:

1. Supporting the formulation of product liability prevention policy.
2. Institutionalizing the flow of product liability information.
3. Notifying top management of the need to alter designs, change quality control methods, recall products, and take other product liability prevention activities as the need arises.
4. Getting the information needed to produce safe products.
5. Monitoring company-wide programmes for product liability prevention.
6. Offering guidance and assistance to lower-level product liability prevention committees (e.g., those in the individual plants).
7. Drawing up product liability prevention educational programmes and checking on their effectiveness.

Most Japanese companies that practise company-wide quality control have central QC committees or TQC headquarters to draw up quality control plans and see that they are implemented effectively. These organizations are frequently able to handle product liability prevention as well. At the same time, product liability prevention audits can readily be incorporated as part of the quality control audits done regularly at the better companies.

5.5.3 Consumer Relations

Because product quality is so important, there are a number of consumer organizations that conduct their own product testing and announce the results. At the same time, the mass media have become more aggressive about publicizing defective products and letting people know when something is unsafe. Such activities, valuable in their own right in the cause of consumer protection, can also spur companies to greater product liability prevention activities.

It used to be sufficient for the sales department, upon receiving a complaint, to notify other departments of the problem so that action could be taken to prevent its recurrence and at the same time to see that the dissatisfied customer got a replacement product. Since the sales department is primarily concerned with meeting its sales targets, however, it sometimes happens that the department is lax in processing such complaints and that things are not done as promptly and as thoroughly as they should be. Likewise, because the company does not have any clear-cut policy on handling accidents, the contradictory reactions from different parts of the company exacerbate consumer dissatisfaction. It is thus important that the company be consistently consumer-responsive and that this consumer responsiveness be communicated to consumer organizations and the mass media.

As a result, many companies have taken to establishing consumer relations departments, consumer service centres, and other sections specifically to interface with the market. Some companies have even taken the old public relations department, charged it with liaison with consumer bodies, mass media, community groups, governmental authorities, and other organizations, and renamed it the department of social responsibility.

While such corporate responsibility departments cannot be responsible for the entire job of product liability prevention and customer relations, they can serve a very useful function in (1) making the rest of the company more aware of the need for product liability prevention, (2) ensuring that accidents are dealt with promptly before they develop into major disasters, (3) helping top management make decisions quicker, (4) enabling the company to respond faster, and (5) enhancing the company's reputation for reliability.

The customer relations department is also responsible for coordination with other departments, particularly the sales people, and for publicizing product liability prevention within the company. Its duties include:

1. Collecting information on the activities of consumer groups, research being done in universities and other research institutions, and governmental legislative and regulatory tendencies so that the company can anticipate and avoid problems over pricing policy, defective products, misleading advertising, pollution, criticism or erroneous reports in the mass media, strengthened regulations, and other areas of concern.

2. Creating a central office to respond promptly to questions and complaints from consumers, possibly including, as is done in some department stores, the establishment of a special staff able to conduct product testing and forward the results of these tests to consumer groups and mass media concerned about quality, pollution, and other problems.

3. Establishing the channels of communication with consumer groups and the mass media, providing public information, cooperating with product testing, and attending meetings with these organizations to explain the company's efforts to produce safe, non-polluting, and top-quality products.

4. Coordinating company efforts to take the initiative on governmental regulation, including testifying at hearings and otherwise helping to influence the directions such regulations take.

5. Maintaining close contacts with community and governmental leaders, researchers, scholars, and other opinion leaders.

6. Drawing up brochures and other information that will help the company respond to questions from consumers.

7. Holding seminars and other educational programmes for the rest of the company, subcontractors and distributors, and others concerned about the consumer movement and the company's own consumer responsiveness.

8. Drawing up manuals on crisis-management procedures to be followed in the event of an emergency, product recall procedures, and other quick-response procedures, clarifying the organizational structure for each kind of response, and seeing that everybody knows who is to do what.

5.6   Product Liability and Quality Assurance

Part of the quality assurance effort, quality control has traditionally emphasized producing products that have the functions needed to satisfy customer requirements, and there has been a tendency to slight safety considerations. Quality control has been more concerned with producing products that are easy-to-sell and easy-to-use than it has been with producing products that are absolutely safe.

In automotives, home electrical appliances, and numerous other fields, the target today is to achieve reject rates of less than one in a million. Today, we need the same level of advanced quality assurance activities in ensuring product safety. There are five important points here:

1. While quality control has traditionally placed the emphasis on analyzing the causes of defects and seeking to ensure that they not recur, product liability seeks to prevent problems before even that first occurrence by anticipating the possible causes of defects and correcting them before they happen.

2. Reliability engineering is needed to ensure that the product is problem-free throughout its useful life, but this must also be coupled with production technology and other technologies to explicate the causes of defects.

3. In conducting reliability engineering, it is important that this not be seen simply as quality control but that it be utilized to get at the causes – which means going beyond process analysis to establish the interrelations within and among quality characteristic sets (the relations among the finished product's quality features, the sub-assemblies' quality features, and the components' quality features as well as the relations among the use characteristics, the inspection charactertistics, control characteristics, design characteristics, and more) and assigning weighted importances to these characteristics. The importance of this weighting and quantification of quality characteristics – what I have termed quality analysis – is now beginning to be fully recognized, as are the implementation possibilities of quality deployment.

4. Although QC has traditionally been concerned with production preparations, purchasing, production, supply, and like areas, product liability prevention goes beyond these fields to also include product planning, design, prototype production, research, distribution, advertising, public relations, sales, instructions for use, post-sale service and maintenance, and final disposal in a cradle-to-grave concern for the product throughout its entire life. Just as it is now recognized that the sales and administrative divisions also need to participate in company-wide quality control activities, so do these people need to take an active part in product liability prevention.

5. While the people on the production line and other front-line positions obviously need to make every effort for improvements through their QC circles and other small-group activities, the focus in product liability prevention is on improving and foolproofing tools and work procedures to prevent careless mistakes. The same might just as well be said of administrative mistakes.

Given this, the main activities in advanced quality assurance are:

1. Establishing and deploying quality policy.
2. Explicating quality assurance activities (including drafting quality assurance tables, quality assurance activity charts, and the like).
3. Evaluating quality at every step (including design reviews and the like).
4. Ensuring design quality (such as by deploying required quality characteristics, developing parts, and standardizing technologies).
5. Recording and analyzing important quality problems (quality analysis).
6. Conducting stratification control of important safety parts and important processes.
7. Performing initial flow control.
8. Propagating quality (including the developing of the quality table, the quality assurance table, the table of QC processes, and the table of service quality).
9. Preventing mistakes (foolproofing).
10. Anticipating and heading off trouble (including defects, accidents, high material costs, late deliveries, and more).

11. Managing crises and changes.
12. Clarifying the control points in keeping with daily schedules (such as with PERT).
13. Conducting quality audits, product quality audits, and quality assurance system audits.
14. Collecting and analyzing quality assurance information.

6

Policy Management and Cross-functional Management

Company-wide total quality control has two objectives. One is quality assurance, which is, of course, the primary objective of quality control. The other is establishing a management perspective on quality control and creating what I have called practical administrative management.

Promoting quality control through practical administrative management requires policy management and cross-functional management, i.e., clarifying policies and checking and acting on these policies. This is why it is so necessary to ensure that a company's policies are clearly understood and that there are specific and effective management plans to carry them out.

In our discussions of management's role in Chapter 2, we touched upon the significance of policy management and cross-functional management for total quality control. In this chapter I will go into greater detail on practical applications, albeit at the risk of some repetition.

6.1 Policy Management

6.1.1 Policy Management and Day-to-day Management

Day-to-day management involves the application of the PDCA control circle for the fulfillment of divisional functions (goals).

1. Once a goal is set, the means of achieving this goal must be incorporated in the division's duties. Functional deployment is a useful tool for this specification (see Section 3.4 for a discussion of quality control functions), and functional deployment should be carried out to determine exactly what operations are actually required. Because a number of different things will have to be done to carry out the division's functions, there should be a list of control items for evaluating the degree of effectiveness of these operations and control programme to ensure that they are performed

correctly (setting control standards). Unfortunately, many divisional duty descriptions include activities that serve no purpose in fulfilling the division's stated function.

2. Carry out the divisional operations. Keep track of the division's progress, making sure that it does not fall behind its own schedule.
3. Check the results against the list of control items and take whatever action is necessary when there are problems and deviations.
4. When the division is failing to fulfill its functions even though it is operating in line with its official duties, these duties need to be restated to better suit its functional goal.

Day-to-day management involves maintaining the establishing pattern of operations while also instituting changes when necessary. Day-to-day management is performed at the divisional, sectional, and even the individual levels. At the individual level, for example, there should be control items against which the individual is constantly checking his own performance in a personalized form of quality control. When every individual in the company does this, you have the ideal form of total quality control. In addition, these individuals should seek to standardize procedures so that the wealth of accumulated individual experience can be applied throughout the company.

Policy management involves deployment to ensure that corporate directions, goals, and plans are clearly understood throughout the company, from top management all the way down to the lowest-level employee. It also extends to ensuring that there is a continuous application of the PDCA circle for ongoing evaluations of activities and feedback on policy effectiveness. The ultimate goal of policy management is to break out of conventional moulds and achieve significant progress through analyses of current problems and flexibility in responding to changing circumstances.

Needless to say, policy management is effective only when day-to-day management is being consistently applied.

6.1.2   Focal Points for Policy Management

Setting policies, developing and carrying out their practical applications, reviewing results, and getting meaningful feedback for establishing revised policies requires a clear understanding and effective application of the following important matters.

6.1.2.1 Setting Goals

As already pointed out, you need policies pointing directions and shaping the corporate culture, setting goals, and outlining ways to achieve these goals.

1. The most important thing in setting goals is to define what the company is trying to achieve. This means you have to have a firm grasp on where the company stands at any given moment, have to know where it wants to go, and have to be able to set appropriate goals. In many cases, goals are set willy-nilly without sufficient attention to this kind of groundwork. The result is a long-term plan with no basis in reality and no real grasp of how

various external factors (e.g., discount rates, exchange rates, and commodity prices) may affect progress toward the targeted goal. Thus no one really knows if the policy has proved effective by plan or by accident, and no effort is made to review methods and approaches to see where they can be improved. In establishing a long-term plan, the first step is to clarify the gap between present circumstances and the desired state and then to detail specific methods and tools for closing this gap.

2. It is best if goals can be quantified. A vague directive to improve the quality assurance system does not tell how this should be done and does not even provide any guidelines for judging whether the improvements have been achieved. Even if it is difficult to quantify the goal, you can still set negative goals such as making sure that a certain problem does not recur. Whatever goal you set, it should be set in such a way that everyone will know whether it has been achieved or not.

3. Goals must take into account both what is necessary and what is possible. As noted elsewhere, policies should neither be arbitrary directives nor weak compromises. If a goal is obviously impossible — such as tripling sales at a time of declining sales — no one is going to bother trying to achieve it. Yet it is equally meaningless to set a goal that is too easily attained. Corporate policy should be something that has been understood and agreed upon by everyone in the company at all levels and throughout all divisions. And once a goal is set, every effort must be made to devise and implement effective ways of reaching the agreed-upon end.

4. Conventional goals are no longer sufficient for companies that want to keep up, much less get ahead, in today's harsh business climate. Today there is a need to aim for daring and challenging targets, but there must be at least a 70% probability of achieving such targets if your efforts are not to prove futile. At the same time, it is important not to fall into the trap of thinking you have achieved a lofty goal simply because you have stated it.

5. Doubling sales and increasing profits are natural management concerns, but they are not, in and of themselves, the kind of policy management that is required in TQC. TQC is aimed at getting all employees to work together toward a common goal. More important than corporate profit is consumer benefit — which means product quality. Management that does not include this kind of quality management is not TQC policy management. There must be a quality policy with product quality as its goal.

6.1.2.2 Establishing Priorities in Implementation

Every division must have its own goals. But unless there is clear guidance on how to go about achieving these goals, they will either not be achieved or, even if they are achieved, it will not be clear how they were achieved and how the same happy results can be achieved again. It is not enough to simply set a goal and tell your people to go to it. Following should be kept in mind in this regard.

1. The distinguishing characteristic of quality control is that it involves looking for causes and correcting or changing these causes rather than simply treating

the effects. You begin by pinpointing good and bad effects, finding their various causes (analyses), and ferreting out the most important cause (audits). If the cause and hence the effect have been bad, you find a way to eliminate or correct this cause; and if the cause and its effect have been good, you find a way of institutionalizing it. As the business climate changes, new methods need to be devised to achieve your goals.

2. In general, just as there are several routes to climb a mountain, you will have several methods of attaining the same goal. If you have only devised one approach, you have not studied the situation carefully enough. Out of the several choices available, you must select the one that is most feasible and offers the best chance of success. This is the process of deciding on priorities for implementation. Some companies, unable to decide on which policies are most feasible and hence should have the highest priorities, end up with policy statements that are little more than lists of targets. These lists are worthless or worse.

3. Ambitious policies are challenging because of the high targets they set, but they must be backed up by specific guidelines on how they are to be fulfilled. It is not enough simply to set goals. There has been a tendency in Japan for companies to set bold targets for quality improvement and the elimination of chronic quality problems. In the process these companies have managed to revitalize their corporate cultures to a degree unimaginable to non-Japanese companies unfamiliar with this kind of quality control.

4. Once priorities have been established, it is necessary to answer the 5-Ws and 1-H: who is supposed to do what when where why and how. By answering these questions you will find you have created an implementation programme. In establishing such an implementation programme, it is important to avoid the danger that nobody does anything until just before the deadline, when there is a mad flurry of activity. Such flurries often leave the goals only partly achieved. The programme should be broken down into stages and should be constantly checked, revised, replanned, implemented, checked again, and so forth. Thus you may start out with a survey, then move on to establishing an organization, setting up daily schedules, implementing measures, and analyzing results. Each step should be reviewed before going on to the next step, and the programme should be open to revision at any stage along the way.

6.1.2.3 Mobilization Planning

Policy management requires the participation of employees at all levels in all divisions. In planning how to mobilize everyone, you need to look at the way corporate policies are communicated, deployed, and shaped in discussion, to review and reassess activities, organizations, assignment of responsibilities, and delegation of authority, and to decide on ways to motivate everyone to cooperate toward achieving shared goals. As already pointed out, policy decisions need to have everybody's willing agreement, and they cannot be dictates imposed from on high or willy-nilly compromises that nobody likes. The following are the points to be remembered in mobilization planning.

1. Policy decisions are not easy to convey. When I have asked division directors, section managers, and department heads to explain their company's policies, I have been appalled at how few are able to communicate these policies articulately. And among those few who can state corporate policy, there are wide discrepancies in interpretation. Policies and the reasons for them should be stated clearly in writing and, if possible, explained in special briefing sessions. Time should be set aside at such meetings to allow for ample debate and questions and answers to ensure that there are no misunderstandings. Everyone is prone to interpreting policy statements to suit his or her convenience, and in some cases, people will have their own ideas as to how these policies should be implemented. Some people, for example, may even decide that the way to achieve the goal of lowering costs is to compromise on product quality.

2. In implementing policies there is no excuse for ignoring things simply because they are not listed. Policy statements will only cover the most important matters, but there are many things – the previous year's unachieved targets, for example – that should be worked for even though they are not specifically mentioned. If the division director had to write out every single item that each section was to work on, he would end up with a long, unwieldy list. And even if this were possible, it is better that the policy statement not be too detailed, lest the drafter should appear to be usurping jobs and authority that are not rightfully his.

3. There will be certain policy matters that require cooperation from other divisions. In such cases, there is a tendency to assume a defeatist attitude, complaining that something can't be done because some other division is supposed to be taking care of it and hasn't done anything yet. In working out policies, the first step is to clarify what your own division is supposed to be doing. Once that is done, you need to consider whether your division's failure to do something might not be causing problems for other divisions. Rather than being defeatist and complaining about what other people are not doing, is there anything *you* should be doing that you aren't?

4. QC circle activities should be spontaneous and geared to seeking out and solving the circle's own problems. As such, they need to be distinguished from policy management activities. Nevertheless, there is a natural progression as the QC circle gains experience to move from solving small, localized problems to tackling larger issues that may prove beneficial to the company as a whole. Accordingly, it is advisable for someone in a management position to be able to explain corporate policy to the QC circle and let the circle members chose on their own those themes they find most interesting. As long as the QC circle is a part of TQC, its activities should not be limited to making improvements or saving money. The company side should make every effort to explain what it is trying to do through TQC, but the QC circle should not be used solely to serve management ends. TQC encompasses

activities in which everyone participates to achieve goals that everyone understands and agrees with.

6.1.2.4 Budgeting

Many companies that have policies run into another problem when they fail to set aside money for implementing these policies, or when the budget process takes no account of policy implementation needs. Several proposals should be drafted suggesting ways in which policy can be implemented, and these drafts should include estimations of their effectiveness and of how much they are likely to cost. These proposals should then be reviewed and one selected. Only then will you be able to put your policy management into action.

6.1.2.5 Planning Management

Once a plan has been decided upon, you need to consider what should be done and how different activities will interact, how progress should be managed (stages of progression, scheduling, and revisions), and why the previous year's policy goals were or were not achieved.

Section 3.4 explained why it is important to set up control items for policy management. These control items are not the policy goals. Once measures have been chosen to achieve these goals, plans must be made and carried out for their implementation. The control items are those items against which these implementation activities are checked to see whether implementation is taking place as planned and whether the company's activities are helping to attain its policy goals. The figures that have been established as goals only indicate the final results, by which time it is too late to make revisions and corrections in how things are being done. Plans and activities need to be reviewed at an earlier stage, and this means you need control items. Control items are used to check on the effectiveness of policy measures; if the implementation activities are seen as the causes of the achieved goals, then the control items are checks on the causes to enable you to make the necessary adjustments before their effects are seen. Causes and effects are closely intertwined and it is necessary to distinguish between them. Thus the control items help to identify where action needs to be taken.

Since policy is something that is communicated from the upper positions in the company to the lower positions, control items should also take the same route in the form of job-specific control items charts.

6.1.2.6 Comprehensive Control Planning

Policies include long-, medium-, and short-term policies, divisional policies, functional policies, and project policies. Within functional policies you will have different policies for different goals, e.g., quality policies, cross-functional policies, and quality assurance policies. Sometimes you will not need all of these policies, and they can be set up on an ad hoc basis as needed. More important than trying to establish policies to cover every single eventuality is to devise an effective system of managing and implementing policies.

Figure 6.1 illustrates a policy control circle. In comprehensive control planning,

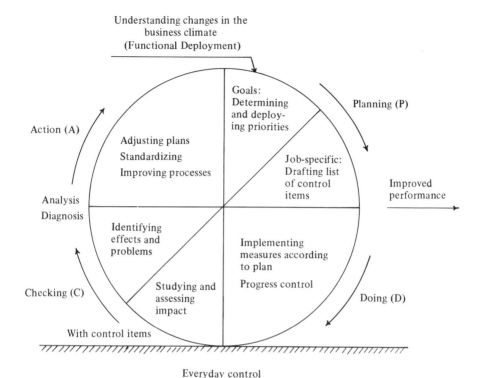

Figure 6.1 The Policy Control Circle

it is necessary to clarify the interrelationships among the various policies, such as those listed above, establish and implement a policy control system, and devise and implement a policy supervision system. Very few companies do this kind of comprehensive planning on a regular basis, but everyone should.

Although there are still numerous problems to be tackled in policy planning, it can still be highly effective when everyone from top to bottom is involved.

6.1.3 Policy Control Systems and Check Lists

6.1.3.1 Policy Control Systems

Policies are communicated from top management to divisional directors, from divisional managers to section managers, and from section managers to department heads. Implementation plans are drawn up at each level, and progress in enacting the plans is checked daily, with new instructions being issued as necessary. A policy should be implemented only after there has been thorough discussion among top and middle management people on how it should be developed. Policies should be products of agreement, not lackluster compromise or dictatorial orders.

Figure 6.2 is an example of a policy control system. Note the check lists of each division, section, and department.

Just as a policy should be implemented, checked, and revised in keeping with a clearly defined system, a daily schedule for policy control should be followed. Scheduling delays can result in the company president's policy being formulated after those of the division and section directors, or in the new year's policy being formulated without a sufficient review of the previous year's policy achievements and failures. These kinds of problems are evidence that the PDCA circle is not working as it should.

The 5-Ws and 1-H are important factors in charting the policy setting, deployment, implementation, and control (checking and feedback) system shown in Figure 6.2. Policies should be implemented following the prepared system chart and activities lists, but there should be no hesitation about revising the chart and check lists whenever necessary. The ability to revise intelligently means you are following the causes and results. Policy control regulations should be institutionalized and various documents (such as policy drafts, policy statements, policy deployment flow charts, implementation flow charts, policy control charts, and implementation results reports) prepared to ensure efficient and effective implementation.

These documents should provide the following kinds of information:

Policy Draft: The previous year's policies and actions, degree of attainment, problems generated by discrepancies between goals and actual achievements, causes discovered through analyses, measures to correct these causes, changes in circumstances, limiting conditions, and how all this affects this year's policies.

Policy Deployment Chart: Top management's policies, check items carried over from the previous year's policies, work allocations, this year's policies, goals, measures, deployment to lower-level policies and instructions, and requests to other divisions.

Implementation Chart: Items to be implemented, points to be careful of in implementation, control items, who is responsible for what, schedules, monthly progress charts, and actions implemented.

Policy Management Chart: Items to be implemented, control items, control data (document names and person responsible for document), and control method (frequency, control limits, and actions).

Implementation Results Report: Implementation status, item revisions, reasons for revisions, results, problems (reasons and causes), future problems and trends, and requests to other divisions.

Remember that all of these documents are supposed to encourage people in analyzing problems, making plans, conducting checks, and taking appropriate action.

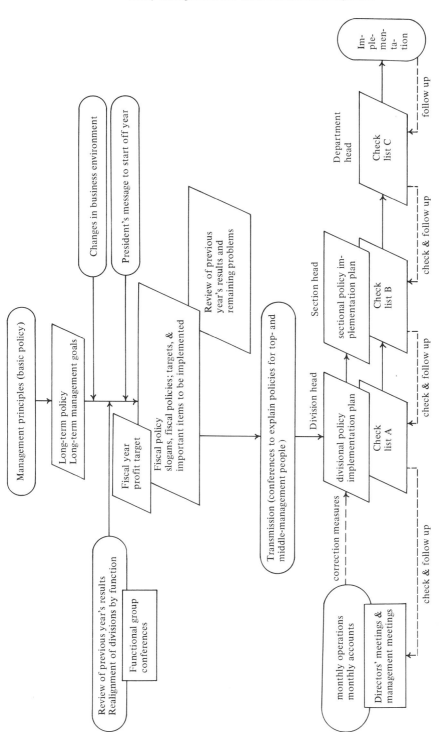

Figure 6.2 Policy Control System (Courtesy of Tokai Rika Denki Seisakusho)

6.1.3.2 Policy Check Items

Check the following items in line with the important points outlined by policy management and carry out the necessary reforms.

◇ Have you made a thorough study of problems carried over from the previous year and any changes in the business climate?

◇ Have you specified your goals in concrete terms?

◇ Have you assigned goals to different divisions and discussed them thoroughly with people at every level in the corporate hierarchy?

◇ Are your priority items well-defined?

◇ Will taking care of these priority items mean you have achieved your goals?

◇ Is there a better way to achieve your goals?

◇ Are you keeping the information channels between top management and people lower down in the organization open to facilitate the implementation?

◇ Have you defined and answered the 5-Ws and the 1-H?

◇ Have the cost of implementation and cost effectiveness been studied? Are sufficient funds available?

◇ Are plans specific, have responsibilities been assigned, and does everyone understand the plans and objectives?

◇ Has a detailed schedule been set up for carrying out these plans?

◇ Have such control standards as control items, control data, and control methods been sufficiently clarified?

◇ Are control data being used?

◇ Is action being taken when it should? Are records being kept?

◇ Are plans being revised as necessary?

◇ Is policy management being carried out the way it is supposed to be?

◇ Is policy being checked to see whether it is achieving its goals?

◇ Is policy management being audited?

◇ Is the policy management system being revised as necessary?

◇ Are policy management methods being standardized and the standards revised as necessary?

Achievement levels should be set for each of the items on this check list, and the composite should be the basis on which policy management progress is judged. For example, for the question, "Are control data being used," you could assign points such as given below.

Answer	Points
Hardly at all	1
Yes, and the PDCA circle is beginning to be applied	3
Yes, and the PDCA circle has been fully applied	5

6.2 Cross-functional Management

6.2.1 Important Points in Cross-functional Management

Cross-functional management has already been defined and top management's role explained in Section 2.3.2, and this was elaborated on in Chapter 4's discussion of quality assurance as one aspect of cross-functional management. Here it is sufficient to review the most important points.

1. Cross-functional management is the management of quality control activities that transcend divisional boundaries, while divisional management is management of divisional activities within each division. If divisional management is the warp of the corporation, cross-functional management is the weft.

2. Cross-functional management is integrated management targeted at certain goals. It might also be defined as management by operational functions (goals).

3. Within the TQC context, cross-functional management's goal is to preserve quality – quality assurance.

4. Cost (C) management and production/delivery volume (D) management are closely related to quality (Q) management; and because Q, C, and D are interdependent, they require integrated management.

5. Among the activities related to QCD control are such cross-functional management applications as product planning management (new product development management), technology development management, and marketing management (orders management).

6. There are also service functions such as personnel management and clerical management.

7. In cross-functional management it is necessary to define each division's responsibilities and to list these among the division's duties. All too often, quality assurance activities are not included among the divisional duties. Quality assurance is needed at every step in a product's life cycle, starting with product planning, design, and prototype construction and ending with product disposal (see Section 3.4).

8. Not all the functions in cross-functional management carry the same weight. In quality control, quality assurance is naturally the most important, and activities geared to lowering costs must be premised on quality assurance.

9. Different divisions will be more closely or less closely related under cross-functional management depending upon what is being managed.

10. Cross-functional management requires establishing functional policies (e.g., quality policies, quality assurance policies, cost control policies) and seeing them through. These policies should be incorporated into annual policy goals.

11. A cross-functional committee should be established to plan, check, and revise all cross-functional activities as necessary. This should not be an ad hoc affair but an established organ of top management headed by a corporate director.

12. Directors should be appointed to functions rather than corporate divisions so that there will be a broad corporate perspective in cross-functional management. Directors will pass on instructions to division heads and oversee functional audits.
13. Cross-functional management should be periodically audited.

6.2.2 Promoting Cross-functional Management

Cross-functional management should be instituted in the steps outlined below. Many items in the policy management check list can also be applied here.

1. Establish policies by function. It should be very clear what you want to achieve through cross-functional management. Day-to-day management and policy management are both cross-functional management possibilities.
2. Draw up a chart indicating each function and the divisions that should be fulfilling these functions (see Figure 2.5). Each division's degree of responsibility should be indicated.
3. Start with quality assurance and cost control, and then go on to production volume control and finally to new product technology development management.
4. Make a chart showing the different functions that the consumer, top management, corporate divisions, and parts and materials suppliers are responsible for at each step in the product's life cycle (see the quality assurance diagram shown in Figure 4.2). This chart should show clearly how different responsibilities interrelate and should trace a feedback route for complaints and revision suggestions. The tools and documents necessary for this kind of system management should also be listed.
5. List the activities required at each step and the items that need to be guaranteed within each step (assurance items). These lists should also specify the kind of work to be done, who is supposed to do it, and who is responsible for the results.
6. In addition to establishing this system, cross-functional management should take up priority projects. In quality assurance, this could be seeking out and correcting the source of common complaints; in cost control, solving a knotty cost problem such as that created by a product that will not be competitive unless its production cost is drastically reduced. These kinds of projects very often require cooperation among several divisions and may necessitate setting up special project teams with representation from all divisions concerned. Insufficient contact between divisions can often hamper cross-functional management, and project teams help to alleviate this problem and make cross-functional management more effective.

6.2.3 Cost Control

In planning a new product, it is just as necessary to ascertain the product's profitability as it is to ensure that it satisfies quality requirements. For this, cost assurance activities need to be carried out in parallel with quality assurance activities. An outline of the steps in this kind of process is shown in Figure 6.3.

The PDCA circle can be applied equally effectively to cost control, i.e., cost planning, cost maintenance (budget control), cost improvement, and so forth. Cost control policy should be directed at lowering costs while maintaining quality. Product quality should never be compromised in the interest of cutting costs. Cost control can be applied to many of the same areas as quality assurance, including materials, parts, equipment requirements, and work processes. It must therefore be planned and carried out in close conjunction with quality assurance activities.

As with quality assurance, planning is the first and most important step in cost control. And effective planning demands that a thorough cost analysis of products already being produced be made and this information used as a guide in deciding on a new product's costs.

The relationship between costs and quality must also be explored in cost planning. Check on how costs will vary with changes in the quality characteristics listed on the quality deployment chart. Your emphasis here should not be on what is most economical from the manufacturing point of view but what is most economical for the consumer.

Some companies have been very successful at cutting costs because they have prepared cost data on materials and parts and analyzed how these data relate to individual quality characteristics.

Cost control as a part of total quality control cross-functional management is more than simply a cost operations system and must include cost evaluation systems and cost information dissemination systems. Quality analysis, process analysis, and other statistical analyses performed as a part of the quality assurance process can be extremely useful in establishing and revising costs.

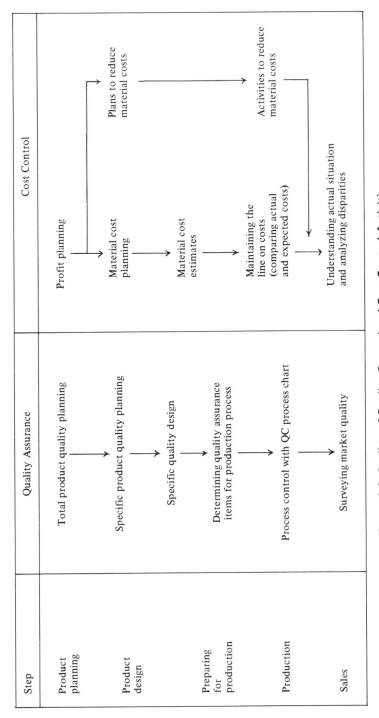

Company-wide Total Quality Control

Figure 6.3 Outline of Quality Control and Cost Control Activities

7 | Quality Control Education

One of the major tasks in introducing quality control into the company is the dissemination of the quality control concept through employee education and training. So important are education and training activities that the people in charge of quality control are likely to find them taking most of their time.

7.1 Importance of Quality Control Education

You will run into many obstacles in trying to introduce quality control into the company, not the least of which is the lack of agreement on what quality control is. Quality control is control aimed at assuring product quality, and keeping track of work quality is one of the approaches to achieveing this end. Despite this, some people mistakenly assume that TQC, because it does not include the term "statistical" in its name, is a non-statistical approach to quality control.

Two of the more basic approaches to introducing TQC are emphasizing control as a part of practical administrative management and emphasizing work quality in an effort to get office as well as plant workers involved in the process.

Much of the kind of quality control I advocate has little to do with statistics, but there is certainly nothing wrong with stressing statistical tools in introducing quality control into the factory. Unlike such vague concepts as management and control, statistics provide specific, solid data, stimulate worker interest, and are easy to understand, especially for technicians and engineers.

Success with the statistical approach can smooth the way for the introduction of other quality control concepts, but failure can make it more difficult, and you thus should be careful in how you go about using statistical tools.

In educating employees about quality control, be careful that you do not over-stress the importance of statistical tools and theory. Your primary aim should be to teach practical approaches to quality control applicable to the particular circumstances on each shop floor. In the simplest terms, quality control involves maintaining, improving, and developing new quality levels. Workers will need to know about:

1. *Maintaining quality*
   How to use a control chart to detect abnormal conditions, how to cope with abnormal situations, how to create standards, criteria, and regulations, and how to decide on control items and control methods.

2. *Improving quality*
   How to make a cause-and-effect diagram and how to do such process analyses as stratification, sampling, and correlation analyses.

3. *Developing new product quality*
   Quality deployment, quality analysis, experimental planning, etc.

In general, people find it easier to understand the concept of improving quality than that of maintaining it. Because it is so visible, considerable effort is spent on improving quality such as through QC circle activities, and many people fail to appreciate the importance of maintaining quality.

7.2 Education by Job Type

What a person needs to know about quality control depends in large part on his position and level within the company. Some of the different levels are outlined below.

7.2.1 Top Management

The company president and directors should not only have a grasp of quality control, how it works, and what it is intended to achieve but should also know how to use such tools as the control chart. It is not easy to tailor an educational programme for top management and someone often has to be called in from outside to do this, since an appropriate teacher is unlikely to be available within the company. Even then, it is questionable whether such an educational programme can attain its intended goals.

This question of how to educate top management on quality control is likely to be a major headache for anyone put in charge of quality control. Regardless of how successfully line workers are applying quality control, regardless of how well division directors and section chiefs understand the concept of quality control, and regardless of whether or not a quality control organization has been established, TQC's effectiveness will ultimately depend on top management's attitudes and policies, and educating top management must be a top-priority item in introducing quality control.

Although presidents and directors are extremely busy people with little time for quality control issues, they are very likely to have strong opinions based on their own experiences and beliefs. In educating top management on quality control, you should (1) keep lectures short, (2) submit reports and recommendations, (3) arrange for top management people to attend meetings and lectures on quality control both inside and outside of the company, and (4) supply reading material directed specifically at top management.

1. *Lectures*

    One of the more effective ways of getting top management to learn about quality control is to invite a quality control specialist to give a series of short lectures or to simply talk to top management people. While this specialist may be someone from inside the company, it is generally better to find someone from outside the company, which is, in fact, the more common approach. This specialist should, of course, be well versed in the statistical tools used in quality control, but even more important than that, he should be someone with experience in general applications and quality control management. An uninterrupted span of time should be set aside for the specialist's lectures, all phone calls, visitors, and other interruptions being shut out.

    As pointed out earlier, there is no shortcut to understanding quality control. Quality control has to become a gut feeling as much as an intellectual perception. It is best understood through practice rather than theory, a point that needs to be strongly impressed upon top management.

2. *Reports and recommendations*

    Every opportunity should be taken to submit reports and opinion briefs on events within the company, as well as inviting the top management people to attend quality control meetings, large and small. Top management people tend to be more interested in results than processes, and they want to know what the economic impact is. Reports should be succinct, with plenty of clearly understood diagrams and charts showing processes as well as results in monetary terms.

    In this day and age, just about every company has an established route for employees to convey suggestions and opinions to the top echelon of the company, and company presidents and directors both want and need this kind of feedback.

3. *Study groups inside and outside the company*

    Even the simple act of attending quality control study groups, discussions, and lectures can often prove stimulating for top management.

4. *Reading material*

    Unfortunately, there is little appropriate material available, and you may end up making your own collections of clippings, articles, and books. Once you have this material, it should be circulated among top management personnel. People are likely to claim that they understand the subject perfectly in discussion, but they are suddenly not so sure when it comes time to actually apply what they've learned. This is natural, and it would be unreasonable to expect top management to understand quality control after reading a few books and attending a couple of lectures. Repetition is necessary, and quality control directors, division directors, and plant managers who complain that top management doesn't understand what needs to be done often have only themselves to blame because they have not done all they could to educate top management.

The "gold in the mine" approach, is one way to explain the importance of quality control to top management. Using this approach, you (1) point out that the company and its plants have a "gold mine" of profit-making potential that can be tapped if only a wide range of quality-related problems and issues can be solved, (2) explain that this hidden "gold" is to be found throughout the company, (3) inform that some problems have already been successfully solved, (4) demonstrate how quality control concepts have actually been applied in real-life situations, and (5) suggest specific proposals for introducing and implementing quality control.

Facts and figures are the most pursuasive arguments to convince top management. It is not enough to simply list problems that need to be solved. Use statistics and data to show what these problems are costing the company and what the company can gain by resolving them. Provide detailed and specific proposals for how problems should be approached and solved. The important thing here is to make your presentation appeal to the technical and business instincts that top management has honed through years of experience. You must make top management realize its responsibility for quality control. If your arguments are solid, top management will be able to see for itself the important role it must play in promoting quality control.

7.2.2 Middle Management and Employees

It is generally accepted that all technical people will need to have a working understanding of the statistical tools used in quality control and their underlying training concepts. Schools are beginning to teach these concepts, and introductory training programmes for new employees that concentrate on the statistical approach last anywhere from a few months to a year in some companies.

While the technical people obviously need to know how to use the statistical tools, it is dangerous to put too much emphasis on statistics. You cannot have effective quality control when a small group of people spend all their time on esoteric facts and figures that mean little or nothing to the other workers on the shop floor, and such a situation may actually set the cause of quality control back. The last thing you want to do in instituting quality control is to create an elite corps of statisticians. Unfortunately, some people who have dedicated considerable effort and time in learning mathematical statistics tend to consider themselves superior to their coworkers, an attitude that can kill the cooperative work atmosphere that is essential to quality control.

Middle management people have years of experience, and they are likely to be much more skeptical about things than line workers. It will not be easy to convince them of the importance of quality control. Some managers will stress concepts and approaches to work, others will demand concrete results, the sooner the better. Although quality control is a diagnostic concept rather than a method of treatment, many companies think quality control will enable their technical people to stay abreast of new technologies and their administrative people to manage better. This is not what quality control is about, and it may take some time before you can get middle management to understand that quality control involves seeking out problems, diagnosing their causes, and eventually correcting the causes of mistakes. It will be particularly hard to get the middle management people in clerical and administrative divisions to realize that they play a significant role in product quality assurance.

An in-house course of study in quality control for division and section heads should include the following.

Subject	Hours
Quality control concepts	12
Control charts	3
Statistical tools	6
Implementing quality control	24

Technicians, engineers, and line workers need to be instructed in
    Quality control concepts
    Control charts
    Statistical tools and approaches (tests, inference, correlation, and distribution analysis)
    Analysis and testing
    Implementing quality control

The availability of relatively inexpensive microcomputers and sophisticated calculators vastly simplifies statistical analyses and the drawing of Pareto diagrams and control charts. Computers have now become a common fixture in most offices and everyone, whether technician or clerical worker, should know how to use them.

7.2.3 Quality Control Staff

The quality control staff are the people in a plant's quality control division and the people charged with administering and implementing quality control within the company's various divisions. As the closest thing to quality control experts, these people should be selected with care, for their attitudes and aptitudes will have a profound impact on how effectively quality control can be introduced and implemented. Any organization is only as good as its people, and this is true also of the quality control organization. In TQC, quality control staff are usually recruited from administrative and clerical sections and divisions. Once TQC is firmly established, it may be necessary to set up a TQC promotion division with quality control and quality assurance sections and departments, but at the initial stage the first consideration is finding the right people rather than creating new boxes on the organizational chart.

The quality control staff people must be politically astute in the best sense of the term, (1) cooperative, (2) diligent and able to get things done, and (3) people with shop floor experience.

As you have probably noticed, there is no need for the quality control staff to be statisticians. Plant workers are likely to either balk at someone who is overqualified or to defer completely to that person and not exercise any initiative on their own. Either case is counter-productive. In many cases, the people directing quality control have attained their positions by default, and no thought has been given to their suitability or effectiveness. Far from promoting quality control, some of these people actually obstruct its effective implementation. The qualifications for quality control supervisory personnel deserve more careful attention.

In teaching these people the statistical tools required for quality control, it is just as important to explain *why* these tools are used as *how* they are used. There was a period in which extensive studies were made on sampling. In many instances, these studies were initiated after quality control activities revealed crucial problems in sampling practices, but in many other instances companies that were unsure of how to apply company-wide TQC chose instead to rely solely on the seemingly easier aspect of sampling. Studies and analyses of sampling and other quality control measures are, of course, always useful, but all too often no one bothers to think about the reasons for such studies and what they are intended to achieve.

7.2.4 Line Workers

Training Within Industries (TWI) and other educational and training programmes should be used to familiarize all line workers, including workshop supervisors and group leaders, in quality control concepts, statistical tools, control charts, and everything else that is a part of quality control implementation. A growing number of plants are preparing their own instruction manuals and textbooks.

Worker training and education must be adapted to local cultural mores and customs. What will work in Japan may not work in other countries, and different approaches may have to be taken for different regions even within the same country. Whatever the approach, the subjects that must be covered are work standards, work procedure manuals and charts, control charts, and other areas having to do with improving product quality and work procedures.

There has recently been considerable emphasis on educating QC circle leaders and QC circle members in how to improve their processes and why such improvements are so important. This is all well and good, but every care should be taken not to forget the equally important, albeit less dramatic, need to maintain quality.

The most important thing for line workers is that they be able to follow standard work procedures and use control charts, and it can actually be detrimental to give them overly sophisticated training.

In training foremen, keep the following points in mind.

1. The foreman has confidence in his abilities. He needs to be trained in how best to apply his long years of experience and intuition.
2. Nobody wants his work load increased. The first step in educating the foreman is to demonstrate where conventional work habits have been inefficient and wasteful and to convince him that quality control will lighten his work load and raise his productivity.
3. The foreman has to recognize the important role he plays in assuring product quality.
4. Most foremen do not think of the company in statistical terms.
5. Quality control education should not be allowed to degenerate into simple instructions on work procedures.
6. The significance of work standards needs to be made clear.
7. The foreman needs to know where his talents can be applied to best advantage.
8. He should be made aware of how quality control is being successfully applied in other industries and the results that are being achieved.
9. Conduct the training programme for foremen in a straightforward manner, keeping your language simple and direct.
10. Make it clear that the company is not toying with quality control as a fad but is taking it seriously as a long-term committment.

7.2.5   Administrative and Clerical Workers

Planning, cost control, purchasing, inventory, labour, and marketing people have traditionally tended to think in administrative terms, and it has therefore been especially hard to educate them in the importance of quality control. Still, statistical applications are gradually being adopted even in these areas, and a growing number of administrative and clerical workers have some familiarity with statistical tools and systems. Computers can further this trend, but administrative and clerical procedures should be standardized for computerization purposes and functional analyses and improvements using statistical tools carried out *before* the company computerizes and automates its office procedures.

7.2.6   Research and Development Staff

Creativity is the prime requisite for new product development, and it should be the goal not only of quality control education but of any kind of education. Deplorably, little attention is paid to this very important point. No matter how many cause-and-effect diagrams you draw or how many distribution analyses you do, they will not be very useful for either new product development or problem solving in making product improvements unless you also have original ideas and concepts to go with them.

Such is not, however, to imply that, for all its statistical tools, quality control depends in the final analysis on brainstorms, intuition, and what is sometimes referred to as a "feel" for QC. These are not matters of chance; they can be taught; and quality control is not the unscientific, esoteric discipline that it has so often been accused of being. There are those who claim that any kind of formal training in control and management will inhibit creativity, but this is not so. The essential element in the scientific approach to ideas is turning the PDCA circle.

7.3   Evaluating Quality Control Education

It is commonly assumed that it is difficult to evaluate the effectiveness of education, but that is only true when the purpose of the education is not clear. Education can be measured by how close it comes to achieving its goals.

Within the company, educational goals will, of course, vary depending on who is being educated and their level of responsibility in the corporate structure. Evaluation methods have already evolved for QC circles. Since the QC circle is already familiar with the tools and methods for solving problems and making improvements, the degree to which each person within the circle understands these methods and tools can be measured using checklists and judging by their reports at QC circle meetings.

More difficult is evaluating the educational level of quality control staff. Tests can be administered to find out how much they know about quality control tools and methods (although there is debate even about the effectiveness of such tests), but no matter how much theory a person may know, this is useless if he or she doesn't know how to apply it effectively. Quality control is meaningful only when it is being applied. One company claimed that it tailored its quality control education programme to meet its employees' needs, but it turned out that all they had done was to circulate a questionnaire asking employees what procedures they did not fully understand and to beef up their educational programme to explain these procedures better. This is not the kind of approach that is going to foster initiative and creativity.

Far better is the approach taken by another company, where employees sent to participate in the company's education division's quality control education course are assigned specific problems to solve upon finishing the course. Six months after the course has been completed, their section chiefs report to the head of the education division on how well they appear to have absorbed the lessons of the course. This is a very effective educational system. The person attending the course takes it seriously because he knows he will be evaluated later, the education division gets feedback on how effective the course is, and the section chiefs are given a unique opportunity to learn the value of quality control.

In the basic quality control course offered by JUSE (Union of Japanese Scientists and Engineers), participants are required to have their superiors assign them specific problems to be solved, and the JUSE lecturers work with participants individually to help them learn how to solve these problems.

7.4   Setting Up a Quality Control Education Programme

There are a number of points to remember in setting up a quality control education programme for your company.

1. The level of the programme will depend on the type of company and its particular requirements, but no matter what the level, there should be separate courses for plant managers, department heads, technicians and engineers, administrative and clerical staff, line workers, and other job categories.
2. Courses should be conducted simultaneously for all divisions and job types within the company.
3. Educational methods should be standardized and quality control instructors trained in a specially designed programme.
4. The goal of quality control education is not to impart theoretical knowledge so much as it is to encourage people to see implementation approaches. Follow-up will always be necessary.
5. Actual situations within the company provide the best material, and every effort should be made to relate the quality control statistical tools to actual situations.
6. Even while they are taking quality control courses, workers should be encouraged to use the methods and statistical tools they are learning about on the job.

However the courses are actually set up and structured, they should (1) aim at enabling people to understand the concept of quality control, (2) avoid an overemphasis on statistical tools and methods, important though these are, and (3) use actual case studies from within the company to emphasize the need to improve and standardize technologies and technical standards through quality control.

8 Making Employees More Quality-Conscious

8.1 Dissemination

Training and educational programmes are, by their very nature, restricted to a limited number of people. It is thus necessary to devise additional means of disseminating corporate policy regarding quality control. Some possible approaches are:

1. *Slogans*
   Employees can be encouraged to submit their ideas for quality control slogans and a prize given for the winning entries. The prizes may be small, but they are important for the recognition they entail and as motivating factors. These quality slogans should be used not only within the company but outside the company as well to publicize the company's commitment to superior product quality.

2. *Newsletters*
   In-house newsletters provide an ideal forum for discussing quality control. A regular column can be set aside for quality control topics or special issues on quality control can be published periodically. Many companies regularly publish journals and other printed matter on quality control. These publications are most effective when they contain spontaneous contributions from front-line employees. Some companies have even mailed educational material on quality control to their employees' families as a means of generating pride in the company's work.

3. *Pamphlets*
   Liberally illustrated, pamphlets can act as effective supplements to regular publications and be used as part of the regular educational programme. At some companies, such pamphlets are available at plant entrances along with safety brochures and other free reading material.

4. *Exhibitions and displays*

   Displays of defective products, each labeled with the cause of the defect, what it was costing the company, and how it was corrected are a direct means of generating employee quality-consciousness. Charts and diagrams illustrating quality control concepts and statistical tools can also help employees to visualize and better understand the whole quality control process.

5. *Posters, bulletins, and in-house broadcasts*

   Pareto diagrams, histograms, and control charts posted on bulletin boards keep people up-to-date on quality control activities. If your company has a p.a. system in its plants, it can be used to broadcast periodic progress reports, reminders, and warnings.

6. *Lectures, quality control congresses, and meetings*

   Regular lectures and seminars on quality control topics provide very direct and effective means of disseminating quality control concepts, and yet few such opportunities are provided in most plants. Time should be set aside for such lectures and seminars, since many line workers never have the chance to learn more about their work outside of their own particular job, and it is a good idea to repeat the basics frequently. Films, slides, and other audiovisual aids can be used to make presentations more interesting.

7. *Quality control contests*

   Foremen and supervisors in workshops throughout a plant can hold quality control contests. Workers would be given a specified length of time in which to devise and implement improvements in their own work areas, reports would be submitted on the results, and the supervisors would award prizes to the people who came up with the best idea or were most successful in implementing an improvement. In Japanese plants, worker improvements often extend to improvements in installations and production equipment.

   Every division should create its own quality control records, but when a particular method of record-keeping proves especially effective, other divisions should be encouraged to learn from and use the same system. Exemplary flow charts, organization charts, analysis case studies, foolproof techniques, and other devices that have been used to good effect should be displayed for all to see and adopt.

8.2   Raising Quality Consciousness

A special effort must be made to make workers aware of quality and its importance if quality control is to really take hold − and this should be done simultaneous with or even before quality control systems are introduced. The worker needs to be convinced that quality control is as much to his own benefit as it is to the company's benefit. There is not, and should never be, a conflict of interest between quality control needs and the needs of the individual.

In promoting heightened quality consciousness among workers, it is imperative that top management demonstrate its dedication to quality control. If this is done, employees will naturally follow management's lead.

Still, no matter how convinced top management is of quality control's importance, its concern will be to no avail unless the same conviction has permeated throughout the company.

Middle management's job is to thoroughly assimilate top management policy, to provide the necessary support for these policies, and to help convey these policies to the rest of the company. It is generally accepted that middle management people will work hard to make improvements within their own departments even if this proves detrimental to other departments. While this kind of competitive spirit is recognized and even encouraged, top management will need to step in at a certain point to ensure that quality control requirements are met uniformly throughout the company and that everybody is cooperating on them. In the process, however, care must be taken not to discourage middle management or to have it mistakenly think that its own objectives must be sacrificed to achieve quality control objectives. Its objectives should coincide, not conflict, with quality control objectives.

QC circles have proved extremely effective in stimulating interest in quality control among foremen, line workers, and other front-line people in manufacturing. Yet statistical methods and other QC tools are only as good as the people using them. No matter how advance computer and automation technology is, the effectiveness of this technology always depends on the people using it. This is why the human element is so important to TQC.

The Western system in which management creates standards to be blindly followed does not contribute to good quality products. Workers who reluctantly do only what they are told within their allotted time cannot produce good quality products. Good quality products are produced only when everyone is willing to put his all into his work.

Still, modern, sophisticated equipment makes it impossible for everyone in the workshop to work at his own pace and in his own way like the craftsmen of old. This is where the quality control circles come in. QC circles provide a forum for people in the workshop to exchange ideas and to stimulate each other to do better work. As of September 1984, Japan had more than 180,000 registered small-group QC circles with a total membership of over 1.59 million. If you add in the unregistered circles, the number is probably even greater.

8.3   QC Circle Activities

8.3.1   The Purposes of QC Circle Activities

QC circles may be formed for many reasons, but their main purposes are:

1. To promote leadership and quality control capabilities among workshop foremen through self-education.
2. To heighten worker morale and ensure that quality control is implemented

throughout the company by promoting quality consciousness and encouraging a voluntary and spontaneous approach to solving problems and making improvements.

3. To act as an integral part of TQC and the focal point for quality control and quality assurance directions set by the company president and plant manager.

Given these basic purposes, QC circles should

1. Be permanent organizations working on a daily basis.
2. Be as spontaneous and voluntary as possible, with circle members overseeing daily control items and doing studies to improve processes and correct nonconformance.
3. Follow up on decisions made concerning past records, rationalization, complaints, and defectives, with their projects registered with the company.
4. Get everyone involved in rotating the PDCA circle under the guidance of the circle leader.
5. Study quality control.
6. Meet and cooperate with other QC circles in the company.
7. Conduct exchanges with QC circles in other companies.

The zero defects (ZD) movement started by the United States military and later introduced into Japanese industry had the same goal of promoting quality consciousness among workers, but it was primarily a theoretical and psychological movement and did not provide the specific tools and methods that are integral to QC circle activities. Only through the implementation of concrete quality control techniques can a goal such as zero defects be achieved.

QC circles take the initiative in seeking out problems and applying quality control tools to solve them. Today you will find QC circles working very successfully in corporate marketing and administrative divisions, and even in banks and hotels.

As one of the distinguishing characteristics of Japanese-style quality control, QC circles have come to be recognized worldwide for their motivating drive and emphasis on people rather than technologies or systems. These QC circles play a prominent role in Japanese-style TQC, and an increasing number of Western corporations are studying the Japanese QC circles' achievements and introducing similar programmes into their own operations.

As an organized activity, the QC circle provides a valuable forum for self- and mutual-education. In other countries, the tendency is to draw a clear demarcating line between white-collar professionals and blue-collar workers, with blue-collar workers expected to simply obey the professionals' instructions. Management will find, however, that it is much more productive to have production line workers participate actively in quality control.

Defects can be caused by management or by shop floor workers. Failure to provide the required guidance and standards results in management-caused defect. Failure to adhere to standards and mistakes on the production line yields worker-caused defects. It is not uncommon in tracing worker-caused defects to find that they actually stem from incorrect standards and other management-caused defects. In many cases, of course, only the floor worker has the knowhow required to create certain standards, and it is to be hoped that workers will take the initiative in revising and improving standards as necessary. This is what QC circle activities are all about.

There are many publications explaining the formation and activities of the QC circle and I will not go into any great detail on the organizational problems here. Instead, because mistakes in the way QC circles are promoted can lead to major problems, I would like to point out some of the main pitfalls and how to avoid them.

8.3.2 Points to Consider in Conducting QC Circle Activities

QC circles are widely acknowledged to be very effective, but their effectiveness can be diminished and they can even block quality control if they are not introduced or employed correctly. Listed below are several factors that need to be considered in forming QC circles.

1. QC circles should never be treated as infallible oracles whose every improvement proposal must be immediately institutionalized without any kind of preliminary checking or testing. If the company does not have any provision for testing results and disseminating successful improvements throughout the corporate structure, this can only mean that management does not take QC circles seriously.

2. There are many questions about QC circles that have to be answered. What do you do in an industry such as construction where almost everyone is a skilled professional? How do you balance the need for initiative with the need for policy control? What has to be done for TQC besides setting up QC circles? All of these questions need to be answered before you can introduce TQC into your company successfully.

   In the early stages, workers are likely to be quite willing to tackle problems immediately relevant to their own specific activities, but ways must be found to broaden their perspective and to direct them toward the company's broader quality policy objectives with the same initative and enthusiasm.

3. In Japanese companies, all workers are simply called employees, whether white collar or blue collar. This classlessness should extend to QC circles as well. Making rank distinctions among circle members runs counter to the cooperative spirit of the QC circle. Working in teams in which they exchange ideas can be just as beneficial for white collar workers as for their blue collar counterparts. It is irrelevant whether these teams or groups are called QC circles or not. The important thing is that they have the same cooperative spirit.

4. A common tendency that should be avoided is to over-emphasize source control, paying more attention to new product development than to maintaining quality levels for products already on the line. Because there is so much stress laid on improvements in quality control, we often forget

the importance of maintaining quality.

It is a basic QC principle that workers adhere to standards established by their immediate supervisors, but workers may forget this tenet in their zeal to make improvements.

5. Dedicated QC personnel who work hard to educate their coworkers in the merits of quality control are to be commended. They should take care, however, that their own work does not suffer as a result. Once QC circles have become firmly established to take care of quality maintenance and minor improvements, QC personnel should feel free to plow that time back into their own work or to move on to other plans and activities.

6. QC circles have much to contribute to good management-labour relations as long as they are not abused by management, used to provide stopgap measures to cover up management negligence, or utilized to step up the demands on workers.

7. The benefits derived and money saved from improvements instituted by the QC circles should be to the circles' advantage.

8. Care should be taken in teaching QC circles how to use Pareto diagrams, cause-and-effect diagrams, and other statistical tools that the QC circles not end up having more form than substance. An overemphasis on procedures can easily obstruct the development of new technology and discourage people from submitting new ideas of their own.

9. One of the reasons Japanese companies have been so successful with QC circles is that their employees are very well educated and conscientious workers. Today, however, the number of part-time and temporary workers is rapidly increasing, and this trend can be expected to create new problems in QC circle organization and implementation. Consideration will have be given to how these people can participate in quality control activities.

10. QC circles are voluntary, and circles are, in principle, free to chose their own projects. However, circles should be careful that they do not end up concentrating on trivial issues and ignoring more important issues affecting corporate policy issues.

Given these dangers, there are a number of factors that need to be kept in mind in conducting QC circle activities.

1. No one is likely to disagree with the statement that workers should adhere to standards set by their superiors. In the actual work process, however, there will be instances in which only the person doing the job can detect the cause of a defect. Accordingly, some workers must take an active part in setting standards. Workers naturally have a role to play in articulating work and product quality standards, and this is emphasized in QC circle activities. On the other side of the coin, QC circles need to be constantly aware of what can happen when workers fail to follow established standards.

2. QC circles generally start out working on minor immediate problems. This is fine when they are still learning the quality control ropes, but once they have mastered the concepts and tools of quality control, they should move

on to bigger policy issues and cooperate with other QC circles in making improvements in whole systems.

3. As Juran has pointed out, management and QC personnel can concentrate on bigger, more forward-looking issues once the QC circles take over the job of making small but important improvements in the workplace. In fact, it is one measure of the QC circles' effectiveness that they free management to plan for the future. In fact, there are even cases in which successful QC circles have highlighted management failures and forced management to do its job better.

4. Japanese workers are to be admired for their single-minded drive, but they should not follow directives blindly. Rather, all workers need to be trained to judge things for themselves, if only to avoid misunderstandings.

5. The QC circle is probably the best way of getting everyone involved in management and promoting peaceful and cooperative management-labour relations. In this sense, the QC circle can prove instructive for top management as well as for regular employees.

6. There should be an equitable distribution of the benefits accruing from improvements made through QC circle activities, but these should be thought of in a long-term perspective rather than as short-term rewards. You do not need to reward every idea and every saving, but it should be clear that the employee will prosper along with the company.

7. Part-time and temporary workers master their jobs more quickly when the QC circle helps them by preparing work procedure charts and other tools to simplify their jobs. If you have less-educated people running your QC circles, it is all the more important that you train them in how to draw up and use these materials.

8. There are well-defined procedures for conducting QC circle activities and reporting on their results. This makes it easier for everyone to quickly grasp the significance of quality control and what it is intended to achieve. Reports are structured according to the PDCA circle, though they will usually start with the checking stage, and are therefore easy to follow. Reports made by middle management people are often restricted to a discussion of what has been done with no explanation of why this was done or what was achieved. Theirs are simple work reports, rather than the more informative QC stories. Middle management could learn a lot from QC circle reports.

The QC circle is one of the best and easiest ways of teaching people about quality control, and this is why so many companies start TQC by introducing QC circles into the workplace. Even in the service industries, where cross-functional management might be more useful, the lack of experience compels companies to start with QC circles modelled on those found in manufacturing, and they are by no means wrong in taking this approach to TQC.

It would be regrettable, however, if they never went beyond QC circles or assumed that all TQC was only administrative reforms. The result would be a failure to implement TQC effectively. Problems arise when TQC is adopted without any clear policy guidelines from top management and without defining the important roles to be played by top and middle management. I know of companies where top management only began to apply TQC when workers compalined that the whole burden of quality control was being dumped on them. The QC circle is only one element of TQC, and it can only function effectively in the TQC context.

9 | Quality Control Activities

Corporate management is involved in (1) maintenance, (2) reform, and (3) development. As such, it is charged with maintaining the status quo while at the same time destroying the status quo. Maintenance is basic to all other activities, since neither reform nor development is possible where there is no known status quo to build on, and a discussion of quality control maintenance activities is thus a good place to start this chapter.

The quality standards decided on before a product is made and the quality features built into a product in the manufacturing process are quite different and should be considered separately — the pre-production standards called design quality and the production standards called manufacturing quality. Design quality is also known as standard quality or specifications quality. Manufacturing quality is often called conformance quality because it is judged by how well the product conforms to its original design.

People often talk about good quality and low cost, but this is only an abstract concept and requires specific and concrete standards to be of any use. You cannot have standard quality until you have defined what you mean by good quality and low cost. Likewise, it is meaningless to refer to "international standards" unless you spell out exactly what these standards are.

In defining your "standard quality," it is important to remember that standard quality must be defined in terms of your company's current capabilities. All too often designers design new products totally oblivious to their own company's production capabilities. This not good design quality. It is wish-list quality. Standard quality should be clearly differentiated from the research and development target qualities.

9.1 The Quality Control System

TQC covers a broad range of activities, but I will restrict my discussion here to the quality maintenance activities in the production process. The heart of all quality control activities, quality maintenance is implemented through quality analyses, process analyses, and the establishment of work standards. Given below are factors of quality maintenance activities.

1. *Deciding on standard quality*

   Deciding on standard quality requires that you consider (1) consumer requirements (sophistication and cost) and (2) manufacturing requirements (technology and control devices).

   You will obviously be limited by your own technology and cannot adopt external criteria wholesale without making certain adjustments. Production technology constraints may force you to create a product that does not meet others' criteria, but it is also possible that a sophisticated technology will enable you to produce something that exceeds expectations.

   Since the manufactured product is intended to be sold, the consumer's needs should be given first consideration, but it is seldom possible to satisfy all of these wants. How far you go to satisfy consumer needs depends in large part on questions of reputation and marketing strategies. Thus standard quality decisions should be made by management based on information on consumer needs acquired through market research and combined with data on your own manufacturing capabilities and limitations.

   A handbook or work manual listing standard quality features is called a quality standards book.

2. *Establishing work standards*

   The first step in establishing work standards is to decide on the processes required to manufacture products to standard quality specifications. This means you have to do process analyses to clarify the relationship between a product's quality indices and manufacturing factors. Instruction books on work standards are called work standard manuals.

   Quality indices indicate a product's quality level. In fact, they could also be called effect values, since there is a clear cause-and-effect relationship between the manufacturing process factors and the quality indices. There are numerous factors that can cause quality indices to fluctuate, some more important than others, and it is neither practical nor desirable to attempt to control all of the manufacturing factors. Rather, you should turn your attention to the few that have a major impact on quality indices, and it is sufficient to control these key factors to ensure stable product quality. Process analyses will help you to detect these major factors, and work standards will explain how these factors are to be handled.

3. *Working to standard*

   Working to standard means adhering to specified standards within the manufacturing process. The work standard manual will dictate various key factors for different processes, and it is these key factors that should be manipulated. For example, the work standard manual may stipulate that the temperature for a certain procedure must remain between 150°C and 160°C. If the temperature drops below 150°C, it may be corrected by opening a steam valve; and if it goes above 160°C you may need to close a valve. In either case, you are making an adjustment to maintain predetermined standards. These standards, and how they are to be maintained, should all be explained in the work standard manual.

4. *Measurements*
Having made your adjustments, you need some means of judging the results so you can see if they conform to the standards. If, for example, you were adjusting the temperature for a synthetic material manufacturing process, you would need to analyze the composition of the material, the quality indices, to judge whether or not it conformed to standards.

5. *Control standards*
The final manufactured quality will seldom exactly meet the predetermined standard quality. Although the goal is to meet standard quality all the time, the finished product usually does not quite conform to the standards. Even within the quality control process, the product's quality indices are not always checked against the original quality standards. Instead, they are compared against standards that vary according to the manufacturing conditions prevailing at a particular time. In rare cases, the control standards may actually be of a higher grade than the quality standards because of improved working conditions.

In any case, it is necessary to establish control standards as well as standard quality requirements. There should be documentation explaining how to set control standards, how to perform control activities, and what the standard procedures should be. It should be noted, however, that such control is only control in the narrowest sense of the term, and is perhaps better called checking.

6. *Checking quality indices against control standards*
Checking against control standards will help to reveal the absence of certain quality indices and indicate where defectives are most likely and why.

7. *Taking action to eliminate causes of nonconformance*
It is possible that you are meeting all the required work standards without actually maintaining control over all possible trouble points. Depending on the situation, such oversight can have dire consequences. As soon as you have traced the causes of nonconformance, you should be instituting measures to eliminate them. This is what is meant by taking action.

If the cause of a problem is found to exist throughout the production line, work standards will need to be revised. If the problem is not chronic, it should be corrected and a record made of what had occurred, and how it was rectified. The important decision to be made here is whether work standards need to be revised or whether it is sufficient to simply maintain a record of what has happened. Everything possible should be done to ensure that the same problem does not recur.

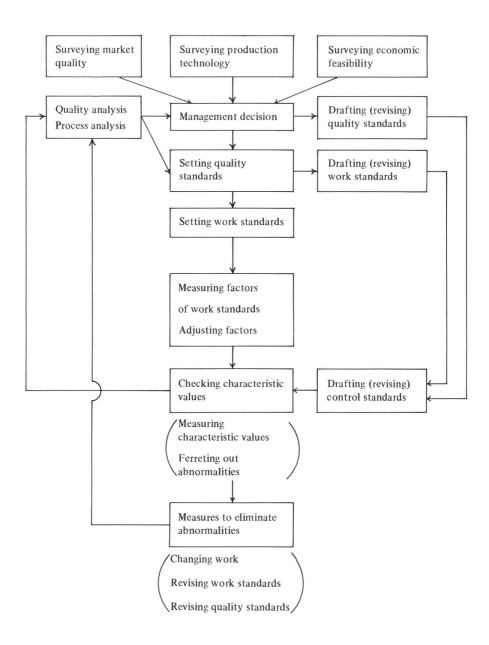

Figure 9.1 The Structure of Quality Control Activities for Quality Assurance

I have diagrammed these primary quality control activities in Figure 9.1. As used in this diagram, the term quality analysis refers to deciding on quality characteristics, stipulating quality indices, and establishing standard quality.

9.1.1 The System Approach and the Project Approach

The styem approach to quality control involves establishing work standards for every step of the way, from design to the end product. These standards include explanations of how to check for abnormalities, how to trace their causes, and how to correct them.

The project approach concentrates on specific quality problems, seeking out priority problems and correcting them.

The system approach is more usual, but a project approach may prove more effective in many cases. Still, the project approach is unlikely to cover everything, and it is important to maintain the system approach as well. Conducting activities to meet a policy objective is a project approach, but in your haste to achieve quick results you may forget that keeping up the system, though less dramatic, is just as important. And once the problem has been solved, it is all too easy to breath a sigh of relief and forget all about the need for institutionalization to ensure that the same problem does not recur.

Quality control should be an all-encompassing grid, projects being the vertical lines and systems the horizontal lines.

9.1.2 Quality Control Activities

Quality control activities include:

1. Quality planning and designing quality: deciding on the quality required for new products and new product types, and establishing, revising, and eliminating criteria.
2. Purchasing and storing materials: materials control, inventory control.
3. Institutionalization.
4. Analyzing and controlling manufacturing processes.
5. Checking on quality and taking measures to correct nonconformance: inspection and processing of defectives, complaint processing, quality audits.
6. Equipment and installation management: constructing and installing equipment, preventive safety measures, measurement procedures.
7. Personnel management: placement, education and training.
8. Management of outsourcing and sub-contracting.
9. Technology development: new product development, research management, technology management.
10. Diagnosis and supervision: auditing quality control activities and supervising quality control operations.

Quality, volume, scheduling, and costs must be carefully monitored throughout even while the primary focus is on product quality.

9.1.3 The Quality Control System and Quality Engineering

9.1.3.1 Quality Control System

Feigenbaum called the TQC activities required for setting and achieving standards a quality system and defined this quality system as a network of control procedures for manufacturing a product according to predetermined quality standards. These are procedures for

1. Pre-production quality evaluation.
2. Product and process evaluation.
3. Quality planning for purchased materials.
4. Evaluating and controlling product and process quality.
5. Feedback of quality information and data.
6. Quality measurement.
7. Training and direction in quality control and upgrading capabilities.
8. Post-production quality services.
9. Quality control functions.
10. Researching special quality qualities.

One of the most important aspects of quality control is that of defining the quality control activities for which each division is responsible and ensuring that there is an active exchange of quality information among all divisions.

Interdivisional quality control activities (functional activities) involve quality assurance, cost cutting, new product development, and more. A well-structured quality system will outline each of the steps in a product's life cycle — planning and development, manufacture, supply, use, and, finally, disposal — explaining quality control procedures for each step. This is an integrated, comprehensive system in which quality control measures at all of the steps are working toward the same goal.

Yet today's TQC has outgrown Feigenbaum's quality control system. In modern TQC, quality control is important from a product's very beginnings to the day it becomes obsolete. I have already covered interdivisional (functional and cross-functional) quality control in Chapter 6.

9.1.3.2 Quality Engineering

I have been stressing the importance of quality engineering (QE) for over twenty years now. Basically, quality engineering is an engineering system that brings together existent technologies and applies them for the process of quality control and all other control technologies. Traditionally, the study of statistical tools has been the basic approach to quality control, with little systematic research being done on quality factors themselves. Aware of this gap, the Japanese Society for Quality Control has begun to encourage research on quality in the hope that these efforts will produce a systematic and scientific discipline of quality engineering.

I have outlined my understanding of quality engineering in Figure 9.2. As Feigenbaum pointed out in his explanation of quality systems, there is need to

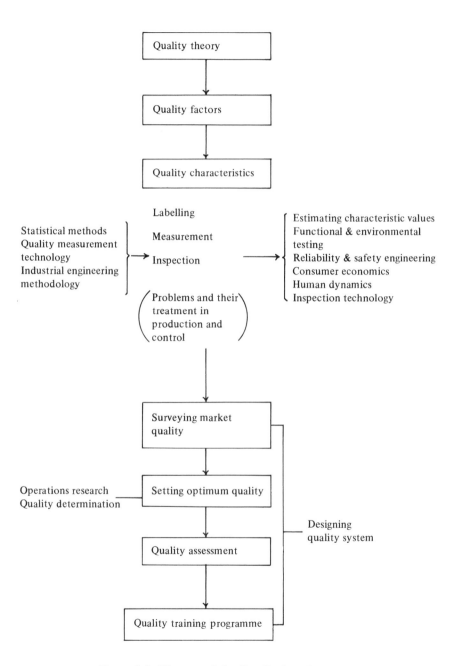

Figure 9.2 Diagram of Quality Engineering

develop better techniques for measuring quality. A product's dimensions and durability naturally need to be measured, but we also need to know how to convert the product's quality or use characteristics into substitute characteristics that can be quantified. We also need to do more studies on this aspect of quality control, as well as on how to make a quality conformance design and how to formulate the basic theoretical underpinnings for quality evaluation. In Japan, engineers and technicians in design, production, manufacturng, and other divisions are beginning to look into this subject to a certain extent, but not in a really systematic or organized fashion.

The typical quality assurance department concerns itself with quality problems and with maintaining and improving quality assurance systems, but is generally not involved in any systematic study of quality itself. In Japan every division, whether production technology, manufacturing, or purchasing, would have its own quality functions, but in the United States a company such as IBM might have a single quality control division under a director of operations that combines all of these quality functions. This organizational structure probably stems from the fact that QC is a specialist's job in the United States, but I believe the Japanese system of having all divisions within the company share responsibility for quality control is more effective. Where the Americans lead, however, is in having both quality engineering and quality system divisions, as shown in Figure 9.3, that not only cover conventional quality assurance but also conduct research on quality. The American QC division conducts research to find solutions to specific quality problems and also does research on quality measurement technology, a field in which Japanese quality control lags behind.

Quality assurance is every division's concern, which is why your quality control committee should include representatives from every division. Still, technical analyses of product quality must also be made, and the quality engineer still does not play as large a part in this as he should in Japan. It is the quality engineer's job:

1. To collect quality-related information from the marketplace. This is often assigned to the marketing division, which seldom does as thorough a job as the assignment's importance warrants. The quality engineer needs to decide exactly what kind of information he needs, how to get it, and how to analyze it.
2. To help the planning and design divisions establish quality standards after studying consumer needs, production capabilities, and quality policies.
3. To plan, evaluate, and reform manufacturing methods with the cooperation of all divisions — marketing, research, design, purchasing, and inspection — as well as outside suppliers.
4. To work together with the divisions concerned in studying quality measurement systems and how to improve inspection, packaging, and shipment.
5. To research quality functions after the product is shipped and to study after-sales services.

6. To conduct quality education for the consumer as well as the company's salesmen.
7. To plan, evaluate, and reform quality assurance systems.

There should be quality engineers in every division, design, manufacturing, marketing, services, and more as well as the quality assurance division, and these people should be cooperating across divisional lines to solve their shared problems.

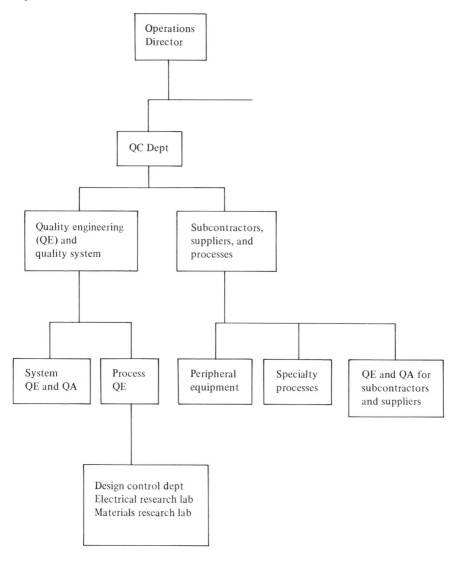

Figure 9.3 Organization of the QC Department

9.2   Quality and Cost

9.2.1   Quality Design Costs

Standard quality features include those that result from manufacturing processes and those that are inherent in the nature of the product itself. It is the latter by which the product's quality is graded, and yet such quality indices as product life, safety, ease of use, warranty, and overload safety margin are all too often overlooked.

The cost of meeting standard quality requirements depends somewhat on manufacturing conditions. If product quality indices are set considerably higher than necessary, as is frequently the case, you can economize on materials. Sometimes high quality grades are maintained solely out of habit, even when such high grades are not required for the product's intended use. Placing unnecessarily strict toleration limits on machine processing margins can result in unnecessarily high production costs.

Manufacturing costs should, of course, be considered in designing a new product's quality features. You should be asking yourself the following questions.

1. Can this be made with cheaper materials?
2. Will this material always be available?
3. Is this material easy to store?
4. How long will the manufacturing process take?
5. How expensive will product inspection be?
6. Are inventory and shipment easily taken care of?
7. How expensive will the packaging be?
8. Will maintenance and replacement parts be readily available?
9. Can standard parts be used?
10. Is it easy to repair?

9.2.2   Quality Manufacturing Costs

The costs of quality in the manufacturing process are different from those for design. Sophisticated designs tend to be expensive while sophisticated manufacturing is usually inexpensive. Eliminating defectives, for example, helps to cut manufacturing costs.

The costs of quality in manufacturing derive from

1. Making the product comply with established standards.
2. Inspections.
3. Quality control.
4. Other avoidable costs.

The first three costs listed above cannot be avoided, but there are many manufacturing costs that could be reduced or eliminated altogether, and it is extremely important to ferret these out at an early stage. There will always be unnecessary costs. Some obvious ones are:

1. Waste material.

2. Unnecessary labour and other costs spent on waste products.
3. Labour, materials, and other costs spent on repairing defectives.
4. Extra work generated by defectives.
5. Extra manufacturing capacity necessitated by defectives.
6. Extra inspection costs.
7. Inspection costs for defectives.

One of quality control's primary goals is to reduce or eliminate all such unnecessary costs.

9.2.3 Quality Costs

9.2.3.1 Manufacturer's Costs

Feigenbaum used the term quality costs to describe the costs incurred in achieving a certain degree of product quality and described three types of quality costs that should be avoidable.

1. Failure cost: This is the cost of defectives and materials that do not meet specifications; the loss incurred as a result of scrapped materials and products, repairs that have to be made to defectives, and the lowered work efficiency that results; and the cost of covering discounts for lower-quality products and of responding to consumer complaints.

   Failure costs are sometimes divided into (1) internal failures and (2) external failures — internal failures being the loss incurred as a result of manufacturing quality failure and external failures the loss incurred as a result of design quality failure.
2. Appraisal cost: The cost of testing and inspecting to maintain quality standards.
3. Prevention cost: The cost of preventing the occurrence of defects through analyses, institutionalization, education and training, measurement instrumentation, upgrading of manufacturing equipment precision, and so forth — in sum, the cost of QC.

While prevention costs account for most quality control costs, it is possible, according to Feigenbaum, to significantly reduce failure and appraisal costs by spending just a little more on prevention.

9.2.3.2 User's Costs

The product's user must contend with the following costs.

1. Electricity and fuel costs incurred in using the product.
2. The costs of stoppages.
3. Misuse costs.
4. Maintenance and repair costs.
5. Troubleshooting costs.
6. Obsolescence costs.
7. Pollution costs.

It is actually more important to reduce these user's costs than it is to economize on the manufacturer's costs. Altogether, the user's costs incurred from the time the consumer first used a product until the product is no longer used is called the life-cycle cost. Unlike disposable products, consumer durables should have low life-cycle costs, even though their original purchase prices may be high. A low life-cycle cost is to the customer's advantage, and much of good quality management is geared toward cutting user costs and increasing user benefits.

With the present need to conserve on energy and other resources, the consumer needs durable goods that can be used efficiently for a long period of time, but there may be some products that are better as disposables because it costs more to service them than it does to purchase another one. It is the manufacturer's job to supply both cheap, disposable products and costly durable goods with low life-cycle costs. Then it is up to the customer to decide which to purchase.

The consumer looks for quality and will naturally seek a high cost: benefit ratio. Figure 9.4 shows how six manufacturers compare in the market for a certain kind of equipment. Plotting cost and benefit data on a chart this way, company D found that its products had relatively low cost: benefit ratios. Further research showed that there was a close correlation between market share and the product's cost: benefit ratio.

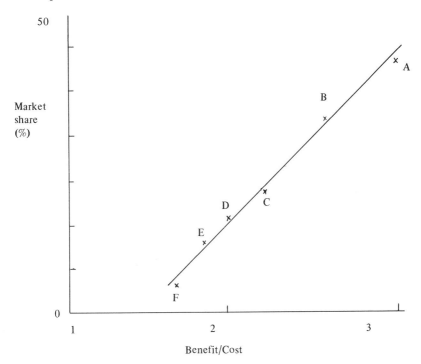

Figure 9.4 Product Competitiveness

Cost and benefit indices were calculated using the following formulas.

Cost = Depreciation cost + operating cost + maintenance cost

Benefit = that benefit derived from the product produced using the manufacturing equipment (e.g., if the equipment is a printing press, this is the printer's profit derived from printing on this press) X production speed (printing speed) X effective working life

Once company D realized that consumers were naturally gravitating to products with the higher cost: benefit ratios, it initated a study to find out where its product fell short and where improvements could be made to increase its market share.

As this example clearly illustrates, market research involves investigating user costs and comparing those for your own product against those for your competitors' products.

9.2.3.3 Social Costs

A manufacturer's costs need to be considered in relation to the quality costs to the consumer, but there is a third set of costs that must be considered for many products: the social costs. In this age of product liability, the manufacturer must include these social costs in the cost of making a product. These include:

1. Litigation fees and insurance costs.
2. The costs of recalling and reworking defectives.
3. The costs incurred in responding to consumer complaints.
4. The costs of documentation and advertising to ensure the product's correct use.
5. The costs of making everyone in the company more aware of product liability.

An estimate of these costs will show you how much you should be investing in quality control, and should make painfully clear that stinting on quality control can be ruinous for your bottom line.

9.2.4 Quality Loss Distribution

If all of the product's quality characteristics are equally responsible for the losses incurred as a result of poor quality, you would obviously have the very expensive and almost-impossible task of improving quality in all areas equally. However, it often happens that certain factors and certain characteristics are responsible for a disproportionate percentage of the quality losses. It is therefore important to ascertain how much product loss is associated with each factor or characteristic. Where are the important problems?

The people producing a product are likely to know it inside and out, and they will probably be able to recite a long list of possible causes for defects, including irregularities in the raw materials, less-than-perfect equipment, and many more. There are so many things that have to be done that you end up doing nothing. Some pessimists even claim that the sheer number of possible problems means that it is impossible to reduce the number of defects. Others want to correct these problems but they don't know where to start.

In actuality, however, it is very unlikely that you will find all of the causes equally responsible for defects in the product. For example, one fluorescent bulb manufacturer discovered that 80% of its defects were generated by its glass tube manufacturing process. Major quality losses are typically caused by minor quality characteristics. The fact that the causes of defectives are not evenly distributed and that defects can usually be attributed to just a few factors makes quality control much easier because it enables you to set priorities for your quality problems as discussed in Section 2.2.2.

9.3   Industrial Production and Statistical Tools

9.3.1   Making the Right Judgments

Everyone assumes that quality control is being taken care of, yet all too often it is not. Why not?

In every job we have to do, we have to make judgments. For example, if you are working with a furnace, you will measure its temperature, and, if the temperature is too high, take steps to lower it such as by cutting back on the fuel supply. Then you will check to see that the temperature has dropped to the correct level. To take another example, in trying to decide which of two reaction vats are better, you will measure the quality and volume of the batches from each vat and base your decision on the results.

Every measurement is followed by a judgment, and then another measurement and another judgment. In the Deming Circle, the next step after manufacturing is judging the quality of the finished product. You have to take measurements and make judgments to produce products that will satisfy consumer needs as economically as possible.

Of course, everybody knows this, and most manufacturers make a major effort to be as accurate as possible in their measurements and judgments. Precision instruments and complex chemical analyses have been developed and put into widespread use for this very purpose, but there was very little guidance on how to make correct judgments on the basis of the voluminous data available — until the advent of quality control. In many instances, the final judgment is left up to the specialist or technician who makes his decision on the basis of gut feelings. Based on years of experience, this kind of gut feeling or sixth sense is not something to be scoffed at, but there is always the danger that such judgments will be clouded by person biases and assumptions. Yet the need to see things clearly without bias or prejudice is basic to any scientific endeavour.

The conventional approach in random-sample testing has been to assume that the characteristics revealed by testing one sample unit are the same as would be found in all units of the same product coming off the same manufacturing line. Yet product characteristics are by no means uniform. No matter how carefully you try to make two metal rods exactly the same, for example, their diameters will never be exactly the same. It is unrealistic to expect every single unit to be identical in mass manufacturing. No matter how sophisticated or precise your manufacturing equipment, it is regulated by people, and human beings cannot create two things that are exactly the same. Thus the conventional wisdom has also been the conventional fallacy as people assumed that sampling individual products and lots would enable them to judge the quality of all of a factory's output.

We need to think in terms of quality dispersion, the concept that there will necessarily be deviations in a plant's production output. Until relatively recently we did not know how to measure this dispersion, or how to measure the quality of a group of products rather than of an individual item. Today, however, we know that there are statistical tools that can be used for a high degree of accuracy in making quality judgments, one of the most effective being inductive statistics that can be used to judge the quality of a group of items on the basis of samples. Statistics provide the substance for effective and meaningful quality control, which is why statistical quality control (SQC) must always be at the core of any kind of quality control.

9.3.2 Quality Control Steps and Statistical Tools

Statistical tools are useful at every step of the way in quality control. In market research aimed at identifying consumer needs, statistics are used to infer what the majority of consumers want from the wants expressed by just a few consumers. In establishing quality and work standards, you must first decide whether they should be based on previous manufacturing results or on the results of new experiments and tests, but you will be depending on statistics in either case. In basing your standards on previous results, you will be using process analysis to trace causes and effects, and in basing standards on new experiments you will be doing factory tests and experiments and analyzing the results statistically. Statistical tools such as control charts will help you see whether the manufacturing is being carried out to standard or whether the standards need to be revised. Sampling will only tell you whether a single item is up to your quality standards, but statistical tools will tell you whether all the products on the line are being manufactured correctly.

Statistical tools are important at every stage of quality control, but they are not the goal of quality control. Used correctly, statistical tools can be extremely useful; but used incorrectly, they may even be harmful.

In the narrowest sense of the term, statistical quality control is the process of measuring a product's length, weight, shape, components, colour and other physical characteristics. Yet statistical tools need to be used to quantify many other things having to do with working conditions (such as temperature, pressure, and working time), with labour (such as the number of workers and their wages), and with costs (such as production costs and losses) if you are to judge industrially manufactured products with widely dispersed quality characteristics correctly. The same methodology can be applied to these areas as is used for the quality control of products. In its broadest application, quality control should be carried out for production volume and costs as well. Everything in industrial manufacturing that can possibly be measured can and should be subject to quality control.

Effective quality control must be based on facts, and statistical tools ensure that you have the correct facts you need to make correct judgments. There is no way you can interpret the facts accurately without statistical tools, which is why they are so essential to quality control.

Management decisions also need to be based on facts and a statistical approach. Top management may not make the actual statistical calculations required, but it should recognize the value of statistical information and tackle problems from a statistical point of view.

9.3.3 Dispersion in Quality Characteristics

Statistical tools were first introduced into quality control as a means of judging the extent of quality deviation among products. There are many reasons industrially manufactured products will not be exactly the same. Materials will not all be the same, manufacturing machines and other equipment do not always function in exactly the same way every time, and the people who operate the equipment do not work in exactly the same way. At any given time there will be a certain degree of variance in any given production line.

Most deviation in quality results from chance causes, most of which you can neither identify nor do anything about. Yet some of the variance derives from assignable causes that can be traced, such as failure to adhere to work standards, equipment malfunctions, and other correctable factors. These are our primary concern. Statistical tools will help you to distinguish between the chance and assignable causes so that you can concentrate on resolving the assignable causes and maintaining consistent quality levels. Statistics will separate unusual deviations with assignable causes from the random deviations that remain within the acceptable tolerance limits for quality control. This state of quality maintenance — when the assignable causes have been taken care of and you have only random variation within tolerance levels — is called the control state.

Of course, maintaining quality is not enough and you also want to improve quality. Deciding whether a higher temperature will improve a product or whether temperature changes do not make any difference used to be left up to the specialists or technicians, who made the decision on the basis of past experience. Using statistical tools, however, makes it possible to take a more objective approach.

9.3.4 Reliability

With the advent of complex telecommunications equipment, missiles, and other sophisticated precision equipment, reliability has become more important than ever. A product's reliability is judged by the probability with which it will function correctly under prescribed circumstances and for a prescribed period of time. For systems or objects, reliability is operation reliability, which is based on its inherent and use reliability. There are many statistical tools to measure the likelihood a product will malfunction and to judge its useful life span, and numerous other methods of enhancing product reliability have been devised.

Reliability research first began with electrical and other kinds of machinery, but it is equally applicable in chemicals, metals, and other manufacturing industries as an integral part of quality control. An understanding of reliability engineering is useful for effective quality control, and the malfunction analyses that are a part of reliability studies are one aspect of quality analysis. For further information on reliability engineering, let me refer you to the many excellent texts that are available on the subject.

9.4 Problems in Implementing TQC and How to Solve Them

Some people complain that, "We don't seem to be getting anywhere with quality control. We seem to have come up against a brick wall." But there is generally a good reason that quality control has failed, and management would do better to look for the causes than to give up on quality control. Why is quality control proving highly effective in so many companies, while others complain that it does nothing for them? All too often quality control's failure is a failure of management.

What are some of the major problems you are likely to run into in introducing and promoting TQC?

9.4.1 Uninterested Top Management
While top management may be very ready to call for TQC to be introduced and promoted and perfectly willing to pay for employees to attend quality control seminars and workshops held outside of the company, it often does not recognize the need for management itself to actively participate in quality control, to set quality control policies, and to conduct quality audits. A quality control programme in which top management does not participate is like a chicken without its head, spending a lot of energy getting nowhere. Top management's apathy and failure to participate in quality control usually happens because middle management has failed to explain the importance of quality control or to outline ways in which top management can participate.

9.4.2 Middle Management's Failure to Recognize its Role in TQC
As already noted, middle management plays an important role in quality control. It is middle management's job to promote quality control throughout the company and to provide the necessary quality control tools. Division directors, section directors, and their staffs all have different functions to fulfill in quality control, but they should all thoroughly understand their jobs and know how to do them

9.4.3 Unclear TQC Targets
Many companies have only give vague reasons for implementing quality control.

"It will help to boost profits," they say. Or "we're doing it because everyone else in the industry is doing it." In other cases, companies will have admirable, lofty goals such as to reform the corporate culture, but they have no idea how they expect to do this, what the corporate culture is and why it needs to be changed, or what kind of a culture they hope to create. It is obviously impossible to have effective TQC with such vague motives.

The planning in the PDCA circle has to be based upon a check of the current state of affairs. You need to know where you are having problems now and what kind of problems you expect to crop up in the future to know what kind of quality control you need. Everyone in the company, from top management down to the lowiest employee, must understand exactly why quality control is necessary, and this is where quality control management policy comes in.

9.4.4 Lack of Product Quality Policies

What kind of quality are you aiming for; what problems exist now, how should they be corrected? If you are striving to meet the so-called "international standards," how does your product stack up against its international competitors, where does it fall short, and where is it superior? It is not unusual to find that no attempt has been made to answer these and other quality questions. But you cannot possibly set goals and define directions for where you want to go unless you know where you are now. Quality policies are needed to provide guidance, but they often don't exist.

9.4.5 Failure to Clarify the Scope of TQC Activities

TQC is supposed to be an activity in which every division in the whole company participates. Yet while each division may be working to improve its particular operations, such as streamlining its documentation and accounting, seldom do different divisions cooperate to maintain a consistent quality level. Even though everyone is engaged in QC, it is not TQC because they are not working together toward a common quality goal. In true TQC, everyone is participating to everyone's benefit.

9.4.6 Lack of a Clear-cut Programme for Implementing TQC

TQC requires some form of management, and all your quality control endeavours will be for naught unless you follow a proper programme. It is necessary to divide your activities into steps, analyzing what you have done at the end of each step and making the necessary reforms before you go onto the next step. Each step should be built upon the results achieved or not achieved in the previous step.

9.4.7 Too Much Stress on Theory and Too Little Effort to Learn the Methodology

There is so much debate about TQC theory that it tends to eclipse attention to how it should be practised. Everyone will have heard about TQC, but they won't know anything about its methodology, particularly its statistical tools, or how to apply them effectively. Conversely, knowing all there is to know about the statistical tools, but nothing about how they relate to policy control, control standards, cross-functional management, and the many other quality control systems will not lead to very effective quality control either. You have to have a balance between theory and practice.

9.4.8 Ritualized QC Activities with Little or no Meaningful Content

Setting up a complicated system and demanding all kinds of forms and other documentation may feel like implementing quality control, but it is not. You are more likely to be simply imposing meaningless regulations and generating extra paperwork. You need to organize quality control to achieve a well-defined end, and the only paperwork you should require is the minimum absolutely essential to achieving this end. Ritualistic quality control devoid of substance is to be avoided at all costs.

9.4.9 Assuming that TQC is Limited to QC Circle Activities

Management people in companies with active QC circles assume that they already have TQC because they have all these great QC circles. They are wrong. While QC circles are proving just as effective in non-manufacturing service industries as they did in manufacturing, it would be wrong to think that nothing more is required for quality control. Quality control is everybody's job: every division, every level; every manager and every worker. Workers on manufacturing lines should obviously be conducting quality control activities, but the people in product planning, research and development, and every other staff area should also be involved. Top management leadership is even more important in these divisions than it is on the plant floor.

9.4.10 Lack of Interest

Every company has its strong points and its weak points. Even a company that is flying high now has no guarantee that it will not come crashing down later. The people in top management have generally attained their position after many years in middle management, but they may find that what worked for them as middle management will not work now. The rapidly changing business climate may demand radically different responses. Yet, out of touch with shop workers and the nitty-gritty of daily operations, corporate executives often fail to develop nilty-grilty a sense of crisis. A sense of urgency, an awareness of TQC requirements, and determination to meet the challenge of implementing TQC are essential ingredients for success. The attitude corporate executives take toward TQC will reveraberate throughout the company organization.

9.4.11 Problems in TQC Headquarters

In implementing TQC, it is customary to set up a TQC promotion centre at headquarters. But all too often this promotion centre is not the driving force it should be, and it may actually obstruct TQC. The people in the TQC promotion centre should naturally have a thorough understanding of quality control, but if all they do is criticize and point out mistakes without offering any constructive assistance, they will generate animosity and forfeit any chance of company-wide cooperation that might have existed. The TQC promotion centre's job is not to issue orders but to assist the various corporate divisions in systematically analyzing their problems and in finding solutions. You cannot "order" people to be interested in their work.

9.4.12 Incomplete Understanding of What You Want to Achieve with TQC

Reports from companies that have successfully implemented quality control make it clear what they expect to achieve with quality control:

1. Top management policy has been well-defined and is being deployed and implemented throughout the company.
2. This policy is targeted at revealing problems and defining priorities.
3. The limits of responsibility and authority have been clearly defined.
4. There are no administrative or psychological barriers, vertical or horizontal, within the company.
5. Problems are being tackled to rectify their causes, not just to stem the results.
6. The PDCA control circle is rotating smoothly.
7. Action is being taken on the basis of careful analyses of statistical data.

All of these items demand the statistical approach.

9.4.13 Lack of Well-defined and Uniform TQC Terminology

You're not going to get very far with quality control if every division insists on using its own terminology to discuss it. Quality control is based on facts, and data are the language of quality control. Yet every field of endeavour eventually develops its own jargon, just as QC uses terms such as cross-functional management, control points, and control items, and no two companies are likely to infuse these words with exactly the same meanings. It is thus all the more essential that everyone within the company share the same understanding of TQC terminology. One way to ensure the use of uniform terminology is to compile a glossary of quality control terms and circulate it throughout the company. It also helps to have a handbook or manual explaining the various QC tools, such as the QC process chart, and how they should be prepared and applied.

Procedures for introducing and promoting TQC will vary depending upon top management's philosophy, the company's circumstances and problems, and its reasons for introducing TQC. From my own experience, I have found the step-by-step procedure outlined in Figure 9.5 one of the most generally applicable, although you should be careful of the following points.

1. QC circles are made up of the people who are actually making the product, and the circles should help to enhance their work and make it more interesting and meaningful because of the close cooperation among everyone

concerned. Because it yields such immediate and obvious results, many companies choose to make the QC circle their first step in quality control. Still, if top management fails to explain TQC's importance, middle management is likely to assume that the QC circles *are* TQC and to fail to pay attention to TQC's many other aspects. At the same time, it is possible to build up worker resentment if it looks as though they are being made to bear the entire burden of maintaining and improving quality. QC circles are a place to start, but not a place to stop.

2. The same holds true for policy management adopted before the need for TQC has been clearly established. This kind of policy management is likely to end up concentrating solely on expanding sales or increasing profits

---

1. Staff surveys TQC's success at other companies, reads the literature, studies the company's situation, and recommends to president the TQC be introduced.
2. President declares company's intent to introduce TQC.
3. TQC introductory audit (to highlight problems, set TQC goals, and get a good understanding of the problems to be solved with TQC) preferably conducted with the help of an outside expert.
4. Appointment of director for TQC (preferably someone at the vice president or executive director level).
5. Establishment of TQC headquarters, appointment of people responsible for promoting TQC at each location, formation of TQC central committee, and formation of TQC committees at each location.
6. Drafting of TQC promotion programme and recording of priority problems.
7. Clear statement of TQC promotion programme by president.
8. Sending people to outside courses and holding in-house courses in line with the TQC training programme (TQC introductory courses for people at all levels, including inviting outside experts to lecture top management and inviting representatives from companies that have been successful with TQC to come and talk about their experiences).
9. Staff courses to enable people to use statistical methods to analyze important quality problems (perhaps using computers).
10. Declaration of start of QC circle activities and establishment of QC facilitators' group.
11. Registration of QC circles and selection of problems to be studied.
12. Decision on annual plans, deployment of plans, policy control, and scheduling (study sessions including retreats for people at all levels to draft and control policy, preferably with some additional TQC education included).
13. Divisional directors' audits of progress being made on priority quality issues (as needed).
14. Clarification of duties of each division (including TQC duties).
15. Setting of operational and control standards.
16. Beefing up cross-functional management as needed (quality assurance, cost control, production volume control, drafting chart of steps and activities, appointing people responsible for cross-functional control items, and clarifying relations with outside clients, suppliers, subcontractors, retail outlets, service personnel, etc.)
17. President's TQC audit (formation of audit committee of top executives, inviting outside expert, conducting audit, and recording results) to ascertain present state of and identify improvements needed in policy control, analysis of important quality problems, operational control, cross-functional control.
18. Confirmation of the results of the above steps, feedback, and improvement (PDCA for TQC via the TQC audit).

Figure 9.5 Steps in Introducing and Promoting TQC

without doing anything about the quality assurance and organizational improvements that are the heart of TQC.

3. Top management should certainly have a finely-honed awareness of the company's problems, but sometimes it will fail to see the forest for the trees. This is all the more reason that the company should be thoroughly audited to clarify exactly why TQC is needed and what should be done.

9.5   The Deming Application Prize

There are a number of awards for quality control, among them the Deming Prize, Japan Quality Control Award, and JIS Award for Outstanding Performance. For company-wide quality control, the most prestigious award is the Deming Application Prize.

It is a great honour to receive the Deming Prize. Invariably, all prize-winning companies will be found to have introduced quality control very systematically and to have formed top management inspection teams that audit every division and every workplace to see that quality control is being implemented in line with corporate policy. This inspection process is called the president's QC audit, and it is complemented by similar on-the-spot inspections performed by plant managers and division heads. In these companies, process analyses and QC circles alike are incorporated into a system of company-wide quality control.

The company that strives to implement prize-winning-level TQC finds that, in addition to reducing the incidence of defectives, TQC lowers manufacturing costs and stimulates new product development. Because everyone in the company is working toward the same end, everyone gains confidence, workers at all levels work better together, and formerly hidden talents emerge.

Even so, there are still companies that misunderstand the whole purpose of TQC — thinking that QC circles are all you need to have TQC. Forgetting the T, these people end up with individual divisions working hard on their own quality control programmes but not contributing to quality assurance. Even worse, they sometimes end up adopting the forms of statistical methods and documentation without the substance. It is impossible to implement effective quality control without setting specific goals.

Sometimes a company will adopt quality control after it has been tested in a single, model division, but you cannot expect significant results from such individualized quality control. Quality control demands a company-wide effort, and it should be systematically implemented.

Many companies proudly say that their goal is not to win the Deming Prize but to succeed in total quality control and attain prize-level quality. This is very admirable. For these companies, the Deming Prize is simply an indication of the level of excellence they hope to achieve. Yet once they attain this level, they may well want to be considered for the Prize, since the prospect of such public recognition and esteem is an important part of stimulating everyone to do his best for quality control.

Some people have been heard to remark that shooting for the Deming Prize is a very expensive proposition. It is not. The enhanced quality will more than pay for the effort, and the Prize is only an incidental side-benefit. It is only costly for companies that try to undertake quality control education and implement standards all at once for the express purpose of winning the Prize. The company may be asked to pay travel expenses for the Deming Prize Committee to come and inspect its plants and facilities, but other than that the Deming Prize costs nothing. Quality control is a long-term investment that is certain to yield large returns, as demonstrated by the fact that so many companies are implementing TQC and hoping to win the Deming Prize.

Given the Prize's prestige, it can be very useful to set the Deming Prize up as a motivator in implementing quality control, but it should never be the sole purpose. Nor, for that matter, should a company let up on its quality control efforts once it has won the Prize. (This last is not so much a concern, since a company with that shallow a commitment would probably not win the Deming Prize in the first place; but if it did, the Prize would do more harm than good.)

As part of the Deming Prize screening procedure, the Deming Prize Committee looks into the company's long-range plans for continuing to implement quality control. Regrettably, there have been some Deming Prize recipients who slacked off after winning the Prize, as though the Prize certified them for life instead of recognizing their particular efforts that year. In fact, there have been enough such examples that some people consider the Deming Prize the kiss of death for a company's quality control efforts.

A company can win the Deming Application Prize with a score of only 70 out of 100, which should be a clear indication that quality control is a never-ending process that should be continued as long as the company exists. The Deming Prize itself includes repeat audits after the first award has been made, and the Japan Quality Control Award is awarded to Deming Prize recipients who have made the most progress in total quality control in the five-year period *after* winning the Prize.

Figure 9.6 gives a sample checklist of the items used to screen companies for the Deming Application Prize. The company is not expected to implement every single item on the checklist, nor does implementing every item on the list mean that the company is carrying out quality control properly. The most reliable measure of a company's quality control programme is how effective it is on a company-wide scale, and the company should emphasize whatever items on the checklist seem necessary, tailoring its quality control programme to the company's specific needs and capabilities.

Area	Check points	Area	Check points
Policy	1. Management, quality, and quality control policy 2. Policy-making method 3. Policy correctness and consistency 4. Use of statistical methods 5. Policy transmission and dissemination 6. Checking policy and attainment 7. Relation between long-term and short-term policies	Standard-ization	1. System of standards 2. Method of setting and revising of standards 3. Actual setting and revising of standards 4. Standards themselves 5. Use of statistical methods 6. Accumulated technical expertise 7. Use of standards
Organiza-tion and operation	1. Clarification of authority and responsibility 2. Correctness of delegation of power 3. Cooperation among divisions 4. Committee activities 5. Use of staff 6. Use of QC circle activities 7. Quality control audits	Control	1. System for controlling quality, cost, and production volume 2. Control points and control items 3. Use of statistical means (e.g., control charts) and thinking 4. Contribution by QC circles 5. Actual control activities 6. State of control
Education and training	1. Plans and actual accomplishments 2. Quality-mindedness, control-mindedness, and understand-ing of quality control 3. How well education on statistical-mindedness and methods has taken 4. Understanding of effects 5. Education at affiliates (especially subcontractors, suppliers, and sales companies) 6. QC circle activities 7. Suggestion system for improvements and its workings	Quality assurance	1. New product development methods (e.g., quality analysis & deployment, reliability & design studies) 2. Safety and product liability prevention 3. Process design, analysis, control, and improvement 4. Process capability 5. Measurement and inspection 6. Equipment, subcontracting, purchasing, and servicing control 7. Quality assurance system and diagnosis 8. Use of statistical methods 9. Quality assessment and audit 10. Actual state of quality assurance
Collecting and using informa-tion	1. Collection of outside information 2. Passing information among divisions 3. Speed of information transmittal (e.g., use of computers) 4. Information processing and statistical analysis	Effect	1. Measuring effect 2. Tangible benefits such as quality, service, delivery scheduling, cost, profit, safety, and environment 3. Intangible benefits 4. Convergence between expected and actual effect
Analysis	1. Selection of priority problems and themes 2. Correctness of analytical methods 3. Use of statistical methods 4. Relating to company's technology 5. Quality and process analysis 6. Use of results of analyses 7. Constructive use of suggestions	Planning for future	1. Understanding of present conditions and specificity 2. Policies for correcting defects 3. Plans for promoting TQC 4. Relation to long-term plans

Figure 9.6 Deming Prize Checklist

10 Discovering and Analyzing Quality Control Problems

10.1 Methods of Analysis

10.1.1 Quality Control Analysis

Quality control is a diagnostic science rather than a remedial one. To repeat the medical analogy that I used earlier, when we get sick, we take medicine and, if necessary, undergo surgery. This is treatment. In medicine, knowing what kind of drug or surgery is required for what kind of disease is all part of remedial treatment. In industrial terms, remedial treatment would be deciding on the correct temperature and what type of oil to use. Most technology is of the remedial variety.

Preventive medicine is the science of correcting the original causes so the disease does not recur – taking care of yourself so you do not get sick. The same idea holds for quality control. When a defective product appears, its cause is sought out and new procedures immediately instituted to ensure that the same defect will not recur. Of course, the defective product is mended, treated in other words, if possible, but treating the symptoms should not be confused with curing the disease.

Figure 10.1 illustrates the control process. Results are checked, the causes of problems traced, and new work procedures established to ensure that the same problems not recur. This is control, and for control you need to pinpoint defects and seek out their causes. In other words, you need to conduct analysis and diagnosis – the diagnosis being based on the analysis.

For effective analysis and diagnosis, you must

1. Collect the kind of data that will be most useful to your analysis and diagnosis. (Avoid irrelevant data and data based on inaccurate or mistaken measurements.)
2. Pinpoint the defect's primary causes. (There are likely to be several possible causes, but only a few will be primary causes.)

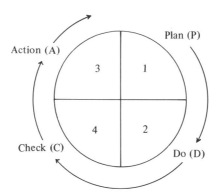

Figure 10.1 The Control Circle

3. Base your interpretation of the data on judgement standards. (Without judgement standards, your interpretation may vary wildly or be completely off-base. Your diagnosis must be objective, not subjective.)

Because the statistical approach provides judgement standards for the correct interpretation of data, it is necessary to apply the statistical approach in seeking out the causes of defective products and other problems, not only in manufacturing but in all work processes (e.g., lagging sales, shipment problems, excessive inventories, delayed deliveries, and high costs), in measuring consumer demand, and in formulating management policies. I touched on this in Chapter 9, but will repeat some of the more important points here.

Statistical data

1. Give you an overall picture of the organization (preventing you from making flawed judgements based on isolated data.)
2. Show how different data interrelate (revealing cause-and-effect relationships and helping you see the primary causes of problems.)
3. Show you changes taking place over time (thus helping you distinguish between normal and abnormal fluctuations.)

Depending solely on intuition and experience rather than statistics is fraught with danger:

1. You may end up spending a lot of time and energy trying to correct a minor quality fluctuation while more urgent problems remain hidden.
2. You may fail to identify the primary cause of a problem and hence fail to correct it.
3. You may take the wrong kind of action because your measurements are incorrect.

10.1.2 Analysis and Diagnosis Tools

There are several basic tools you will need to do analyses and diagnoses. Known as the seven QC tools, these are amply covered in other QC literature and I will only introduce them here.

1. Stratification
    This is the process of stratifying data according to their different character-istics and causes. For example, customer complaints could be stratified by what the complaint is about (e.g., defective product, insufficient quantity, incorrect shipment, damaged product, and delayed delivery), by the source of the trouble (e.g., factory, warehouse, and sales outlet), or by the division responsible (e.g., design, manufacturing, inspection, distribution, sales, and services). Doing this helps to clarify the problem and makes it easier to solve.

2. Pareto diagrams
    When defects are lined up by how much they cost the company, you will usually find that only a few problems account for most of the expense. These are called the vital few, and the remainder are the trivial many. Going back to my health analogy, there are many diseases but only a few are fatal. Your quality control endeavours should be concentrated on the vital few problems, and to help you find them draw a graph showing cumu-lative cost on the one axis and the types of problems along the other axis. By connecting up the points on the graph you will draw a curve called the Pareto curve. Figure 2.1 is an example of a Pareto diagram for one company's products.

3. Cause and effect diagrams
    These are diagrams of quality control problems and their causes. Figure 10.2 shows some of the possible causes for declining sales.

4. Histograms
5. Graphs and control charts
6. Check sheets
7. Scatter diagrams

10.1.3 Procedures for Analysis and Diagnosis

Go through the following steps in conducting analyses and making diagnoses.

1. Seek out problem points.
    Use the Pareto diagram to find out which problems are most important and then collect the relevant data on these problems. Histograms and control charts will help to clarify the nature of the problems.

2. List possible causes.
    Applying your knowledge and experience, draw up a cause and effect diagram. Surprisingly, specialists tend to be distracted by a single possible cause, and the best approach is to get together as many people as possible in a brainstorming session at which everyone throws out ideas. These ideas can be sorted later by process and category. Remember that the cause and effect diagram simply shows all possible causes and does not tell you which are the primary causes.

3. Identify the primary causes of the problem.

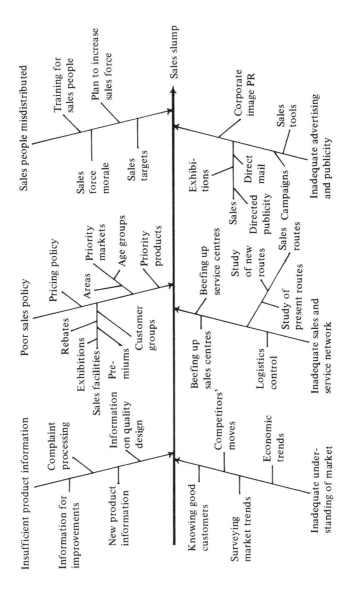

Figure 10.2 Sample Cause-and-effect Diagram for Sales

Use stratification, sampling, correlation analyses, and other statistical methods to isolate the primary causes.

4. Devise measures to correct the problem.

It is not always economically feasible to tackle some causes, and you must begin by deciding which causes will be worth the time and money spent to eliminate them. There's no point in devising measures that cannot be implemented.

5. Implement the corrective measures.

Nothing is going to change unless corrective measures are implemented, and you should be as courageous as possible in their implementation. Basing your actions on statistically substantiated diagnoses will make them easier to carry through.

6. Check the results.

You need to know whether your measures have been effective. If at all possible, this effectiveness should be measured in monetary terms.

7. Institutionalize the new measures.

New standards should be established to ensure that the same problems will not recur.

10.2 The Importance of Analyses in Quality Control

Quality control involves (1) maintenance, (2) improvement, and (3) development. To maintain quality, you must first decide on a product's manufacturing quality (standard quality), establish work standards that will achieve this quality, and set up a control system to check on work procedures. I have already discussed the quality control system required for this in the preceding chapter.

As shown in Figure 9.1, you must carry out quality analyses in order to decide on a product's standard quality, and to establish work standards you need to make process analyses.

To improve product quality, it will be necessary to analyze the current product's quality, looking into its production processes and the various related quality control procedures to identify problem points. Solving these problems will help to eliminate defects and ineffective operations.

Development refers to new products and operations, but it is just as important to have a thorough understanding of current products and operations as well as of production, technology, and management capabilities.

All these kinds of analyses are important to quality control. Analyses used to be primarily limited to process analyses using statistical tools, but analyses should extend beyond manufacturing processes to all of the quality control operations and procedures and should draw on information from outside the company as well as from inside. And while statistical tools can be very useful, you should be aware of the problems that may occur in applying these tools and should apply them in a well-organized and systematic way. Finally, it is important to establish new policies on the basis of what has been learned through analyses.

The quality analysis and process analysis that appear in Figure 9.1 involve the following.

1. Quality analysis
   (1) Selecting quality characteristics.
   (2) Taking quality characteristic measurements.
   (3) Checking on the relationship between finished product quality and parts' quality.
2. Process analysis
   (1) Checking on the relationship between quality characteristics and their causes.
   (2) Selecting those causes having the most effect upon quality characteristics.
   (3) Measuring the degree to which the primary causes affect quality characteristics.

In the following sections I will discuss how to diagnose quality, processes, and quality problems.

10.2.1 Three Approaches

1. Analysis based on past data
   In this method, no changes are made in work content or procedures or in how data are collected. This approach applies to any data acquired under these conditions. What we generally refer to as studies would fall under this category.
2. Analysis using categorized data
   In the first approach, you will be handicapped by not knowing the quality of the data you work with. In this second approach, no changes are made in either work content or procedures, but the procedures for collecting data will vary depending on what you want to know. Various means that can be adopted for this purpose include numbering and labelling lots and using radioisotope scanning.
3. Experimentation (experiments in the marketplace and factory as well as in the research laboratory)
   This approach involves the deliberate changing of factors and standards under carefully controlled conditions. And because work content and procedures are changed, you will also have to change the way data are collected.

When these three approaches are applied to different factors, they will vary in significance as shown in Figure 10.3. For example, in terms of cost, the third approach will be the most costly and the first the least costly. Thus Figure 10.3 suggests that the second approach is the best. Work conditions and procedures are not changed and instead data is collected in different ways for different categories. This way you know the source of the data and it will be easy to trace the causes of change because any changes in the data indicate changes in conditions. Diagnoses can only be made correctly with accurate data.

(1)	Cost	$(3) > (2) > (1)$
(2)	Impact on market and production	$(3) > (2) > (1)$
(3)	Accuracy (volume of information with same data)	$(3) > (2) > (1)$
(4)	Universality	$(1) = (2) > (3)$
(5)	Time (since started collecting data)	$(1) = (2) > (3)$

Figure 10.3 Comparison of Factors

10.2.2 Analyzing Past Data
Analyzing old data has the following disadvantages.

1. It is not always clear what the data mean.
2. The data might be false or incorrect.
3. Data are difficult to correlate.
4. Standards might not be uniform.
5. Data might not be very reliable.

Despite these drawbacks, even uncertain data can provide valuable information if handled correctly.

When quality control is first introduced into the company, it is common to prepare control charts showing the possible causes for quality characteristics based on the company's technological knowhow up to that time. This may raise quality consciousness among employees or reveal mistakes in measurements, but it does not in and of itself fulfill the true purpose of quality control. The causes analyzed may not be the primary causes or may interrelate in unexpected ways making the control charts useless.

Your first concern should be with finding the actual causes of your problems. A factor overlooked up to now may turn out to be the primary cause. Tracing the root causes of problems and examining the possible problems you've thought of so far are two different processes, analogous to using the tools you've been given and discovering completely new tools. To make these discoveries you need to move in several directions at the same time seeking out new concepts.

The genius achieves this through inspiration, but the rest of us must rely on statistical deduction, and for this we must begin by analyzing past data whatever its quality. Any predictions of potential defects in a new product, for example, are of necessity based on this kind of analysis of past data for old products and on the measures that were implemented to prevent the recurrence of quality problems.

In analyzing data be sure to

1. Make a thorough study of the problem characteristics using histograms,

graphs, and control charts to track changes in quality characteristics.
2. List all the possible causes you can think of for the problem.
3. Investigate the relationship between problem characteristics and their primary causes, checking the graphs for interrelationships and the control charts for abnormalities.
4. Stratify characteristics by their causes and compare the relationships between and among categories.
5. Experiment with different groupings, data volumes, and sampling intervals to heighten control chart accuracy.
6. Apply other statistical methods to your analyses.
7. Always act on your findings and check to see how effective this action is.

10.2.3 What to Do with Your Analytical Results

A report on analyses results that only covers statistical facts and figures is inadequate. The whole purpose of analysis is to seek out the causes of a problem and eliminate them to increase profits. No analysis is meaningful unless it ties into concrete economic benefit.

Your analysis report should include an explanation of the purpose of the analysis, a summary of results, the names of the people responsible for the analysis, the period of the analysis, and the methods used (inspection, estimation, technological and economic studies, remedy proposals, and a prediction of the remedy results).

A set of temporary standards should be drawn up on the basis of the analysis results, and after these standards have successfully gone through a trial period, they should be established as permanent standards. Experience and knowhow help in defining quality characteristics and the primary causes of quality problems, but you will need to implement cross-functional management on a regular basis to ensure a broad base of experience.

10.2.4 Specific vs. Common Technological Problems

It should be noted, however, that the purpose is not simply to solve the specific technological problem. For example, an analysis may reveal that the primary cause of a quality problem with a certain kind of metal was that it was being processed at the wrong temperature. Once this cause has been pinpointed it is a simple matter to correct the temperature setting, as long as the same kind of metal is being processed. This kind of analysis and problem-solving is characteristic of the QC circle and is to be commended to the extent that it is effective.

On the management level, however, an analytical approach is needed that will help to resolve problems related to model changes, new products, and new technology applications. In the metal processing example, the temperature change solution will not necessarily apply to other kinds of metal. You need a more broad-ranging solution applicable to common technological problems. These common technological problems might also be referred to as control technology elements, and their analysis would involve trying to find out where the information was insufficient or where the checking failed to be carried out properly. These elements are common causes of problems no matter what the product, and correcting them will also serve to ensure that the same problems do not occur with new products. Taking action on control elements and methods of implementation is an effective means of preventing problem recurrence. The primary difference between QC circle improvement implementation and management-level improvement implementation is in this difference between specific and common problems. In management-level quality control, analysis results need to be applied evenly and broadly.

10.3 Market Quality Surveys

10.3.1 The Purpose of Market Quality Surveys

The market survey is broadly defined as collecting, recording, and analyzing sales-related data. More narrowly defined, it is restricted to data collection and the process of researching and analyzing these data is called market analysis. It is further possible to make market predictions or estimates on the basis of the analysis results.

The purposes of a market survey are to acquire data to help you decide the following.

1. What to sell: This includes investigating the marketability of a product, seeking ways to improve the product, testing products, diversifying products, researching packaging and naming consumer preferences, studying rival products, and deciding on price.
2. Where to sell: This includes locating markets and deciding how extensive a sales network is required.
3. Whom to sell to: This includes surveying consumer purchasing power, types of customers, their purchasing habits, and demand levels.
4. How to sell.
5. When to sell.

The loop of factory production begins with accurate information on market quality and ends with feedback on the product's own quality characteristics after the product has been sold to the consumer. Production's concern doesn't end when the product is shipped from the factory. Even products that have passed quality inspection in the factory may end up defective by the time the consumer gets them. By the same token, inadequate handling procedures can lead to defective products getting mixed up with products that have passed inspection, and poor storage conditions and improper handling in shipment can lead to defective products being distributed. Inadequate and confusing instructions may also prevent the consumer from using a product correctly. Complaints are one kind of feedback from the consumer, but there is no guarantee that all the problems with a particular product will be revealed through customer complaints, and it is up to you as the manufacturer to take the initiative in checking on the quality of products that have reached the consumer.

10.3.2 Methods of Performing Market Quality Studies

While the market survey is focused on investigating distribution systems, in the final analysis it is always the consumer who is the ultimate target. Never forget that your market is in essence a collective group of consumers, and the most important part of any kind of market survey is its consumer survey.

In planning a market survey you must first clarify exactly what you intend to achieve. Some examples of market survey goals are:

1. Selling a new product.
2. Improving a product already on the market.
3. Opening a new market.
4. Finding out how price affects consumer demand (price elasticity).
5. Finding out how quality affects consumer demand (quality elasticity).
6. Finding out how well a product is meeting consumer needs and whether there is anything hindering salespeople's efforts to sell the product.
7. Measuring market size by product type and estimating the market's growth potential.
8. Evaluating the competition's strengths.
9. Estmating present and future consumer needs and planning sales strategy.
10. Analyzing the effectiveness of various sales promotion efforts.
11. Testing the effectiveness of sales strategy, product display techniques, and advertising.
12. Checking on distribution conditions, especially inventories.

Samples are one way of learning the consumer's quality requirements. Another technique is to regularly buy products already on the market (especially those of rival manufacturers) and test their quality levels.

10.4 Complaint Surveys

10.4.1 Opening New Markets

I have already said that consumer needs are the foundation upon which product quality is designed. Here I would like to stress the fact that the manufacturer can help to shape these needs. Even though the consumer may initially be inclined toward a lower-quality product, the consumer can be persuaded to buy a slightly more expensive product if the manufacturer can effectively demonstrate that a higher quality product is in the consumer's interests in terms of better durability or performance. This kind of consumer education is what I would call true customer service. Ample consumer education should be one of the manufacturer's primary concerns.

You can find out whether it is possible to influence consumer needs and to what degree by distributing samples in a market quality survey.

The same approach should be taken in opening up completely new markets for new products. Both arrogantly forcing your own quality standards onto the consumer and pandering to vulger tastes are doomed to end in failure.

10.4.2 Complaints

Consumer complaints are an important source of feedback on product quality. You can improve a product's quality design, upgrade technology, and even enhance your company's reputation for reliability by investigating the nature of the complaints. Unfortunately, the tendency has been for individual salesmen to sweep complaints under the rug, placating bothersome consumers with rebates and other stop-gap measures that contribute nothing to analyzing the nature of the complaint or unveiling its causes. In some places, salespeople are actually commended for their efficiency in settling complaints this way.

Elsewhere, people in management who happen to come across a customer complaint often make a big fuss, conducting their own personal probe into the matter and alienating a lot of employees in the process. In either case, important quality information can be lost or ignored, leaving nothing that the company can refer to in designing improved quality features.

Complaint processing is a crucial part of quality control. In culling information from complaints for quality designing, you should keep the following points in mind.

1. Complaints vary widely, but most of them are concerned with product quality problems. Problems do occur, of course, when an insufficient number of a product is delivered or when delivery is delayed, but for the most part complaints will be about quality. For example, some 50% of complaints regarding export products have to do with quality problems.
2. Complaints are not always justified. Some consumers will complain in the hope of getting a discount, getting the product replaced with a newer model, or getting something else from the company. The manufacturer must always be on the lookout for such bogus complaints. It is also possible for complaints to stem from the consumer's failure to follow instructions properly. It is always necessary to investigate complaints carefully and to weed out these kinds of problems from the more legitimate concerns.
3. There is no guarantee that there will always be complaints about defective products. Consumers seldom bother to complain about inexpensive products (like safety pins), while you can almost be 100% certain that there will be complaints about relatively expensive items. For products between these two extremes there may or may not be complaints, and the complaint ratio is likely to fluctuate considerably. Figure 10.4 showing the ratio of complaints by product price in an American market survey illustrates this phenomenon. The consumer survey provides an important assistance in finding these unvoiced complaints.
4. Complaints should never be investigated by a single individual but should be studied in a systematic fashion through established routes.

10.4.3 Tips Regarding Complaint Processing

Complaints are always difficult to process since they inevitably involve accuser and defender. Try the following for smooth and successful complaint processing.

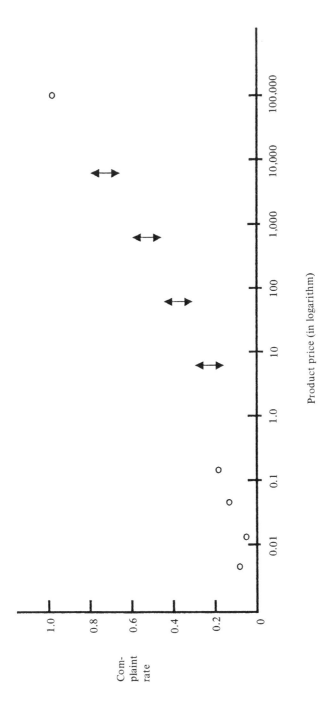

Figure 10.4 Comparison of Product Price and Complaint Rate

1. There should be a system for processing, investigating, and reporting on complaints. Everyone in the company should know about this system and consumers should be told whom to direct their complaints to.
2. Every division and section should know what it is supposed to do when a complaint comes its way.
3. Every division and section's responsibilities and authority regarding complaints should be clearly defined. Manufacturing divisions and sections, for example, should not be held responsible for design problems.
4. Market surveys to investigate sources of complaints and learn more about market needs should be a regular part of the company's activities.
5. In investigating a complaint, it is important to learn how the consumer inspected and used the product in question.
6. Complaints should be processed promptly and measures undertaken to solve the problem and ensure that it will never recur.
7. All complaints should be recorded immediately and seen through to the end. No complaint should be allowed to be left hanging.
8. A complaint processing committee will help to spur on complaint processing. It can also define divisional and sectional responsibilities regarding complaints and ensure that complaints are directed to those divisions and sections most directly concerned.

10.4.4 Items to be Covered in Complaint Processing

In processing complaints following items should be covered.

1. Product name.
2. Initial screening: who made the complaint, who processed it, and where.
3. Product history: where it was made, how it was shipped, and when it was purchased.
4. Product volume or quantity and price.
5. Nature of complaint.
6. Causes and corrective measures implemented.

After a complaint has been processed it should be analyzed. This can be done through:

1. Sampling surveys.
2. Establishing date of manufacture and manufacturing conditions.
3. Inspection records.
4. Inspections of other products in the same lot.
5. Analysis of a test product manufactured under exactly the same conditions as the defective product.

10.5 Analyzing and Diagnosing Quality Problems

The first step in implementing quality control is to decide on the product to be manufactured, i.e. deciding on the design quality. Next comes an analysis of quality problems aimed at eliminating the causes of defective products. This kind of analysis should be done at the earliest design stage if manufacturing quality is to be maintained. The process of seeking out and analyzing quality problems and their causes is called diagnosis.

10.5.1 The Diagnosis

Quality diagnosis involves:

1. Seeking out quality problems (see Section 2.2.2).
2. Creating and implementing a fact finding programme for quality problems.
3. Analyzing the relationships between the finished product and its parts and materials and between its use characteristics and quality characteristics (quality analysis).
4. Analyzing past manufacturing data.
5. Deciding on measures to be implemented on the basis of diagnosis results.
6. Analyzing new product quality (see Chapter 11).

10.5.2 Measuring Product Quality

Before you can judge a product's quality, you need to measure its quality characteristics. Certain points should be kept in mind in doing this:

1. A product's quality is not its quality at the time of shipment.
   Many manufacturers assume that their product quality is guaranteed just because they have stringent inspection procedures prior to shipment. They are dangerously wrong. Product quality is never going to be the same when it reaches the customer as it was during the pre-shipment inspection. There are several reasons for this.
   (1) Inappropriate handling after inspection may result in defective products being shipped from the plant.
   (2) Poor inspection procedures may of themselves let defective products through or even damage the products that are being inspected.
   (3) A product will inevitably change over time. To find out how it changes so that you will know what the product quality level will be for the duration that it is used by the customer, you must conduct storage tests and product life tests.
2. The manufactuer's quality requirements and the consumer's quality requirements are not always the same.
   (1) Things that the manufacturer considers defective may not be considered faulty by the consumer.
   There are functional and non-functional defects. For example, a scratch on a roll of photographic film is a functional defect, but poor printing quality on the box that the roll of film comes in is a non-functional defect. Every effort must be made to prevent functional defects, even those that the consumer may be unaware of, but the consumer will only be annoyed if efforts to correct non-functional defects raise the cost of the product. A check should be made to ascertain that inspection items are relevant to the product's intended use. There are instances in

which completely irrelevant testing is done simply because the inspection procedures allow for greater volume of inspection over a shorter period of time.

(2) Inspections are often conducted under irrelevant conditions.

Problems arise when the purchaser's inspection conditions and the manufacturer's differ. This is particularly important in inspecting functional features.

There is, for example, the problem of fading distance in visual inspection. Scratches and other defects in metal-plating will not be visible at a certain distance, which is why the actual distance and lighting conditions for the inspections should be specified.

3. Complaints are an invaluable aid to learning the customer's quality requirements. There is no guarantee, however, that customer complaints will find their way back to the manufacturer, and the fact that there are no complaints is no cause for complacency. Customers seldom bother to complain about cheap products. At the same time, you need to know the source of a complaint and its validity. Often salespeople will pass on a customer's complaint to the manufacturer without checking on it, even cooperating with the customer to frame the complaint. Upon investigation, it may well turn out that the customer was not using the product correctly.

10.5.3 Analyzing Quality Problems

A variety of numerical values (charactertistic values) will indicate a single product's quality. For example, a piece of cloth will be evaluated by colour and pattern, weave structure, sheen, texture, stretching characteristics, wrinkling, susceptibility to dirt, transparency, and more. The important thing is to know which of these characteristics are important to the consumer. There will be characteristics that interact with each other, such that if one is of good quality the other will be too, and vice-versa. The ratio of one value to another may also be significant, since some are more important than others. The more characteristic values there are the more complicated this becomes.

Deciding what the characteristic values should be to maintain a required quality level is a very difficult process requiring quality analysis.

There are a number of points to be careful of in performing quality analysis:

1. There will be numerous quality characteristics to be considered, but the consumer will actually only be concerned with two or three of them. Extensive market research and thorough complaint processing are needed to identify these two or three characteristics.

2. While consumer needs are diverse, it is possible to filter out the particular quality requirements of any one stratum by stratifying your consumers.

3. Of all the faults in a single product, only two or three are directly responsible for making the product defective. The emphasis in process control should be on these two or three factors.

4. Imprecise and unquantifiable quality definitions will lead to complaints. For example, stipulating that a product should be "as smooth as possible"

is not going to help in judging whether it is smooth enough. For quality characteristics that are difficult to quantify, you should provide samples and stipulate detailed inspection procedures as well as conditions. These instructions should be as specific as to state, for example, that inspection must be made by the naked eye at so many meters from the product under very specific lighting conditions. The consumer should also be careful to inspect the product under the same kinds of conditions. Finally, if it is still impossible to pin down the product's quality with any meaningful terminology, it may be necessary to define the product's quality in terms of its condition of manufacture, e.g. the raw materials used and manufacturing processes.

5. Remember that quality in the broadest sense also includes production cost, and this should be factored in at the design stage.

6. The consumer's quality requirements will change over time. Just because a product has been inspected once does not mean it should not be inspected again later.

Analyzing quality problems is much too broad an area to be covered by a single individual. The quality control committee should discuss responsibility allocation for quality analysis among representatives from every corporate division.

10.5.4 Regulations for Quality Analysis and Diagnosis
Quality analysis and diagnosis should be conducted at regular intervals according to standard procedures. Regulations should cover the following items.

1. Purpose
   Important quality problems should be defined and recorded, analyzed and diagnosed, and finally corrected to improve product quality.

2. Things to be done and decisions to be made
   Have every division submit a list (with a Pareto diagram attached) of what they consider critical quality problems.
   Stratify these problems. (Are they, for example, corporate-wide concerns, divisional concerns, or specific to particular offices and branches?)
   Decide on how these problems should be registered, who is responsible for their analysis and diagnosis, what the procedures for analysis and diagnosis are, and who is going to do or coordinate the work.
   Calculate the cost and benefits of resolving these quality problems and decide on whether the solution of specific problems should be made policy for this business year.
   Set up a schedule and procedures for reporting on results.

10.5.5 The Quality Troubleshooting Team and Analysis System
Some quality problems are of concern only to specific divisions and others affect several or all divisions. Critical quality problems inevitably involve several divisions, as already pointed out in Section 2.2.2.

Solving these kinds of interdivisional issues will require forming teams of people familiar with the required analyses methods from all the affected divisions. Within the factory, this kind of team would be directly responsible to the plant manager.

A team made up solely of young workers will not have the authority to zero in on critical interdivisional quality problems or to implement its findings, even though it may be well-versed in the actual analyses procedures. The person who is given control responsibility for such analyses and diagnoses should be someone with the necessary authority.

One company I know of put its technical division head in charge of technological problems and its accounting division head in charge of overseeing the analyses and correction of financial problems. These were both very good choices because they had the necessary stature within the company.

It is possible to resolve certain critical quality problems as part of quarterly or business-year policy, but critical issues may take several years to resolve, and it is recommended that such problems be handled separately from corporate fiscal policy.

I have heard of companies that publish analytical examples as practice problems in statistical methodology for their employees. While this is all very well and good, particularly at the early TQC stages, it should not be forgotten that the purpose is to solve critical quality problems, not simply to apply certain statistical tools. One approach to ensuring that the appropriate statistical methodology is used is to have people well-acquainted with the quality control statistical tools instruct people in the various divisions.

For your quality analyses and diagnoses to be effective, an analysis system needs to be devised that provides guidelines in selecting critical quality problems, gathering the required quality information, deciding what data should be analyzed and how, when and what statistical tools should be used, how solutions should be implemented and institutionalized, and how different divisions should cooperate in the process.

In diagnosing the effectiveness of a quality assurance system, you need to confirm the principal quality complaints, seek out what should be done but is not being done at each stage within the system, find out what kind of data is not being applied correctly, find out what items are not being checked sufficiently, and otherwise clarify and analyze the technical problems common to the whole system. Having pinpointed the system's weaknesses, you can then make the necessary corrections. If this is done, analyses and diagnoses can be effectively incorporated into the overall quality assurance system.

11 | Quality Control at the Design and Development Stages

11.1 Research and Development

The research division tends to be one of the most uninterested and uncooperative divisions in the whole company when it comes to quality control. Yet the research and development people have one of the most important roles to play in developing new products, standardizing production, identifying the causes of defects, and improving product quality.

Research and development people tend to scorn quality control because:

1. They believe research requires inspiration and inspiration is not to be had in the midst of standardized, organized, and regulated control activities.
2. They do not see how control can be applied to the custom-made products that they deal with everyday.
3. They perceive research as a highly individualized activity immune to the usual organizational rules.

Yet research and development is not by nature antithetical to quality control. Inspiration is born of data scrupulously collected and organized and looked at afresh in the light of careful analysis of past experience.

Research can be divided into basic research and applied research. In many cases, basic research is taken to mean ferreting out and applying technological breakthroughs made overseas in the belief that it was more expedient and more cost-effective to build upon imported technology and knowhow. However, as long as a company or country is dependent on foreign technology, you can never hope to take the technological lead and will always have to import new technologies. Long known for their reverse engineering, Japanese companies have recently come to realize that this puts them at a disadvantage in the long run. Although original research may appear extremely costly and wasteful at first, it eventually helps to push the company to the head of the technological pack and ultimately leads to considerable profit.

Basic research does require original thinking, something only the individual can supply. But the collection and analysis of data to spark the individual's inspiration can be done most efficiently and effectively by the organization. At the same time, individual inspiration and creativity can be enhanced by a grounding in quality control. Many times, the individual who participates in a group effort to solve a problem finds the interplay of ideas stimulates him to be more creative. Still, the essential role played by the individual spark of genius in basic research must be acknowledged, and no group of mediocre individuals is likely to get very far without the catalyst of genius. Nor, for that matter, will a committee effort prove effective if the committee members just go through the motions and fail to recognize their individual responsibilities.

Corporate research, unlike research conducted at universities or public-funded institutions, is concentrated in applied research specifically directed to contributing to and maintaining the corporation's technological lead. Companies invest in research because they expect it to pay off for the company. It is thus necessary to define the research targets and the research budget before research starts and to scale back any research that is outspending its budget. Research is an activity to be managed like any other.

11.1.1 Types of Research

Research is generally divided into the following three categories:

1. Basic or pure research: Also called fundamental, background, and target research, this is directed at pushing back the frontiers of knowledge. As such, it is looking at things in terms of decades.
2. Applied research: Also called raw material research, product research, waste utilization research, technical and sales service research, and even market research, this is directed at creating new products or processes for specific purposes and at setting technical standards.
3. Process or product development research: This is research directed at applying known principles to improve a process or product, or at finding new applications for known products and processes.

11.1.2 Research Control Activities

1. The process steps are:
   (1) Deciding on a research theme.
   (2) Collecting information and data.
   (3) Drawing up a research plan.
   (4) Deciding on the final research proposal.
   (5) Directing and carrying out research.
   (6) Reviewing and applying research findings.

2. Research control is performed by a control or technical section within the research division. Research control involves:
   (1) General outline: Definitions, goals, and range of application.

(2) Organization: A control structure showing authority and responsibilities, division structures and their authorities and responsibilities, groups organized by subject and their authorities and responsibilities, production management and its authorities and responsibilities, various committees and their authorities and responsibilities, chief researchers and assistants and their authorities and responsibilities, liaison among research and testing organizations, and liaison among research and testing organizations and other divisions.

(3) Research and testing policies: Research policy, long- and short-term plans, plans by item, supplemental plans, and research and testing plans for mass production.

(4) Implementing research and tests: Supplemental research and tests, laboratory tests, intermediary tests, tests for mass production, relationships among testing stages, and changing research and test plans.

(5) Research results and reports: Standards for evaluating research results, relationships among research results and other factors, preparing and submitting reports, compiling, evaluating, and applying reports.

(6) Inspecting research and testing activities: Special inspections, regular inspections, and document inspections.

3. Selecting research themes

Proposals for research themes should originate in the planning, design, production, and marketing divisions. In actuality, however, the bulk of research proposals for new materials, products, and production processes come from the research division itself. In the United States, 45% of all proposals originate in the research division, and 65% of these result in actual research projects.

It is essential that you maintain control over the types and numbers of research projects. Too many projects will only lead to overwork and poor results. Keeping an inventory of corporate resources, a subject I will go into greater detail later on, is another important part of research control.

4. After completing a research project:

(1) Decide whether or not to publicize findings.

(2) Submit patent applications.

(3) Make application studies.

(4) Apply the results.

Yet before this can be done, it will be necessary to answer the following questions.

(1) Have the data been collected correctly?

(2) How were measurements made?

(3) What are the characteristics of the raw materials used in research experiments and tests?

(4) How were experimental conditions controlled?

(5) Have the results been evaluated objectively?

11.1.3 Evaluating Research and Development Projects

Evaluating research and development projects involves essentially the same process as evaluating new product development. Since research is considered an investment item by the corporation, results must be judged by what returns they yield. Important in creating R&D policy, setting project priorities, and spotting and correcting problems, evaluations are generally made at three stages: before starting a research project, at an intermediary stage during the project, and after the project has been completed.

The final, post-project evaluation is intended primarily as a review of the way the project was carried out and its effectiveness. As such, this final evaluation should itself be a long-term assessment with a long-term perspective to match the project's estimated payoff period.

11.2 Product Development and Design

11.2.1 Steps in Product Development and Design

New product development goes through the following steps, with steps 3 through 8 often repeated.

1. Conceptualization and proposal.
2. Background research and data collection.
3. Research and development.
4. Building product prototype.
5. Planning and designing equipment and processes for mass production and acquiring the necessary materials and supplies.
6. Quality design.
7. Planning mass production.
8. Standardization for mass production.
9. Application research.
10. Test marketing.
11. Formulation of marketing strategy.
12. Post-sales marketing research (quality inspection and quality audits).
13. Redesigning quality.

With the possible exceptions of steps 1 through 3, all of these steps apply equally well to small-volume production, single-item production, and even made-to-order production.

Quality control activities related to new product development and design involve nothing less than company-wide total quality control due to following reasons.

1. Because effective guidance and an explicit management policy are needed, middle management bears a heavy responsibility for conducting the studies, collecting and analyzing the data, and making the forecasts that provide the information and substantiation for a decision by top management.
2. There are numerous steps before mass production can be started, and it takes time to go through them all.

3. Problems are very likely in the intermediary stages, and it usually happens that problems ignored in these stages turn up again in mass production.
4. An increasing number of people will become involved as the mass production stage is approached, and problems in these final stages can threaten the corporation's continued existence.
5. Project members are drawn from nearly every division in the corporation — technical, research, production, purchasing, sales, distribution, advertising, publicity, and administration — and it is essential that they cooperate fully and closely.

It is often mistakenly assumed that quality control can only be applied to mass production, but nothing could be further from the truth. In fact, quality control is less likely to be needed in the mass production of a single item because the possibilities for trouble are fewer. Problems are more likely to crop up in small-volume production of a variety of products, single-product production, new product development, and start-up for new product mass production. Quality control is particularly needed in these situations. Quality control at the development stage has proved highly effective in many cases, and new product development is in many ways a testing ground for the effectiveness of a company's quality control policies.

Traditionally, new product development has been left up to the few researchers and designers considered experts in the company's particular technology. These people tend to have such strong faith in the technology (often technology that they have helped to develop) that they lose sight of the user's requirements and actual production limitations in designing new products. They may also fail to collect important data from other divisions, and in many instances they are left to their own devices with little or no direction from top management. Sometimes these people get wedded to a particular idea that is in neither their own nor the company's interests.

Because much of the technical expertise peculiar to a company's production tends to be in the minds of the people using it, there is often little quantifiable data on process causes and effects or on the relationship among the parts and the whole. Sometimes problems are solved and there is no clear record of what the problem was or how it was solved, in which case the underlying causes tend to remain, leading to repeated complaints about product quality.

It is often assumed that quality control can't be applied to a new product in the development stage because the new product will have different characteristics from products already in production. This is not true, however, since the development steps and the departments involved from planning to production are basically the same for all products. It is important in implementing quality control during product development that:

1. Corporate policy regarding the product to be developed is very clear.
2. The procedures and control activities for each step in the development process are carefully spelled out and standardized.
3. There are standards indicating when one step has been completed and it is

time to move on to the next step.

4. The technical expertise that has been accumulated within the company is sorted through and analyzed so that the relevant technologies and skills can be applied in new product development.
5. Careful control is maintained over the development process with a clear understanding of what kind of information, control methods, and data will be required at each step.

11.2.2 The Development and Design System

A system for new product development and design needs to be set up and implemented. This is done with the help of a quality assurance diagram such as shown in Figure 11.1. As already explained in Section 4.3, it is important in plotting a quality control diagram that:

1. The route for information feedback is clearly outlined.
2. Development steps are listed on the vertical axis and the relevant activities for each step on the horizontal axis, making it clear who or which division is responsible for each activity.
3. Procedures and tools (devices and documentation) and operation rules (criteria and standards) are specified.
4. The items to be evaluated and how they are to be evaluated before going on to the next step in the quality assurance process are specified.
5. The system is revised periodically as everyone becomes more experienced in its application.

Development is usually the first stage in production, and it is imperative that quality assurance, cost control, and production volume control be implemented here as an integrated system, even though they may be handled as interdivisional cross-functional management systems in the actual production stage. Cost and production volume are just as important in planning a new product as product type and quality are.

The quality table explained in the following section is a useful tool for managing the product development system, but as Figure 11.2 shows, it is important to transmit the same quality consciousness throughout the various stages, from product conceptualization through marketing.

11.3 Quality Policy and Development Policy

One of the first and most important steps in creating a new product is that of clarifying exactly what the new product is being developed for. Everyone involved should share the same understanding of the quality level they are aiming for and what they are trying to achieve with the new product. Individual divisions tend to each have their own approaches to and interpretations of quality, and this lack of cohesion results from a failure to analyze the consumer's quality requirements and a lack of consensus in evaluating the company's production and processing capabilities.

Quality Control at the Design and Development Stages

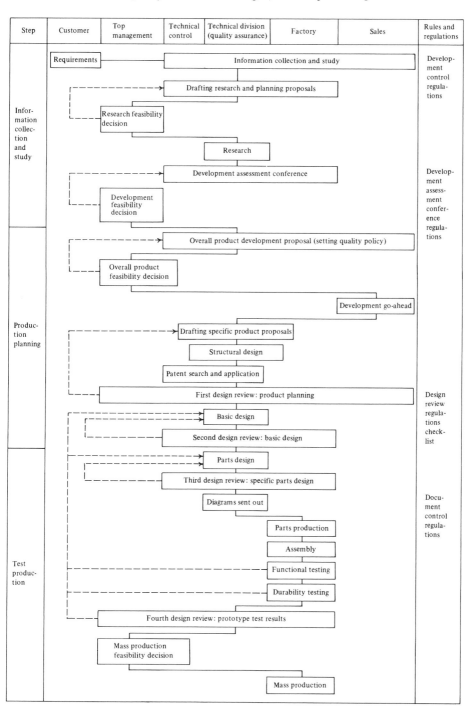

Figure 11.1 Quality Control in the Development and Design Stages

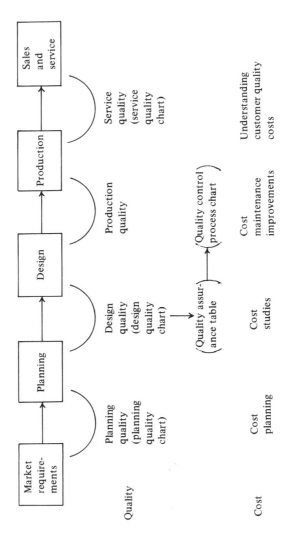

Figure 11.2 Controlling Quality and Costs

Successful product development demands that the company fully exploit its strengths while at the same time minimizing its weaknesses. As a result, it is necessary to draw up an inventory of corporate resources and to analyze the company's strengths and weaknesses. While everyone recognizes the importance of market research, most people forget the importance of analyzing the company's own capabilities and objectives. A careful analysis of the company itself is prerequisite to making decisions on the degree of quality to aim at in a new product, how this quality is to be developed, and what quality and development policies should be devised to guide and define the limits of the product's quality development.

The inventory listing corporate resources will list the company's human resources, materials, installations and equipment, and finances as well as a comparison of how the company stacks up against its competitors technologically.

A technology map like the example shown in Figure 11.3 lets you see where the company stands technologically, and this may also be used to see what new technical capabilities are needed for the new products you want to develop. A new product that plays to the company's technical strengths has a much greater chance of succeeding than one that pits the company against stronger and entrenched competitors. If you find you need a technology that you do not have or are weak in, steps must be taken to rectify this shortcoming as soon as possible.

While still at the planning stage, it is necessary to (1) review corporate resources, particularly to confirm the company's technological strengths and weaknesses, (2) establish a system to make full use of the technology available, (3) fill in the missing technological gaps, and (4) record, analyze, and solve the priority quality problems.

Still, technology will not solve everything. While new technology can create new market needs, developing a new product without regard to market needs solely because the technology is there is a foolhardy venture at best.

As noted by Juran, new product development should begin with (1) a study of social needs, go on to (2) review the new product's economic significance – e.g., will it be cheaper than existing products, what will it cost the consumer in terms of materials and energy, and how can the product's life cycle costs be kept down – and then, and only then (3) seek technical solutions.

Yet too many companies today start out at the technical end, deciding to develop a new product simply because it is technically possible, then looking at the economic ramifications, and not considering the problem of whether the product will meet any real consumer needs until after mass production has begun. No wonder so many new products fail.

Technology provides the seeds to supply market needs. How these two interact is shown in Figure 11.4. You can use this figure to determine which category your new product concept belongs to and to decide what will be needed for its development.

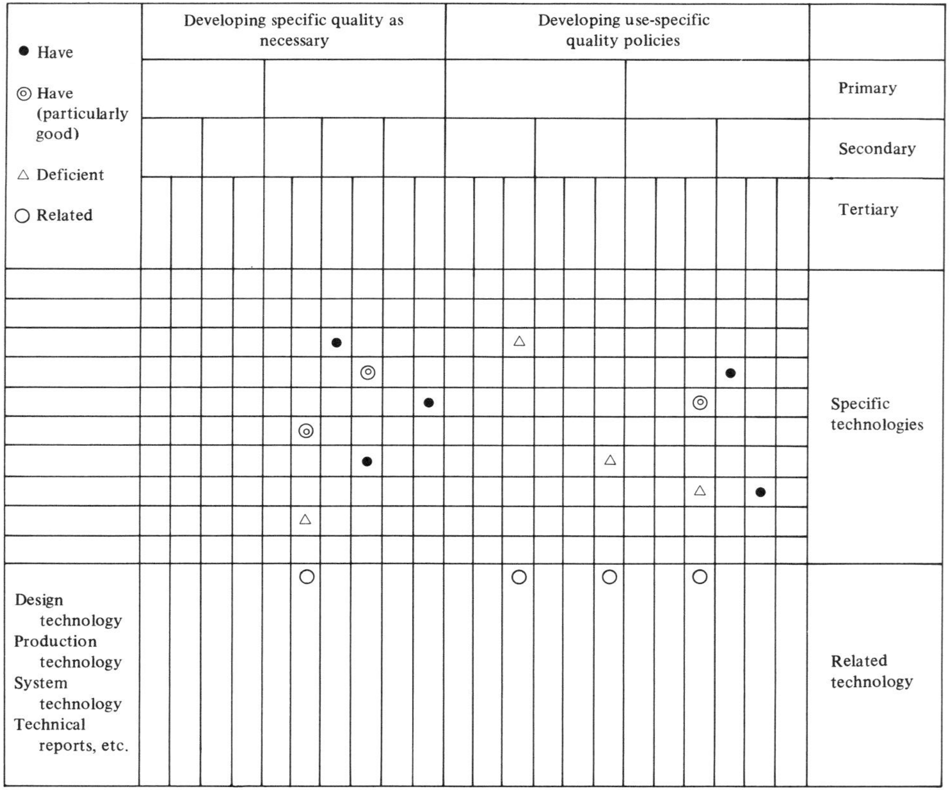

Figure 11.3 Mapping Your Technology

Market / Technology		Technology		
		Current technology	Related technology	New technology
Markets	Current market		Reformulation Minor alterations to improve quality or reduce costs	Replacement Major alterations to improve quality or reduce costs
	Related market	Remerchandizing Making the current product more attractive to current market niche	Improved product Improving on the present technology to improve the product	Product line extension Using new technology to expand the product offerings to the current market
	New market	New uses Developing new uses to sell the current product to new market niche	Market expansion Improving the current product to expand the market for it	Diversification Using new technology to go into a new market niche with a new product

Figure 11.4 New Product Analysis

11.4 New Product Quality Planning

11.4.1 Quality Deisgn

Top management plays a central role in planning product quality. It is essential to have a clear quality policy that can successfully tackle the following issues.

1. All too often a new product's quality charactertistics are decided by just a few people who base their judgements on vague hunches more than anything else. This is especially true when the new product has been proposed by one of the powerful higher-ups in the company, and it is not unusual for production of such a product to begin almost immediately and with very little consideration of its future potential. In other cases, a company may rush to match a competitor's new product without conducting market research on the product or considering its own manufacturing technology limitations, in which case the result is poor product quality, high production costs, and wasted materials and manufacturing equipment. Designing new product quality is a process that should be carried out in a systemic fashion with ample research.

2. While the greater part of new product design can be accomplished with technology and expertise you already have, problems are likely to occur in areas where the new product necessarily diverges from products already being manufactured, such as the use of new materials, a slightly different structure, different components, and processing differences.

3. A detailed, statistical market study of new products that are variations on older products and of new products that are completely new will reveal certain marketing laws. When this information is combined with what you have learned about your competitors, it should be possible to predict future product trends with a high degree of accuracy.

4. Just as conventional knowhow can determine a new product's characteristics, so is it possible to forecast the likely quality level of the new product following the shift to mass production. If you know the quality nonconformance rates in the research laboratory and in the factory, you will be able to estimate the degree of nonconformance that is likely in the factory from your laboratory results. Past production experience and a knowledge of production technology for other products can contribute significantly to new product development.

5. It is impossible to overemphasize how important it is that everyone within the company share the same understanding of the purpose behind a new product development plan. All too often different divisions have different interpretations. For example, one division may assume a new product is being developed to make use of idle equipment in the factory, another might think the new product is intended to cut costs, a third that it is meant to put the company ahead of the competition, and a fourth that it is meant to augment the corporation's existing product lines. This kind of confusion stems from a lack of consensus in evaluating the company's equipment, technology, and human capabilities.

These apparent and hidden resources must be correctly evaluated before initiating a plan for new product development. General Electric's V.P. Gregg has called this the process of drawing up an 'inventory of corporate resources'. Once this inventory has been drawn up, a company's new product policy can be formulated that will keep the company from recklessly embarking on new ventures incompatible with its capabilities. An effective new product policy is one with a firm grasp of the company's strengths and weaknesses.

6. Standards are needed to judge new product feasibility. At a minimum, these standards should take profitability, growth potential, market leadership (whether the product possesses the required functions, has an appealing appearance, etc.), market positioning, and impact on other products into account.

7. It is just as important to stop the production of obsolete products as it is to start the production of new products, and these two functions might well be handled by the same organization.

8. In planning and designing a new product, you need to perform a quality deployment to find the quality characteristics required by the product's potential user and the substitute characteristics to be used in designing the product. Inspection characteristics and control characteristics must also be defined. As will be discussed in Section 11.6, there is still much research and development to be done on quality-related technology (specific and control technology).

11.4.2 Quality Planning

Concomitant with Japan's traditional dependence on imported technology, quality control has tended to concentrate on existing products rather than on quality planning for new product planning and design.

The first step in quality planning is to define what is meant by quality. A product's quality depends for the most part on its fitness for use, but you cannot judge a product solely by its characteristics. For example, in judging an automobile's suitability, there is a whole system of conditions that must be taken into consideration including the road system, the driver, and the weight load, and these factors will largely define the parameters for an automobile's quality.

A product can be classified as mechanical, electrical, or chemical, but these categories generally overlap and interact in a complex system, and it is this system that should be the target of quality control. To give an example of what I mean by this, one automobile company had to recall thousands of cars because of a corroded pipe, eloquent evidence that the automobile is at once a mechanical product and a chemical product.

In judging a product's suitability, it is also necessary to check for harmful side effects. You need to look not only at the benefits — for both the customer and for everyone else who is in any way affected — but also at the drawbacks. Even though it is called a technology assessment, the impact on the environment and natural resources also have to be taken into consideration.

A system can be a group of interacting, interrelated, or interdependent elements forming a collective entity or a functionally related group of elements. Product quality is similarly made up of many quality properties which are functionally related to serve the product's intended purpose. Among the leading quality factors are physical, functional, human, temporal, economic, production, and market factors. For each of these factors, it will be necessary to clarify labelling, measurements and how they were made, and methods of evaluation, and functional deployment based on a product's intended use is one useful approach (See Figure 11.5)

Although quality evaluation at the design stage is still an imprecise operation, one possible approach is to evaluate quality in terms of the tangible and intangible costs to the user after the product has left the hands of the manufacturer, perhaps using the quality tables that I will be discussing later.

In designing product quality, you have to start with a survey of consumer needs. Very often, as already noted, this can be done with market surveys of competitive products and customer complaints.

11.4.3 Quality Policy
Standard quality is not the level of quality you hope to obtain but the level that you have decided will satisfy both consumer needs and your own cost requirements.

11.4.3.1 Points to Consider in Deciding on Standard Quality
Standard quality should satisfy the consumer's requirements, be appropriate to the product's intended function, and incorporate those appearance, form, design, and other quality characteristics that will most appeal to the consumer.

Just because you make a washing machine that will last 50 years does not mean you can charge that much more for it. The consumer is likely to prefer a cheaper machine that lasts only 10 years. A machine that lasts 50 years will be obsolete before the half-century is up. If people are satisfied with a lower-quality product, the wise manufacturer creates a product that meets those standards and not much more.

The next question is whether there is any benefit in sacrificing quality for lower costs. While the manufacturer should not be self-righteously trying to force excessively high quality onto the consumer, neither should be seek to skimp by with the minimum acceptable quality and to pander to uninformed public opinion. A quality policy deliberately geared to producing low-quality products is generally a mistake, but there are rare instances when such a policy is unavoidable:

1. When the available parts or materials are not suited to a high-quality product. While improved production technology may enable the manufacturer to produce low-cost high-quality products, this is not always possible.
2. When the manufacturer does not have superior designers.
3. When the manufacturer lacks the required technology and experience.

Physical factors	Appearance features (height, width, length, weight) Dynamic features (speed, attraction, strength, fragility) Physical factors (permeability, insulation, heat-resistence, stretchability) Lighting features (transparency, translucency, luminosity) Sound features (tone, clarity, volume, sound/noise ratio) Information features (verbosity, information volume, accuracy) Chemical features (corrosion-resistance, non-flammability, non-explosiveness) Electrical features (insulation, conductivity, leakage)
Functional factors	Efficiency (energy efficiency, handling ease, level of automation) Safety (non-toxicity, foolproof design) Feature diversity (diversity of uses, combinability for diversity) Portability (portability, installation) Customer range (for amateurs, for experts)
Human factors	Impression (Expensive quality, name recognition) Exclusivity (custom-made, imported, natural) Familiarity (traditional, new product) Sensual quality (finish, feel, taste, friendliness) Fulfillment (intellectually fulfilling, information-fulfilling) Propensity to excessive quality (service, specifications not found on competition)
Temporal factors	Lasting value (heat resistance, dust resistance) Time factors (permanence of effect, speed) Durability (useful life, breakage rate, ease of repair) Disposability
Economic factors	Benefits (low cost, inexpensive maintenance) Frills and extras
Production factors	Workability (few processes, few repairs and adjustments, does not need specialized technology, work standards flexible) Raw materials (wide quality tolerance, easy to store, easy to inspect, have process capability) Earnings (strong earnings, easy to adjust, easy to adapt to other products)
Market factors	Product life (trendiness, seasonal) Selection (wide selection) Reliability Reasons for purchase (Select on own, influenced by opinion leaders, influenced by others) Life cycle (long life cycle, short but profitable life cycle)

Figure 11.5 Quality Factors

In the final analysis, only when these three problems are resolved can a manufacturer set high standard quality levels.

11.4.3.2 Quality and Price

The manufacturer faced with rising costs has three quality policy choices on price:

1. Leave the price as is and lower product quality.
2. Leave the price and quality as are and accept a smaller profit margin.
3. Raise the price and maintain the same quality level.

The first possibility should be avoided at all costs. The consumer does not always notice right away when product quality has been lowered, but once he does notice, he is not likely to notice that quality has been restored until quite some time after the fact. The second choice is the one most manufacturers opt for when they do not expect their costs to remain high for very long.

11.4.4 Basic Data for Quality Design

In designing product quality, you must decide on the kinds of preparatory surveys that will be required, who will be responsible for them, and how the collected information should be analyzed.

Below is a list of the basic quality design data used at one major company. Because it takes a long time to collect and process such data, it should be kept up to date on a regular basis.

1. Characteristic values and assurance level
    (1) Survey of households that have purchased products from the company over the past two years and the uses they have put these products to.
        Location, product volume and purchasing trends, and size of demand.
        Volume of use, applications, reasons for using the product, testing methods, and sampling methods.
        Reasons for not using the product any more, use requirements, additional quality characteristics desired and why, and problems encountered in using the product.
        Complaints on the product to date.
        Comparision with competitive products.
        Desired packaging and shipping methods.
    (2) Market information regarding possible sales expansion, new applications, estimated volume needed, sales price, and range of characteristic values.
    (3) Survey of similar products available (including any product that could be used for the same purpose).
        Production volumes, market prices, trends, and manufacturers (by product type).
        Type of product by application and volume used.
        Lot sizes (production lot, product lot).
2. Range of qaulity characteristics and process capabilities

(1) Quality characteristics.

Monthly average characteristic value and standard deviation.

Correlation between production volume and quality characteristics.

Control charts, histograms, and graphs.

Intermediate quality characteristics in production process, changes in quality of products in storage (relationship to packaging system).

(2) Basic data surveys.

Flow sheet of equipment and installations now in use, survey of process capabilities (quality, volume, cost).

Study of plant capacity (including cost estimates).

Ideal production method and sources of materials.

3. Nature of aberrations and testing methods

Processes, sampling, and standard measurement allowances (aberrations).

Changes in property constants due to impurities and compounds.

Control analysis values and their correlation to product analysis values.

4. Standard inventories

Sales record data, per-day shipment volume, and inventory remaining at end of each month.

Route from factory to consumer and survey of intermediate control conditions. Days required for delivery.

5. Substitute characteristics for use characteristics

Testing methods and review of standard characteristics.

11.4.5 Regulating Methods of Gathering Quality-related Information

In order for your quality-related data to be of use, you need to regulate the ways they are gathered. These regulations should cover:

Surveys of market quality and condition of products sold.

On-going studies of samples of the company's own products and competitors' products (quality levels and prices).

Surveys of production technology and control conditions.

Inspection reports, abnormality reports, statistics on defectives, and analyses of defectives.

Information filing, transmission, and deployment.

11.5 Progress Control and Evaluation during Development and Design Stages

11.5.1 Progress Control During new Product Development and Design

Among the various methods for maintaining control of development progress, two methods in particular ensure that the required task is efficiently tackled and completed within the given personnel, equipment, time, and costs limitations: the PERT (programme evaluation and review technique) and CPM (critical path method) scheduling methods. These two methods approach the problem by first estimating the time it is likely to take to complete each task and then creating a time network on the basis of these estimates. Once a time network has been set up, it is easy to spot the probable bottlenecks and to shift time from easier processes to clear these bottlenecks up before they occur. The whole point of the time network is to eliminate all possible causes for delay, among them:

1. Sudden changes mandated by top management after development has progressed well into mass production prototypes, all because of the lack of a clearly defined new product development policy.
2. Top management's inability to come to a prompt decision.
3. Changes caused by the failure to reach vital decisions as development progresses and other reasons.
4. Improper checking at the completion of each development stage, forcing everything to be done all over again.

Time can be juggled in many ways by constantly adjusting daily schedules, and it is the job of quality control to seek out the causes for delays and ensure that they not recur.

Although the main causes for delays as listed above relate to product quality and cost, they can be taken care of by preparing quality and cost checklists ahead of time for each development stage. The application of such control and assurance checklists is called QC-PERT, or sometimes PERT-QC, and is a proved method.

Another aspect of QC-PERT is the simultaneous progression with product development and quality deployment (discussed in greater detail later, this covers critical characteristics, control characteristics, parts characteristics, quality assurance planning, specifying available and unavailable technology, and planning technology development, and assurance control planning) (See Figure 11.6). An example of this is the construction control chart used in the construction industry to control construction progress, quality, costs, and safety factors.

The important thing is to remember that quality control (including cost and production volume control) should be planned and enacted concurrently with all development and design planning.

11.5.2 Development and Design Evaluations
Two kinds of evaluations are made in new product development, one that estimates expected value and the other the product's actual value.

11.5.2.1 Expected Value
Following are several methods of estimating expected value.

1. The profile method: In this, the product's stability, growth potential, marketability, environmental impact, productivity, and other characteristics are estimated at several stages.
2. Checklist method.
3. Planning point method: This is based on a formula in which the larger the P_N value, the higher the project's priority.

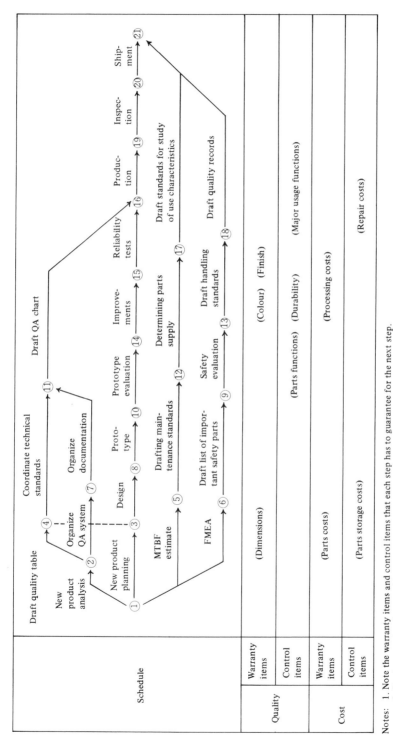

Figure 11.6 QC-PERT

Notes: 1. Note the warranty items and control items that each step has to guarantee for the next step.
2. Do the same for the post-shipment sales and service steps.

$$P_N = \frac{P_C \cdot P_T \cdot HF(C_P - C)L}{B}$$

In this formula, B is the total development budget, L the estimated product life cycle, P_C the product's commercial feasibility, P_T the product's technological feasibility, H annual operating hours, F production speed, C_P product price, and C cost.

4. Current price method (market value method): Premised on annual profits equal to the development investment, the product with the largest P_N value is the priority project.

11.5.2.2 Actual Value

The goal of new product development is to achieve maximum returns taking the product's inevitable depreciation into consideration. Since profit is a function of time t, it can be shown as $P_{(t)}$ such that:

$$\int_0^D \frac{dP(t)}{dt} \cdot dt$$

where you want to aim for the maximum possible value of $P_{(t)}$. Since profit is the difference between total sales S and total costs C, it will be sufficient to maximize $P_{(t)}$ in the equation

$$\int_0^D \frac{d\{S(t) - C(t)\}}{dt} \cdot dt$$

To derive unit cost c from total cost C, use the formula

$$c = \frac{C}{fHF}$$

where f is operating capacity, H annual hours of operation, and F production speed. To find the rate of return on development investment R_I:

$$R_I = \frac{100\ fHF(C_P - C)}{G} \quad (\%)$$

where C_P is sales price and G gross investment.
To calculate the time T_P it will take to recover the original investment:

$$T_P = \frac{G}{(1 - \alpha)\ fHF(C_P - c) + f_D G} \quad (years)$$

where α is the tax rate on the profit and f_D the rate of depreciation.

A good development project is one in which R_I is as large as possible and T_P as small as possible.

11.5.2.3 An Evaluation Example (expected value using the profile method)

A new product's usability can be judged by its external and internal factors. External factors include (1) marketability, (2) demand assessment, and (3) comparison with the competition, while internal factors include (1) production capability (process capability), (2) sales capability, and (3) profitability. Yet each of these factors includes several sub-factors. Under marketability, for example, there are (1) sales network, (2) current production line, (3) quality and price (price comparison with other products of same quality), (4) size and quantity of each, (5) commercial feasibility (as compared with competitive products), and (6) the effect on your other products currently on the market.

Each of these sub-factors should be weighted for probability and importance on a scale of zero to ten. Thus a grade of excellent would be worth 10 points, good 8 points, average 6 points, poor 4 points, and inferior 2 points. By multiplying these excellence scores by the probability estimate for each factor you can derive the expected value of the total product. For example, say there were five sub-factors in the quality and price item, that each had a different excellence score in descending order, and that the probabilities were 0.3, 0.4, 0.2, 0.1, and 0.1 respectively. These could then be listed and the calculations done as shown below.

Sub-factor	Execellence	Probability	Calculation	Expected Value
1	Excellent	0.3	10 x 0.3	3.0
2	Good	0.4	8 x 0.4	3.2
3	Average	0.2	6 x 0.2	1.2
4	Poor	0.1	4 x 0.1	0.4
5	Inferior	0.1	0 x 0.1	0.0
			Total	7.8

And because item three on price and quality has an importance factor of 3.0 (as determined from the data on previous products), this is then multiplied times 7.8 to give a weighted estimated value of 23.4. Doing this exercise for all of the items will enable you to calculate the marketability and finally the estimated value for the entire project. If it is above a certain value, the project is feasible and you should go ahead. If it is below, now is the time to stop.

11.5.2.4 Points to be Careful of in Making Evaluations

There are those who say there are too many variables and uncertainties to make meaningful evaluations in new product and technology planning and development. At best, judgements can only be made on the basis of experience and intuition, these people claim. But they are wrong. It is possible to make meaningful evaluations if you collect all the available data. And even if your evaluation proves to be somewhat off the mark, you will have the data to go back to and find out where you erred. Even if your data seem insufficient, collect additional data from other similar development projects and do repeated evaluations. In time, you will have sufficient information.

The weight of each evaluation criterion will vary with the company's history, experience, business record, and other factors. But even if you do not have definitive weighting standards, begin with rough standards that can be changed as you get feedback and develop a better understanding of the situation.

Evaluations should be done at each stage of new product planning, development, and design. I have already discussed research evaluation in Section 11.1.3 and will cover design evaluation later.

Evaluations should be done not only for new products at the development stage but also for products that are already being manufactured and sold, and you should seriously consider halting production of products that score poorly. This is not as simple as cutting a new product development project short. There are generally fewer people involved in new product development, but when a product is already being manufactured, you will have to consider new job assignments for the line workers, sales personnel, and others whose jobs depend on that particular product. Once it gets going, a product develops an institutional momentum or inertia that makes it hard to stop. Yet reluctance to make this kind of decision can result in continued production of an obsolete product that is a drain on the company's resources and profits.

11.5.3 Control Items for New Product Development and Design Functions
Just because you have set up a development and design system, that is no guarantee that every stage will progress as planned. Effective management of new product development also demands that periodic checks be made to confirm that development goals are being met. Where goals are not being met, you need to find out why and to remedy the situation as soon as possible. Among the items to be checked in new product development are:

1. Feasibility of the original development policy.
2. The costs of the development project in terms of time, money, people, number of meetings, etc.
3. Number of times it has been necessary to backtrack in the development process and the time spent on this.
4. Appropriateness of evaluation criteria at each development stage.

The whole development process is made more efficient and effective when each of these items has been clarified and everyone concerned knows exactly who is doing what, when, and why. This too is one of top management's jobs.

11.6 Technology Development (Specific Technology and Quality Control)

11.6.1 Quality Deployment

Once the desired quality level has been derived from the use for which the new product is intended, it will be necessary to clarify the interrelationships among the product, its sub-assemblies and parts, and among those quality characteristics decided upon at the design stage such as its use characteristics, inspection characteristics, control characteristics (those quality characteristics requiring process control), and design characteristics. All of these quality characteristics relate with one another, and you cannot possibly do effective quality assurance if you overlook these interrelationships.

A quality table shows how product quality is derived from the product's intended use characteristics. Functional deployment is applied in preparing the quality table. Unlike the design analysis approach in which effects are traced backwards to their causes, functional deployment is a process of analyzing everything from the new product's professed purpose to the methodology applied to achieve this end. Simple analysis may be sufficient for products already being manufactured, but the design approach is the most effective means of achieving the same end in the development stage. Figures 11.7 and 11.8 are examples of quality tables.

Not only does the quality table show how various quality characteristics interrelate, it also indicates which specific technologies relate to product quality, stipulates the quality control items for each development stage, and is used in quality assessments and market research. Figure 11.9 shows the quality evaluation, Figure 11.10 is a quality table structured to show the substitute technology characteristics required to achieve the desired quality level, Figure 11.11 expands this to cover substitute characteristics for parts and processes, and Figure 11.12 is used to decide on development methods.

It is obviously necessary to take the product use system into consideration in applying quality deployment to develop the kind of quality that will meet consumer needs mentioned above. This involves quality deployment at every stage including preparation for use (removing the product from its packaging, installing it, inspecting it and making adjustments, and training and practice in its operation), actual use, when the product is idle, after it has been used, and during safety and maintenance operations.

First developed in Japan, quality deployment is being widely applied today as an important part of new product development.

11.6.2 Quality Analysis and Process Analysis

Analyses will have to be done to decide on the respective importance of each quality characteristic listed in the quality table. This analysis of quality characteristics is called quality analysis, and the breakdown analysis conducted in reliability engineering is just one form of quality analysis.

There are those who think technology development has nothing to do with

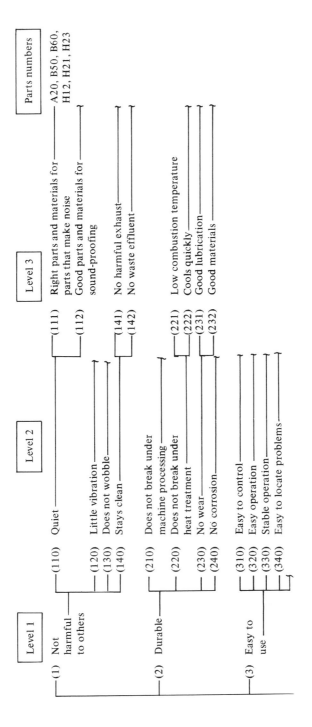

Figure 11.7 Quality Table for Large Diesel Machinery (Partial)

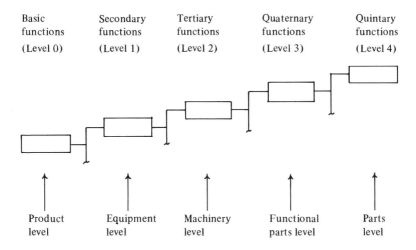

| Basic functions (Level 0) | Secondary functions (Level 1) | Tertiary functions (Level 2) | Quaternary functions (Level 3) | Quintary functions (Level 4) |

| Product level | Equipment level | Machinery level | Functional parts level | Parts level |

Figure 11.8 Correlation between Functions (Quality Characteristics) and Product Structure

quality control, but they are dead wrong. Your company's technical capabilities and quality control are intimately related, and quality control plays a major role in analyzing, organizing, and standardizing the technology you use – and in upgrading technology levels.

The statistical approach is recommended in technology development. This involves:

1. Anlayzing and ranking in terms of importance of the quality characteristics of the product as a whole and of its parts.
2. Quantifying and measuring quality characteristics.
3. Deciding on dispersion tolerance ranges.
4. Knowing the limitations of the available production means and applying this knowledge to design.
5. Analyzing reliability and deciding on the overall system's margin allowance.
6. Applying such breakdown analyses as FMECA (failure mode, effects and criticality analysis; also called FM and EA) and FTA (fault tree analysis).

Process analysis is used in identifying the causes for defects in existing products so that improvements can be made and the problems kept from recurring. As was discussed in Section 10.2.4, there can be specific technical causes for defects. For example, if the temperature for heating a certain metal is found to be inappropriate, all that you need to do is to find out what the appropriate temperature is for that particular kind of metal. A somewhat different approach will be necessary in developing a new product, however, because you have to begin with forecasts of possible problems and then figure out how they can be solved and prevented. In this case, seeking out specific technological causes will not help in the horizontal deployment. If you are going

Stage	No.	Quality Wanted Primary	No.	Secondary	No.	Tertiary	Importance	To own company	To Company A	To Company B	To Company C
Processing	1		11		111		B	Very	Some	Very	Some
					112		A	Very	Very	Some	Very
			12		121		A	Some	Very	Some	Very
					122		B	Very	Very	Very	Very
Use	2		13		131		C	Very	Very	Some	Some
					132		B	Very	Some	Very	Some
					133		A	Some	Some	Some	Very
					134		B	No	No	No	Some
			14		141		A	Very	Very	Very	Very
					142		B	Very	Very	Very	Some

Figure 11.9 Quality Assessment Using Quality Table

Stage	No.	Quality Wanted Primary	No.	Secondary	No.	Tertiary	Importance	A	B	C	D	E	F	G	H
Installation	1		11		111		C	O							
					112		B		O			O	O	O	
			12		121		B		O		O				
					122		B			O					
Use	2		13		131		C	O	O	O					
					132		A			O	O		O	O	
					133		A			O		O			
			14		141		B					O			
					142							O			

Figure 11.10 Conversion from Quality Wanted to Substitute Characteristics

— 196 —

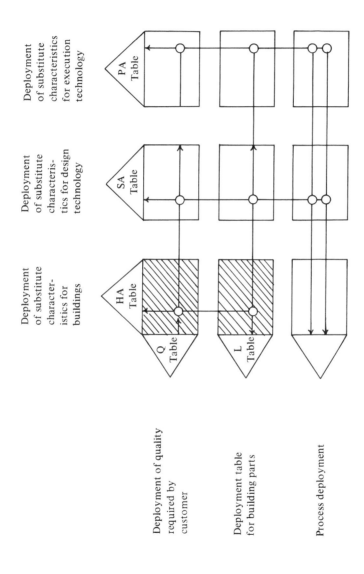

Figure 11.11 Deployment of Substitute Characteristics to Parts and Processes

to be using a different kind of metal, you have no way of knowing whether the heating temperature will be appropriate or not. The approach to take, therefore, is to identify the possible control technology causes through analysis of the kind of necessary information you lack and the additional check points that are required. By incorporating this kind of analysis in your control planning you will be able to prevent defectives before they occur.

The assurance and control items covered under the QC-PERT introduced in Section 11.5.1 are examples of the kind of criteria relating to products already being manufactured that can be analyzed to find the control technology causes for potential defects. It has been my experience that it is relatively easy to move to mass production on a new product when previous products' defects have been analyzed, control technology causes identified and incorporated into a QC-PERT, and the necessary preventive measures applied.

Your basic technology should be the groundwork underlying everything else. The most secure kind of basic technology is one in which causes and effects, elements and the system of which they are a part are clearly quantified and their relationships shown by formulae. In referring to its technology, a company may only be pointing to a rough list of available technology or to subjective technical expertise as defined by the experience and knowhow of the individual worker. This is why it is so important to standardize your technology and present it in an organized and well-defined system that anyone can understand. In the process of doing this you will realize the vital role quality control plays in raising basic and applied technology levels.

11.6.3 Inspiration and the QC Circle

There are those who believe implementing and standardizing quality control will stifle the kind of inspiration that sparks new product development. Quality control and inspiration, however, are by no means contradictory. In fact, scientific studies have recently been done to identify the steps that lead to inspiration, and it has been found that these steps are analogous to those used in the QC circle. From what I have read on inspiration and the creative processes, these steps are simply a rotation of the QC circle: identifying a goal and setting up a plan for its achievement, implementing this plan, reviewing the results, and then devising a new, revised plan. Within the PDCA circle it is particularly useful to draw up checklists for each step.

11.7 Design Review

Just as we conduct product inspections, so should we inspection design blue-prints. This kind of inspection is called a design review, and it is an essential part of ensuring product liability protection and product safety. There are a number of points to be kept in mind in conducting a design review:

1. You need to do a quality evaluation. Product quality is defined by the advantages the product has for the person who uses it, and you need to do a

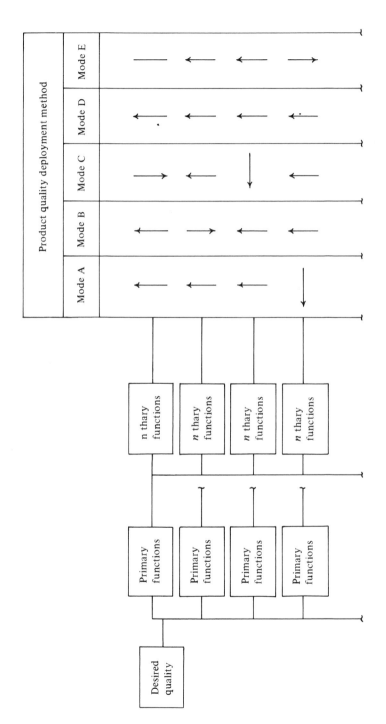

Figure 11.12 Selection of Deployment Methodology

quality evaluation to determine what benefits the new product will offer — not only to its immediate user but also to everyone who comes in contact with its use.

2. The quality charts discussed earlier are useful tools for quality evaluation.

3. A design review should be made by a disinterested third party rather than the designer himself.

4. The most effective design review is that conducted by a panel representing the end users, salespeople, and others involved.

5. Product safety and product liability evaluations will require professional advice from product safety specialists and legal experts.

6. There should be at least three stages in the design review: the design concept review (DR1), the blueprint review (DR2), and the prototype review (DR3).

7. Standards for design review methods and criteria should be established beforehand.

8. A design review should be made once again after mass production has started, and the design review checklist should be revised in line with the findings at this stage.

9. It will not always be necessary to conduct all three design review stages for every type of product. These guidelines should be followed scrupulously for a completely new kind of product, but the final prototype review may be all that is required when you are only modifying one of your products. Still, there should be clearly defined standards for skipping design review steps and records explaining why a specific design review stage was waived.

11.8 Design Change Control

A product's functional and physical characteristics are usually recorded in what is called a configuration. Since a design change will alter this configuration, configuration control (such as the U.S. military's MIL-STD-480 used for altering procurement specifications) is needed in instituting any changes.

Design changes are often made arbitrarily by designers, yet this can easily lead to quality problems and increased costs. To avoid problems, any changes should be preceded by a thorough study of their likely impact and followed up by strong quality control all the way down the line. The original change and all the other changes it causes should be standardized.

There are many kinds of design changes. Some (such as corrections and additional explanations appended to documentation) have no effect on product quality, liability, safety, compatibility, or maintenance. Others, however, can have very far-reaching impact. Thus any kind of design change should include:

1. An explanation of the reason for the change.

2. A statement of priorities.

3. A notation of when the change is to be made.

4. A listing of the impact the change will have (on sub-assembly systems,

parts, personnel, training, functions, systems, supplies, operations, testing, inspection, etc.)

5. A listing of related changes that will be required.
6. Data verifying the need for the change.
7. Authorization for the change.
8. An explanation of how the change will affect raw materials, parts, process capabilities, work standards, tools, inspection criteria, and inspection methods.
9. An explanation of how people will be notified of the change.
10. A thorough check of how the change is made.
11. Recovery and disposal of all old design configurations.

Fluctuations in materials and production costs should, of course, be carefully monitored. I know of one case where a design change in a piece of machinery caused it to become twice as heavy as before and to cost twice as much to build. And this was not discovered until just prior to the start of mass production.

11.9 Building a Prototype

The important thing about prototype production is that it gives you a chance to study the product fully before you go into mass production, and it is crucial that you use this opportunity to the fullest. In creating a prototype it should always be kept in mind that the handmade prototype is distinguished from the mass-produced product by a major difference in process capability. If a relatively accurate forecast is not made of the likely quality difference between the prototype and the mass-produced product, the final product that comes off the line may bear little resemblance to its prototype. This is why it is important to maintain careful process control over the prototype and to accurately judge the potential quality deviation in the production process.

Statistical analyses and well-constructed tests can provide the test data required to judge mass-production quality levels and fluctuations fairly precisely. Tests in which the product is put to actual use are also important. These should be based on analyses of actual application conditions, and bench tests can be highly effective as long as they recreate these conditions and provide solid statistical analyses of the results. Still, even with the most thorough tests, it sometimes happens that unstable quality or serious quality defects are discovered only after mass production has been started. These kinds of problems can be detected and corrected by initial flow control.

Initial flow control is reinforced quality control conducted for a specified period of time in new product prototype production and whenever a major change has been made in production processes or product design. In quality control for a product that the company has been manufacturing for some time, every effort is made to simplify the collection of information on raw materials, parts, production processes, inspection procedures, and market conditions. Initial flow control, on the other hand, purposely involves numerous and detailed

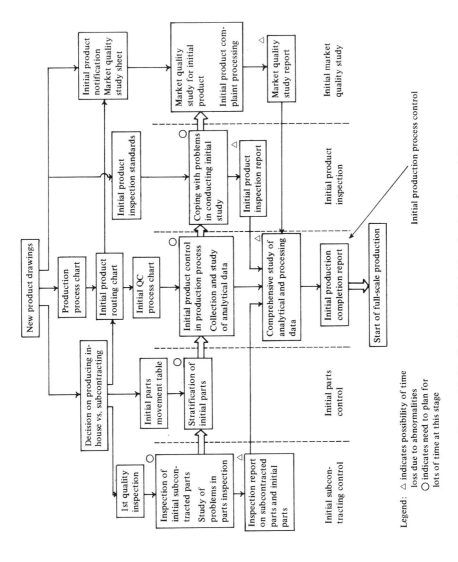

Figure 11.13 Outline of Initial Production Control System

quality check points and the promotion of quick feedback on control findings. Separate quality control flow charts and lists of quality control items are prepared for new products undergoing early initial flow control. Figure 11.13 illustrates the initial production control process.

Keep in mind, however, that initial flow control is no substitute for good quality assurance at the design and prototype stages. Thorough analyses are needed at the quality design stage to enable you to do all the quality assurance you can prior to test production, and initial flow control is directed at catching and correcting those quality problems and fluctuations that simply could not be foreseen.

11.10 Product Liability Considerations at the Development and Design Stage

Important though product liability is for the company that manufactures the same product day in and day out, it is even more important for the company that it must plan, design, produce, and supply a steady series of new products. Product liability fears have slowed the pace of new product development in the United States, and it is clear that only those companies that are able to overcome this considerable obstacle and create new products that meet the needs of the times are likely to survive intact.

Within the context of product liability, quality assurance at the development and design stage must meet the following requirements.

1. Quality and development policies must take product liability into consideration. Top management must be fully aware of the importance of product liability and the need to ensure product safety, and everyone at all levels must work to be sure that top management has the necessary information for setting these policies.
2. The people responsible for new product planning and design should also be fully aware of the importance and legal ramifications of product liability.
3. Because design engineers tend to become immersed in the creative side of their work, the design review process often overlooks or minimizes safety and legal considerations. There should be some system of ensuring that product liability is considered, either by having new product designs checked by safety technicians and legal experts or by setting up a design review division that is completely independent of the design department.
4. In the planning stage, a review should be made of all the possible ways a product might be used and what might happen when a product is used differently from what the designer had intended.
5. Tests should be done to find out what happens when materials for the new product are contaminated or improperly or incompletely processed.
6. A misuse study should be made to determine the product's safety when it is used incorrectly, not just under the optimum specified conditions.
7. Tests should be done to ensure that the product can be used as intended.

8. Prior to the initial trial manufacture of the product, estimates should be made of what could happen if processes are carried out incorrectly or other mistakes are made.

9. Records of all test results, particularly of those made by third-party testing agencies, should be compiled and maintained on the prototype and on the test-run product.

10. Inspections should be done of the facilities and testing methods of suppliers of raw materials and parts.

11. Safety instructions and warnings of the danger in using a product incorrectly should always be included in instruction and maintenance manuals.

Conventional quality control applications did not address these concerns satisfactorily. Don't wait for customer complaints before you address problems. It should be possible to forecast and forestall likely problems by the time a prototype has been made and test-run manufacturing been done, and this kind of preventive approach is at the heart of true quality control.

As already noted in Chapter 5, there has been an increasing number of product liability suits involving design defects, and many problems in product safety have been traced to inadequate design. For example, there was an incident in the United States in which a child was burned when a humidifier fell apart. The case was taken to court and it was determined that poor design was responsible for the humidifier's falling apart so easily.

More and more, designers are being called to testify in product liability cases. In the United States, the manufacturer is held accountable for accidents that result from predictable misues of a product, making it imperative that you check product safety in all conceivable situations. This is an oft-neglected but no less crucial part of quality control.

Most companies' quality assurance systems concentrate on the production stage and fail to consider product safety from the consumer's perspective. In effect, they leave out consumer-oriented quality deployment in preparation for use (removing the product from its packaging, installing it, inspecting it and making adjustments, and training and practice in its operation), actual use, when the product is idle, after it has been used, and throughout safety and maintenance operations. This is very dangerous, not only for the consumer but for the company's very survival.

12 Quality Control in Production and Purchasing

Chapter 11 focused on quality control in the new product development and design stages. This chapter will look at quality control in the production stages. By production stages, I mean all the preparations that precede actual mass production, production itself, and the storage and shipment of finished products. As shown in Figure 12.1, these stages can be further divided into sub-steps each with its own quality control requirements. Of course, the exact procedures for these quality control activities will vary depending on the type of product being produced, whether you are involved in production based on market size estimates, bulk orders, or custom craftsmanship, and other factors. Figure 12.1 lists the quality control activities for a company manufacturing machinery.

Quality control at the production stages is as much the common concern of all divisions as it is the individual responsibility of the technology, production technology, purchasing, manufacturing, inspection, distribution, customer service, and other divisions. It extends over a broad range and should be carried out using the kind of quality assurance activities chart shown in Section 4.3. In this chapter, I will discuss process analsyis, process control, and process improvement, all of which are essential to maintaining and improving quality.

I have included a section on the purchasing division because, even though the purchasing division plays an important role in assuring product quality, it is generally staffed primarily by office workers with little understanding of or appreciation for quality control. Thus I feel a discussion of the purchasing division's quality control responsibilities is in order here.

12.1 Process Analysis

12.1.1 The Importance of Process Analysis

In maintaining quality control, it is first necessary to decide on the product

Median steps	Small steps	Quality control activities
Production preparations	Conveying technical information	* Deploying quality information on development product and design quality and technical information to production and sales & service divisions * Drawing up technical standards * Communicating information on important quality issues
	Production planning	* Confirming quality standards * Drawing up inspection plans * Drawing up process delineations and process plans * Drawing up quality assessment plans * Drawing up purchasing quality procurement plans * Drawing up logistics plans
	Sales planning	* Confirming sales points * Drawing up sales policy * Drawing up advertising and publicity plans
	Service planning	* Drawing up technical service plans * Drawing up service documentation
	Planning basic unit	* Incorporating results of prototype testing in blueprints for basic unit * Confirming important parts * Overall evaluation of blueprints for basic unit
	Process planning	* Deciding process delineations and which done in-house and which subcontracted out * Deciding processes * Procuring necessary equipment * Deciding on suppliers * Deciding on work standards * Drawing up process control standards * Drawing up important process control standards * Drawing up inspection standards * Drawing up inspection work standards * Limited-run production and drawing up control standards for same * Drawing up product assessment standards and checklist
	Preparations for sales	* Ensuring that sales & service people know about the product * Drawing up advertising and publicity materials * Exhibiting product and otherwise generating PR
	Preparations for service	* Drawing up educational materials and technical service documentation * Planning and producing service tools and equipment * Training service people * Drawing up parts list and price list * Drawing up genuine parts list and obtaining parts
Production	Production start-up	* Procuring subcontracted parts * Receipt of initial parts and materials * Processing initial parts and materials * Assembling and inspecting initial parts and materials * Assessing initial parts and materials * Studying things that went wrong on initial production * Rectifying equipment or process capacity shortcomings * Rectifying things that went wrong on initial production * Improving work standards and process control standards
	Normal production	* Training and educating workers * Improving product quality and eliminating excess quality through process analysis and process improvement * Checking interactions among processes * Correcting process abnormalities and preventing recurrence * Improving equipment safety and maintenance * Providing assistance and conducting QC diagnoses for parts suppliers and subcontractors * Product inspection
Mainten-ance & transport	Maintenance & transport	* Preventing product deterioration during storage * Preventing product deterioration during shipping * Checking packing and loading

Figure 12.1 Major Quality Control Activities for Production Process Steps

quality to be produced (standard quality), then to establish standard work procedures that will ensure that this quality is built into the manufacturing process, and finally to decide on the methodology for process control. I have already discussed this system of quality control to some extent in Section 9.1.

Before you can improve a product, you have to know its current quality and the production processes it goes through, analyzing each quality control process to identify the quality problems requiring solution. Building in quality in the production process requires a thorough understanding of the technological conditions for each work process. For example, in heating a certain metal, you must know the required temperature, what kind of heating agent is needed if any, and other factors that will have to be maintained in the production process to achieve the desired product quality. This involves knowing the relationship between the characteristic values of the finished product and the factors in the heating process that lead to these characteristics. You must, in other words, know the causes and their effects.

In identifying the relationship between major causes and their effects, you have to do what is called process analysis. The process's technical requirements are set forth in a manual of technical standards and specific work procedures outlined in a work standards handbook. Sometimes technical and work standards are combined under manufacturing standards, and sometimes work standards are further categorized into work directions, a summary of work goals, time-motion standards, and work procedures.

The word "process" can be confusing, since it often means different things to different people in different contexts. In the context of productivity, process is what the product goes through and the activities that take place in this process are referred to as work. Thus transporting, cutting and trimming, and inspecting, for example, are processes from the product's perspective and are individual work procedures from the worker's perspective. The process is therefore a series of individual production activities.

In quality control, a process is perceived as a series of causes aimed at achieving certain effects, and the process analysis that is undertaken to pinpoint these causes involves:

1. Studying the relationship between quality characteristics (effects) and their causes.
2. Selecting the causes that have the most pronounced effect on quality characteristics.
3. Judging the extent to which these causes affect quality characteristics.
4. Deciding on the optimum process conditions required to maintain the causes having the best effect.

The statistical approach is the most effective in process analysis, and I have already discussed analysis and diagnosis methodology in Chapter 10. It is useless to apply the statistical approach, however, without first carefully analyzing the data, both the data that you already have on hand and the data that you collect new. It is also important to make a thorough study of actual manufacturing processes to identify the relationships between quality effects and their causes.

12.1.2 Effects and Their Primary Causes

An industrial product is a collection of many elements and therefore has many different quality characteristics, each with its own value. Naturally, the combined effect of these characteristics and their dispersion is significant in judging final product quality, but as much attention should be paid to fluctuations among individual characteristic values as to a single representative value. In industrial production, changes in raw materials, production volumes, production conditions, and work conditions can all cause major fluctuations in a product's characteristic values.

Causes can thus be traced to materials, manufacture, measurement, production and measurement methods, workers (men), and machines. These are typically referred to as the 6-Ms, and are sometimes consolidated into the 4-Ms, i.e., materials (raw materials and parts), machines (installations, tools, and measuring devices), methods (manufacturing, measuring, and control methods), and men (workers and management).

Feigenbaum referred to the 7-Ms: market, men, money, management, materials, machines and methods, and miscellaneous, with the qualification that management is a very important factor affecting product quality.

Other factors affecting quality are:

1. Factors that affect quality characteristics independently of all other causes.
2. Factors that directly affect other causes and thereby indirectly affect quality characteristics.
3. Factors that affect quality characteristics when they interact in certain ways with other causes.

In statistical quality control, factorial effects are those effects resulting from the interaction of various factors. In general, the primary factors affecting characteristic values are referred to simply as causes.

The purpose of a quality diagnosis is to seek out those causes that have a major effect upon the product's characteristic values and to control them to achieve the desired quality level. For this reason, you must do the following.

1. Use statistical experiments to clarify which causes have the most impact.
2. Use statistical estimation to find out to how much these causes affect the product's characteristic values.
3. Measure the degree to which the combination of minor causes affects the product's characteristic values.

Having done all of this, you are ready to create or revise work standards on the basis of your findings.

12.1.3 Latent Causes in Chemical Manufacturing Processes

What, exactly, are the some of the major causes that emerge in production processes? By way of illustration, let us look at some of the causes and effects in the chemicals industry.

12.1.3.1 Materials

Many raw material characteristics can affect the finished product's quality. In the chemicals industry, these could include chemical compositions, crystal forms, particle sizes and their distribution, hardness, and tensile strength, and raw material quality can have a particularly major impact on finished product quality in the chemicals industry. It is thus very important to have stringent purchasing division sets arbitrarily high standards and demand specifications raw materials are going to be sampled and analyzed to ascertain quality, and this should involve coordinating inspection procedures and standards with your suppliers to ensure uniformity throughout.

When a company neglects the need for this kind of careful analysis of materials, uneven material quality can be a primary cause of fluctuations in final product quality. On the other hand, you can also run into problems if the purchasing division sets arbitrarily high standards and demand specifications and inspections that have nothing to do with the actual characteristics required by the production and inspection divisions.

Finally, while the materials themselves may be of the required quality when they are received, quality can deteriorate as a result of improper handling. Different lots may get mixed up because they are not clearly marked, or they may be contaminated in the shipment process.

12.1.3.2 Production

Improper or insufficient pre-production preparation can lead to poor product quality. Not enough information may have been conveyed to the work floor, standard allowances may be incorrect, or mistakes can have been made in allotting materials, equipment, and personnel. Specification allowances will fail to provide the necessary guidance when they are too broad or too narrow. In extreme cases there may be no allowances at all, making work nearly impossible.

Other production-related factors that can cause quality problems are incorrect work procedures and a failure to provide the required work environment or equipment.

In batch processing, the residue left by previous reactive substances can affect new batches made in the same reactors. Using recycled materials can also cause quality to fluctuate.

Fine adjustments are required in many processes, but there may be over- or under-adjustment because there are no regulations concerning the degree and timing of the adjustment. Leaving such adjustments up to an automatic control system can result in over-adjustment.

Reaction heat and speed are critical factors in chemical reactions, and they can be affected by the timing and order in which substances are combined. The amount of a substance in the reactor should also be carefully regulated in that it affects the rate of heat diffusion and the speed with which the substances should be mixed.

Excessively uneven quality can be caused by fluctuations in reaction heat, speed, and catalytic functions, most generally by a combination of such factors. You might also have poor quality reactive substances, improper mixing or heat transmission, insufficiently processed substances, overly processed substances, shoddy equipment maintenance, contamination from improper handling of materials during shipment and in the plant, or any one of a number of other problems – all of which will cause your quality to vary.

Work teams are often given conflicting instructions, with the result that there is undesirable fluctuation in final product quality. For example, one team may be told to mix new substances into the reactor vat slowly and carefully while another team simply dumps them directly into the mixture. Discrepancies like this and their resulting problems occur most often when day and night shifts and different work teams relieve each other. Everybody needs to get the same training if you want to avoid this kind of situation, and there should be strong communication links among all workers.

Final product quality can even be affected by a worker's physical or mental condition. Chemicals may not be mixed properly and other mistakes may be made because workers are required to work in difficult, unnatural postures, under poor lighting, when they are tired, and so on.

12.1.3.3 Measurements

Incorrect timing and instrument errors in making measurements can affect quality. As chemical analyses are often long, complicated processes, there is all the more reason procedures should be carefully studied, standardized, and controlled. All too often, the people making these analyses are unaware of the points at which errors are most likely to occur. They need feedback and strong training in what they are doing, and this must not be allowed to be a rote or mechanical operation. Analyses should be fast and based on actual measurements rather than statistical inferences.

Sampling and measuring methods differ considerably depending on whether they are for quality assurance or for process control. If they are for process control, a certain degree of correctable deviation is allowed. For example, reactor readings should usually be in the centre, but they do not have to be exactly on centre as long as the deviation is always the same.

Problems occur when a measuring instrument's scale is either too precise or not precise enough. An instrument may be corroded or covered with residue that affects its readings. It is also possible that an instrument has been incorrectly placed. A pyrometer cannot be expected to give an accurate reading if it is near a cold spot.

In using automatic controls, the factors to be controlled, gauges, and set points should be determined on the basis of experimental trial and error. An automatic control may not be as finely calibrated as required and it may be necessary to incorporate mechanisms for slow relays and placement averages when taking measurements from several points. Temperature control is, of course, extremely important and it is helpful to draw up a control chart showing the degree of temperature deviation allowed.

12.1.3.4 Environment

Heat and power sources are important environmental factors in a chemicals plant. Steam pipes weave throughout the plant and though valves may be at uniform settings there can still be instances of over- or under-heating. Electric power fluctuations also affect product quality, though this is much harder to measure. Three brief power failures spread out over a 30-minute period will have decidedly different consequences than a single 30-minute power failure, and the aftereffects of a power failure can wreck havoc with product quality for some time.

12.1.3.5 Control

Improper control can also upset manufacturing processes. There may be control charts, but their existence is no guarantee that they are used properly and action is taken to correct inadequate processes. In many companies, no attempt is made to detect and control the various causes that can affect product quality, and it is left to shop workers to do the best they can. The control chart can be an efficient tool for preventing mistakes, but it is not sufficient in and of itself. Other preventive tactics also need to be adopted, including colour coding and work process rationalization.

While I will be covering causes and effects in machinery production in the sections on process capability, many of the causes I have described for chemical production are just as applicable for a factory producing machinery. For example, a hydraulically controlled cutting machine can go awry, cutting pieces that are not to specification, because its hydraulic oil is overheated with the machine's repeated use. No matter what you are manufacturing, you should be alert to cause factors and their effect on quality characteristics. A thorough understanding of process acquired through numerous process analyses is essential to maintaining and improving product quality.

12.1.4 Selecting the Principal Causes

1. As you can see, there are numerous factors that can affect the characteristic values of a product. You could probably list ad infinitum the factors that can affect the production of a synthetic substance through chemical reactions, for example. To cite just a few possibilities, there is the composition of raw materials, their purity and water content, crystal size, speed of dissolution, temperature, pressure, agitation speed, the size and type of reactor, and many, many more. All of these factors affect the finished product's characteristic values, but to different degrees. It is neither necessary nor possible to control all of these factors. Rather, you should concentrate on the few key factors that have a major effect upon characteristics values and control these vital few to maintain process stability.

2. If all factors carried the same weight, it would be necessary to control each

and every one. This is impossible – and fortunately unnecessary. In most cases, controlling the principal factors is sufficient to achieve one's goal. The degrees to which different factors affect a product's characteristic values can be measured using the Pareto diagram. The diagram is certain to reveal the two or three factors that must be controlled – the causes having the greatest effect.

3. A product is judged by many quality characteristics. For example, a sheet of metal will be judged not only by its thickness but also by its surface condition and hardness. Still, a few of these characteristics are generally sufficient to define product quality.

4. While a product is usually evaluated by a combination of quality character-istics, such as length, weight, and external appearance, it is difficult to analyze the combined effect of these characteristics. Thus each character-istic value should be analyzed separately. The same holds true for a product that is actually a combination of several elements. Rather than attempt to evaluate the whole, it is generally easier to investigate the characteristic value of each separate element.

5. It will naturally be easier to judge those characteristic values that can be quantified and measured. This does not mean, however, that characteristics that are difficult to measure can be ignored. Even such characteristics can be analyzed. For example,
    (1) Grades can be assigned to colours and odours.
    (2) Two items of a pair can be ranked in comparison rather than attempting to rank several items that are difficult to compare.
    (3) Analyze a substitute value that relates to the characteristic value that you really want to measure but cannot. For example, a product's surface smoothness can be measured using a friction index. Of course, you have to remember that the two values will not correlate exactly.
    (4) A value determined by the condition under which a measurement is made can be used to judge product quality. For example, surface scratches can be scored by the distance away from them you have to be before they are no longer visible.

    Actual measurements will give you more accurate information regarding a product's quality level. Yet in fields such as the chemicals industry, where continuous processes must be analyzed, calculated statistical values can provide a valuable reference in judging finished product quality. You could, for example, derive a characteristic value for a certain chemical through a statistical calculation based on the number of reaction vats that take longer than a given time to synthesize their contents.

6. Just as there are many causes that can affect a single characteristic value, so there are many characteristic values that can be affected by a single cause. Thus it is often possible to achieve the quality level you require by controlling related characteristic values. You could, for example, indirectly control a product's hardness by keeping track of its thickness. In deciding which characteristic values should be controlled, you should choose those

that are easier to measure. But even more important, you should choose the characteristic value that most affects the goal you are trying to achieve. For example, if there is no urgent need to improve product quality, you may decide to make increasing yield your primary goal. If at all possible, you should also consider the comparative costs of various improvements so that you can choose the most cost-effective approach to achieving this goal.

7. Select cause factors that can be controlled. In heating up a furnace, it will be easier to measure the temperature nearest the outside surface of the furnace than the actual temperature at the centre. Another method of controlling temperature in an oil-fired furnace would be to control the valve on the pipe that feeds the oil to the furnace.

Whatever approach you take, your aim should be not simply to find out why the errors occur but to cut down on the number of errors. Knowing why defects occur is no help if you take no corrective action.

12.1.5 Investigating Causes and Their Effects
Spur-of-the-moment inspections to find out the causes of defects can actually be counterproductive. You may overlook critical causes or repeat a process analysis that has already been done. To avoid this, it helps to draw up a list of the important causes and their effects. This list of causes and effects should include the following information.

1. On effects: quality target, specifications, quality standards, consumer needs, comparison with the competition, measurements, sampling methods, measuring methods and instruments, sampling margin for error, measurement margin for error, histograms, control chart, method of preparing control chart, control standards, control conditions, average values, fluctuations, and control index.
2. On causes: work standards, measurements, effectiveness and timing of adjustments, method of making adjustments, adjustment economies, control charts for making adjustments, graphs, process capability charts, and how these various charts and graphs are prepared.
3. On cause-and-effect relations: cause-and-effect diagrams showing the inter- actions of causes and effects and lists of causes that can or cannot be controlled.

The relationship between causes and effects are usually demonstrated in the kind of cause-and-effect diagram shown in Figure 12.2. Some people make the mistake of drawing up a diagram that only shows the effects and not the causes that are thought to lead to these effects. The cause-and-effect diagram will not indicate the degree to which different causes lead to different effects, and you will need to do a process analysis to get this information. It is a mistake to assume that making a cause-and-effect diagram is all there is to analyzing causes. The diagram is meant to be used. After some experience with a job it should be possible to grade the various causes according to the degree to which they affect the end goal, to add new causes discovered through analysis to the diagram, to

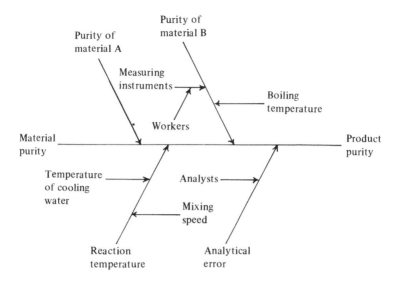

Figure 12.2 Cause-and-effect Diagram

delete not-so-important causes, and so forth. The diagram helps you to organize your knowledge of the process for more effective control. Multiple diagrams should be drawn up for every process that needs to be analyzed.

There is another kind of cause-and-effect diagram that can be useful in the laboratory where it may be necessary to trace the influence of intermediary causes on various effects. An example is shown in Figure 12.3.

12.1.6 Deciding on Optimum Standards for Causes

Once you have found the causes that most strongly influence effects, you need to establish and maintain the optimum standard values for these causes. The statistical approach is the best way of deciding on optimum standards.

While these standards can be set with statistical methods, experimental planning will enable you to change these values until you find the optimum standards. This is important because the factory is bound to have numerous extraneous factors that are not found in the laboratory and that invalidate laboratory standards. Be careful, however, that this process does not lead to too much fluctuation and nonconformance. If at all possible, it is best to determine optimum standards working directly with the production processes and gradually altering processes one at a time. Eventually, you will hit upon the optimum standards to be maintained. Another important factor in setting optimum standards, of course, is cost.

Even when a cause value remains constant, its effect may vary because of the influence of other causes. It is therefore important to keep this fluctuation to a minimum to make it easier to judge what difference your conscious changes

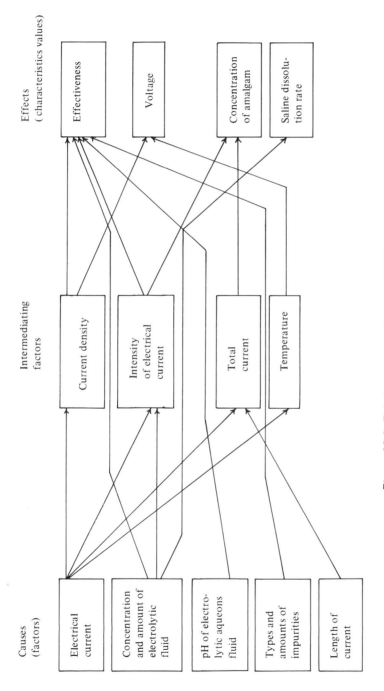

Figure 12.3 Relations among Causes and Effects

produce. Some causes, such as temperature, cannot be isolated from their ramifications, and it is important on these to take the side-effects into account. Remember also that you have to take costs into consideration in setting your standard values.

12.1.7 Process Analysis Methodology

Analyses and diagnoses should not be done arbitrarily by a single division, not even the quality control division. These are procedures that require close cooperation among all divisions and sections, and there should be a handbook of common procedures for the kinds of analyses and diagnoses. This kind of handbook can be referred to by any of several names: analyses standards, methods of tracing breakdowns to their causes, regulations for dealing with defects, and so on. A committee should be set up to decide how to organize the analysis procedure, who should be in charge of it, when it should be carried out, how much it will cost, and how the results will be reported. Only after top management has approved the committee's recommendations should the actual analysis be done, although most of the forms can be drawn up even before approval is received.

Taking this approach ensures that people on the line will not suddenly decide to change processes or work procedures and that analyses results will not be ignored. Mistakes provide invaluable lessons, and creating a framework in which everyone shares responsibility makes it more likely that mistakes will be reported, since no one person will have to bear the blame.

Separate analysis standards should be established for each process, and these standards should include a listing of all the process's characteristic values and their possible causes. Once you know a process's quality characteristics and their causes, how the analysis is to be done, and what control methodology is to be applied, it is relatively easy to plan and implement an analysis and to control cause factors.

1. Major points in setting regulations for analyzing quality problems
   Goal: Collecting information on critical quality problems, analyzing them, and implementing measures for maintaining and improving quality.
   Contents: A quality control committee should decide on an analysis plan, how it should be implemented, and how results are to be reported. Among the things to consider in setting these standards are methods of organizing and analyzing data (in terms of their economic and technological significance), Pareto diagrams, loss calculations, estimates of the funding required to make changes, analysis methods, analysis organization, person responsible, timing, costs, and reporting methods.

2. Major points in setting regulations for factory experiments
   Goals: Minimize the confusion that is likely to be caused by experimental changes of production conditions, make your adjustments in the work standards, and see the process through to its conclusion.
   Contents: Designing the experiment, getting top management approval,

assigning someone to direct the experiment, and informing the materials, production, and inspection divisions of these decisions. Decide what to do about the defectives that will result. Decide on who will be responsible for making measurements, keeping records, and organizing and analyzing results. Organize the QC staff and supply them with the necessary tools. Include specialists in designing experiments. Consolidate results, prepare a progress chart, report on results, and institute the required reforms.

It helps to have the analysis standards include the standard deviations for material balance, energy balance, and cost balance. Although few companies actually carry their analyses this far, these areas warrant careful study.

12.2 Process Design

12.2.1 Process Studies

You cannot control a process until it has been analyzed to trace the relationships between its causes and effects and technical and work standards have been established. The technical standards are required to maintain causes at their optimum levels and the work standards to provide control items with which to check for and correct abnormalities.

The manufacturing process can be broken down into roughly four stages: processing, transport within the factory, inspection, and shipment. The first step in analyzing a process is to clarify its various procedures. It is especially important to define the interrelations among work, materials, components, and the final product. This is done by preparing a flow sheet. In Japan, JIS code Z 8206-1960 gives the symbols to be used to indicate each work procedure on the flow sheet. The equipment and machinery used in a process are also entered on the flow sheet, as are such work condition indicators as temperature, pressure, distribution of materials, and so forth. The direction of flow is indicated by arrows between machinery and work steps. It can also be useful to indicate the direction of energy flow (electricity, steam, etc.). The quality and volume of materials and components should be recorded.

Different factories use different kinds of forms to outline a process's work procedures. Known by various names — production routine, operation sheet, operation detail, and sometimes collectively as process specifications — these do not have to be detailed explanations of how specific jobs are done. The details can be specified in work standards or work directions. Yet it is essential that they include the following, all of which could also be incorporated in a work standards handbook.

1. The materials that will be used in that particular process. Actual material quality should be indicated under material specifications, so that you only need to note here whether the material to be used meets these specifications.
2. The equipment and machinery that will be used, their types, models, sizes, capabilities, and capacities.
3. The flow of materials, including both volume and speed.

4. Process experiments and tests.

The process analysis is performed to decide:

1. What kind of process is most appropriate.
2. What kind of work will be required.
3. What kind of control is necessary.

The first process analysis goal is, in effect, process design, and you will need to study the following items before you can design a process.

1. The production process
   By production process, I am referring to everything from the purchase of raw materials to the sale of the finished product. By contrast, the manufacturing process is more narrowly defined, being limited to the process by which raw materials are transformed into a finished product. A thorough study of the production process will include studies of market quality, price competitiveness, marketability, technology, packaging, shipment, and sales, with the understanding that some of this research will have to be done before you can decide on standard quality.

2. Work analysis
   This includes work methodology, sequence, load, division of responsibilities, organization, environmental conditions, safety and sanitation, work conditions, route analyses, and efficiency studies.

3. Production technology
   Production technology includes studies of production equipment capabilities in each process, operating efficiency, and machinery maintenance.

4. Production control
   Though production technology is often studied, production control tends to be overlooked. Production control will include information on sampling sites and methods, measuring sites and methods, systems of recording data, control charts and other control tools, and the QC flow sheet.
   The QC flow sheet is a particularly important tool for studying processes. It should include indices for sampling and measurement deviations as well as other data as discussed in Sections 12.3.2 and 12.3.3.
   Other control processes that should also be studied are measurement control, temperature control, and equipment control.

5. Process capability
   This I will discuss in the following Section 12.2.2.

6. Process dynamics
   Studies of process cycles, timing, and delays, particularly as related to causes and their effects, are important in, for example, designing automatic control systems.

12.2.2 Process Capability Studies

12.2.2.1 Process Capability Chart

A control chart will tell you whether a process is being controlled or not, but having controls is in itself meaningless if specifications are not being met. You should therefore begin by making a study of how closely a process is adhering to specifications. This is called a process capability study, and it is done using a process capability chart that plots changes in individual quality characteristic values over time.

Examples of process capability charts are shown in Figure 12.4. In chart (a) you can see that though characteristic value fluctuations are not excessive, the average is consistently above the specifications' upper limit. Chart (b) shows a highly volatile process fluctuating wildly between the lower and upper limits. In chart (c), the average is roughly between the two limits, but there are values that dip below the lower limit and others that go above the upper limit.

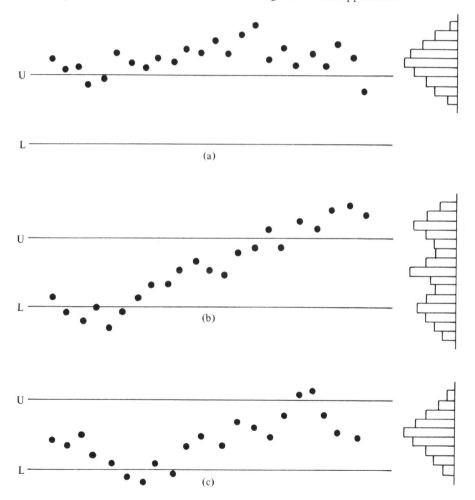

Note: U is the upper limit and L the lower limit.

Figure 12.4 Process Capability Charts

A process capability chart can tell you if you are getting too much fluctuations, but it can also indicate that you are being overly meticulous and getting all of your numbers unnecessarily close to the optimum middle, in which case you might want to reconsider the economics of the process and allow yourself a little more tolerance.

Only after you know that a process is meeting its specifications and is symmetrically stable is it worthwhile preparing a control chart. You may think you are controlling a process, but if quality standards are not being met, your control is obviously meaningless. A process cannot be controlled effectively until it has been thoroughly analyzed and work standards have been established. Of course, it may happen that the process has already been analyzed, in which case you can move directly to preparing control charts, but any new or unanalyzed process should start with a process capability study.

12.2.2.2 The Meaning of Process Capability

JIS Z 8101-1981 defines process capability as

"Pertaining to the specific result inherent in the stable process, the limit of capability that is able to attain reasonably. Usually, this term concerns quality, and when the distribution of quality characteristic values of products manufactured by the process shows a normal distribution, it is frequently expressed by 'mean value + 3 σ,' while it is sometimes by 6 σ (where o is the standard deviation of the distribution mentioned above) only."[1]

You must use the control chart to determine whether a process is stable or not. There are specialized texts on how to prepare and use control charts so I will not go into detail here but will confine myself to explaining the control chart's function.

JIS Z 8101-1981 explains the quality control chart as:

"A chart used to investigate whether a production process is in a stable state or not, or to sustain a production process in a stable state. Having drawn a pair of lines to show control limits, points representing quality or process conditions are plotted, and if the points are within the control limits as well as showing no trend in alignment, the production process is in a stable state, while if a point falls outside the control limits or the points align with trend, it indicates that some assignable cause has existed. If the existence of assignable cause is perceived, the cause shall be investigated and appropriate actions shall be taken to prevent the recurrence of such case to the production process, whereby the process will be able to sustain in a stable state."[2]

Western Electric's 1956 Statistical Quality Control Handbook says that process capability is the normal functioning of the process when the work is being statistically controlled, meaning that it is the capability inherent in the process and the results that may be obtained from the process when it is

---

[1] Japanese Industrial Standard:Glossary of Terms Used in Quality Control, JIZ Z 8101-1981. (1981). Prepared by Japanese Industrial Standards Committee. Tokyo: JUSE, p. 14.

[2] Ibid, p. 50.

operationally free of externally generated obstructions.

This "being statistically controlled" is the same as JIS's "stable state," defined as "A state such that almost all of the plotted points on a control chart are within the control limits as well as showing no tendency in alignment."[3]

Process capability needs to be considered in terms of production volume and cost as well as quality, since you need capability to reach the required production volume at an economical cost, but within the limits of quality control it can be referred to as process quality capability. A process capability study should extend beyond a study of current conditions to pinpoint and correct problems.

Process capability is expressed numerically using process capability values, i.e., quality characteristic values. When these are relatively normally distributed as shown in Figure 12.5 they will be within $+ 3\ \sigma$ with σ equaling standard deviation.

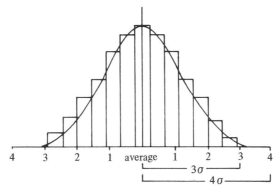

Figure 12.5 Distribution of Quality Characteristics (Normal Distribution)

In practical applications, process capability values should be within a range of no more than six times the sample standard deviation, i.e. 6s. The s is derived from data for roughly 100 recent characteristic values in a production process taking place according to specifications.

While there is never any guarantee that the quality characteristic values will always be normally distributed, you are better off if the values are symmetrical above and below your target value.

12.2.2.3 Evaluating Process Capability

A process capability index is used to judge whether a process has the required capability. This index C_P is derived by dividing the difference between the upper and lower acceptable deviation levels (the deviation allowance) T by the process capability value A (A = 6 s).

$$C_P = T/A = T/6s$$

[3] Ibid, p. 54.

Though quality characteristic values generally remain within the $+3\sigma$ range as shown in Figure 12.5, it is known that there is a 0.27% probability of a value's exceeding the upper limit. Thus, if the upper and lower limits are relatively close to the mean value, the process is stable, though a certain number of defects must be expected. If the upper and lower limits are too far apart at a range greater than $+4\sigma$, however, the data will indicate no defects.

Process capability is evaluated by the indices shown in Figure 12.6. Only when a process is stable enough to derive an average process capability value can you calculate its index. When a process is stable, minor deviations are usually easy to correct.

	Process Capability Index	Assessment	Response
1	$4/3 \leqq Cp$	Pass	Sufficient to inspect at start of operations. Can consider speeding up process or otherwise increasing load.
2	$1 \leqq Cp < 4/3$	Needs watching	Danger of producing defects. Needs watching.
3	$Cp < 1$	Fail	Need to consider changing procedures, changing equipment, and changing tolerance. Inspect total output

Figure 12.6 Process Capability Assessment Standards

A process's capability is interpreted in terms of its average characteristic value and the range of deviation from this average. When the deviations are minor and easily correctable, capability can be evaluated simply by their range of dispersion without worrying about a central average value. Using variance integration, this can be expressed as

$$\sigma P^2 = \sigma \text{ machine}^2 + \sigma \text{ men}^2 + \sigma \text{ materials}^2 + \sigma \text{ methods}^2 \dots$$

The σ machine, σ man, σ materials, σ methods, and so forth in this formula are the values that will account for variance in the process and are called process capability factors.

A machine's process capability cannot be judged simply on the basis of its operational specifications. A certain degree of variation is inevitable even when the same worker uses the same materials to perform the same operation on the machine, let alone when one of these factors varies. These inevitable variations must be taken into account in judging the machine's process capability. This is why the finished product's quality characteristic values need to be derived from data obtained from the actual machine used in the factory, operated by the worker who is normally assigned to it, and using the specified materials and work procedures. If this is true of a process you are already using, it is all the more true of a new process, a new machine, or new materials. If a machine does not have the required process capability, it should either be adjusted as necessary or replaced with equipment that can produce the required results.

By breaking up process capability into its diverse factors, it is possible to estimate the probable degree of variation that will occur whenever one or more of these factors, man, machine, materials, or method, change.

A good example of a process capability study is one made by a factory that checked on all the various process capability factors related to one of its machine tools. By gathering data on the range of variation in the machine tool's vertical and horizontal axes, its blades, and other factors, it was possible to pinpoint and correct excessive deviations, thereby narrowing the range of non-conformance in processed parts.

12.2.2.4 How to Do a Process Capability Study

After you have conducted a thorough process analysis and corrected the major shortcomings in the process, you are ready to make a process capability study. The first step is to gather data on the process's quality characteristics and draw a process capability chart. If the distribution of characteristic values is too far to one side or the other, the machinery being used has not been adjusted properly or is malfunctioning. When the average value shifts in an undulating rhythm, a piece of equipment is probably off-centre or unevenly worn down. Once you've got your diagram, you will be able to isolate and correct problem areas.

In a process capability study you are looking for positive and negative factors. The positive factors are (1) the interrelationship between quality and volume, and (2) process flexibility.

This means you will have to find out, for example, how much a change in materials affects final product quality, what material quality level must be maintained to keep finished product quality within the specified range, and whether or not yield will fluctuate as a result of a sudden fluctuation in voltage.

Conducting a process capability study will enable you to:

1. Speed up processing procedures.
2. Apply rigorous processing conditions.
3. Know how much capital investment is required.
4. Estimate costs for specific products.

The health-conscious person knows his body's normal state of health and tries to follow whatever regimen is necessary to maintain this state. You want to exercise, but you do not want to over-exert yourself trying to do things that are beyond you. In the same way, quality-consciousness requires that you have a firm grasp of your process capabilities so that you can design quality standards that are within your capabilities. Allowing too little margin for variation and setting impossibly high specification standards make defects inevitable. There is no reason, of course, not to improve process capability. But neither can you force rigorous specifications on suppliers and subcontractors who do not have the requisite process capabilities. There should be some degree of cooperation, such that your specifications are within the process capability of the supplier and the supplier will endeavour to upgrade his process capabilities.

12.2.3 Deciding on Manufacturing Methods

The results of process analysis and the various process studies are applied to devising an optimum manufacturing system and creating quality standards, these standards then being compiled into a handbook that everyone involved can refer to. As noted in Chapter 9, there is a distinct difference between standard quality and target quality. There are many ways of indicating standard quality, some of which will be introduced in this section.

12.2.3.1 Standard Quality and Guaranteed Quality

Guaranteed quality is that level of product quality guaranteed to the customer in catalogues, manuals, and other documentation. In this sense, you could refer to guaranteed quality as the product's extra-corporate specifications. These specifications must, of course, meet customer needs. Intra-corporate specifications, those quality standards that must be built into the manufacturing process, are defined so as to allow the permissible inspection margin, as shown in Figure 12.7, such that

Guaranteed quality = standard quality + inspection margin.

When your intra-corporate standard quality specifications are allowed too broad a margin and inspection quality ends up less restrictive than guaranteed quality, you will find yourself having to inspect every single product as it comes off the line and only allowing those that meet the guaranteed standard to be shipped.

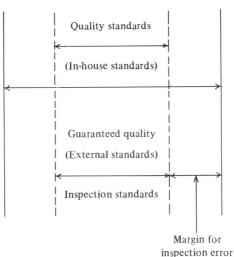

Figure 12.7 Relationship between Guaranteed Quality and Quality Standards

Below are some examples of how specification values might be indicated.

1. For individual products:
   0.56 ± 0.04
2. To indicate acceptable dispersion range:
   $\overline{X}$ = 0.5 (with a range not in excess of ± 0.03)
3. To define inspection limits:
   Not more than 10.8, but passing those products that exceed this limit by less than 2% and do not go over 12.3.
4. When substitute characteristics are not clear:
   When you do not know the substitute characteristics the purchaser requires, it is best to break down his needs into specifics by asking exactly what materials he wants, how he wants to use them, what kind of manufacturing system he has, and so forth. Do not guess at substitute characteristics.

Once standards have been established it is necessary to institutionalize a system of revising these standards.

12.2.3.2 Regulations Concerning Specifications and Standards

Following are the details on purpose and contents of these regulations.

1. Quality standards and control regulations
   Purpose: To define and differentiate standard quality, guaranteed quality, and inspection standards, and to specify guarantee units and sampling methods.
   Content: Should provide a broad range of information encompassing sampling methods, how to collate measurement data, ascertaining significance, types of documentation, how to make revisions, how and where standards and instructions should be filed, review processes, who the decision-maker is and the limits of his authority, who is responsible for control, the method of distributing information on standards and regulations to all parties concerned, and how outdated standards and regulations handbooks are to be recalled, catalogued, and stored.
2. Inspection standards for materials and products from outside suppliers
   Purpose: To avoid purchasing excessively high quality products and eliminate waste in the manufacturing process.
   Content: Specifications, inspection items, inspection method, inspection lot size, what is done with lots that pass inspection, what is done with lots that do not pass inspection, communication channels between purchasing company and supplier, quality specifications and examples, average quality characteristic value and upper and lower limits, sampling methods (methods and equipment used for each quality characteristic), lot size (should be the same as manufacturing lot size, as large as quality can be guaranteed), inspection methodology (all output or with samples and stipulated quality levels for each quality characteristic), inspection standards (what happens to lots that do not pass inspection: Are they returned or accepted at a lower price? Is the supplier required to cover the costs of sorting out defects?),

investigation into the reasons for defects, and how the supplier collects quality data.

3. Regulations regarding materials and parts that do not pass inspection.

Purpose: To prevent the recurrence of defects and to explain what is to be done with defective products.

Content: Who decides what to do with defective lots (return, try to salvage acceptable units, or use for special applications), the effects of defective products on various departments, and how the use of special products is to be supervised (any kind of special application must be experimental by nature, and requires close supervision).

12.2.3.3 Technical Standards and Work Standards

The details are as follows:

1. Technical standards

Technical standards are intended to indicate how a manufacturing process takes place and should specify the kind of equipment used, how measurements are made, and all conditions that may possibly affect the manufacturing process technologically. Technical standards are created on the basis of research on past production technology and feedback on problems that occurred, customer complaints about product quality, and how such problems were resolved. In preparing technical standards, you will need to compile all the data acquired through process analyses and process capability studies in an easy-to-use form. The kind of quality information system that was discussed in Chapter 4 under quality assurance can also be used effectively in preparing technical standards.

2. Quality information regulations

Purpose: To regulate the flow of information related to quality inside and outside the company.

Content: Studies related to customer quality needs: market research, condition of sold products, condition of products kept in storage at the company, competitors' inspection standards, and prices for competitors' products.

Studies of manufacturing technologies: control charts, inspection reports, reports on abnormalities, statistics on defects, analysis of defects, and study of costs.

Control reports: Reports from line workers on quality, costs, and production volume controls, who these reports should go to, when they should be made, who makes them, required document form, and standards.

Records and information reports (the 5-Ws and 1-H): their organization and filing, computerizing, printing, and copying.

3. Work standards

Work standards are detailed, specific instructions on how to perform work processes. As long as work standards are closely followed it should be possible to maintain standard product quality. While technicians knowledgeable in the manufacturing process should take part in creating work standards, it is even more important that you have the active participation of the workers who actually perform the work processes. It is up to them to maintain work standards, and they are not likely to do so if standards are arbitrarily set and imposed from on high. Even if they did try to adhere to such standards, they might easily overlook abnormalities.

Work standards are prepared on the basis of previous work experience and should be organized and compiled in a training handbook which workers study before they set about their various jobs. Yet discrepancies will inevitably emerge once actual production begins, and it is necessary to revise the work standards accordingly. I know of one plant where there are blank pages in the work standards handbook where workers can fill in any information they feel is relevant. Besides making for more realistic work standards, this is a very good way to stimulate worker interest and encourage participation.

Very often work standard handbooks are formal affairs written up like legal documents. This may be necessary for company records, but for the shop floor instructions concerning work standards should be presented in an easy-to-understand format making liberal use of sketches, photos, and other visual materials. One company I know of uses prerecorded instructions on tape, a very practical approach when you are manufacturing one-of-a-kind products and specifications are constantly changing. Having workers listening to tapes over their headphones also means that they can keep their eyes on their work better.

To summarize the purpose and nature of work standards:

Purpose: To clarify limits of responsibility and authority and to free the control staff to concentrate on their real work.

Contents: A detailed outline of each step in the work procedure that is practical and does not allow for discretionary changes, instructions on how to deal with abnormalities, definitions, their formulation, their study, committee decisions, revisions, reports, announcements, formats, custody (including who is responsible for maintaining records), training, confirmation, alterations and discontinuations of product lines (including regular changes), procedures for recalling outdated handbooks, and where and how the original standards handbook is to be kept on file.

4. Equipment, tools, and measuring instruments

With the rising cost of labour, a growing number of companies have been introducing labour-saving equipment into their manufacturing processes. Using robots and automated equipment, however, means that material measurements always have to be uniform, Process capability studies and improvements have thus become more important than ever.

Maintaining stable quality and cutting down on turnaround time have also become crucial as the nature of manufacturing has changed from mass production of a single product to small-lot production of many different products. With this shift to flexible manufacturing, new production processes have been adopted such as one in which a worker operates a number of different machine tools arrayed around him in a U-shaped work area instead of the traditional conveyor belt system. Here too, process analyses and capability studies are essential.

Tools are another area of concern, since they must often be adapted to a variety of products and it is necessary to make sure that tool parts can be changed quickly, safely, and in a foolproof way that minimizes the possibility of damage.

The technology for the quick and accurate measurement of use characteristics and substitute characteristics lags behind that for measuring dimensions and weight. The dimensions appearing on a design blueprint are not the customer's needs. What the customer needs are those characteristics that are essential for the product's correct use. Yet there has been little study made of how to measure these use characteristics. And to compound the problem, the characteristics that are measured in the manufacturing process are not always the ones that most accurately reflect the product's actual use characteristics. There is still ample room for improvement in this field. A method of continuous measuring throughout the production process would be particularly useful, and efforts are being made in this direction. One example is a method employed for checking that the holes on some electromagnetic components are not blocked by blowing air at them and seeing where air does or does not come out the other side. Before any kind of equipment or measuring instrument is used in the workplace it should be tested for its process capability and its margins for error so that every effort can be made to reduce this margin as necessary.

5. Training and assigning workers

No matter how good your equipment and how advanced your technical standards, you will not be able to guarantee product quality if your workers are making mistakes. At one factory producing clock faces it was found that veteran workers were highly productive but were turning out a lot of faces where the central hole was not right. Careful study revealed that the workers had never been told that this was especially important, and were devoting their attention to less-important areas. It was also found that workers' opinions varied as to when the tip of the electric welder they used needed to be replaced. A sample of a worn tip was on display, but it turned out that each worker was judging the wear by a different standard. Obviously, samples alone are not enough. Workers need to be trained in how to look at and interpret the samples.

Effective training means teaching practical applications that are going to be useful to the worker on the job. One diemaking plant has its workers practice with at least 20 different basic forms, a training method that has proved very effective.

On-the-job training involves more than simply teaching a worker his particular job. He should also be trained in the process of improving work procedures and process control. This extends to the QC circle. In fact, it might well be argued that one of the primary purposes of the QC circle is to train workers to be alert, to be more aware of what they are doing and how it is done, and to become expert in quality assurance methodology.

12.3 Process Control

Process control has many meanings. In production control it refers to production planning and progress management aimed at achieving a specified production volume. In quality control it refers to the maintenance and improvement of product quality within the production process. The constant and steady rotation of the PDCA circle of control is basic to any kind of process control.

12.3.1 Control and Adjustment

At one plant, the electric current heating a furnace is reduced when the furnace exceeds a certain temperature and is increased when the furnace temperature drops below a certain point. This is control in the sense of adjustment, and is not the kind of action that is being referred to by the action to be taken in the PDCA circle. In the example of the furnace, the temperature settings and how to adjust them are specified in either the technical or work standard handbooks and come under the PDCA category of doing. In this particular instance, the temperature control process could be automated for greater accuracy and speed.

Automatic control of processes still requires quality control, however. It is necessary, in other words, to establish, through process analyses and process capability studies, how such adjustments should be made and to what degree of accuracy. It is foolish to arrange for precision control of minor factors while ignoring the major factors that affect a process.

To give an example of what this kind of mistaken attention to detail can lead to: The plant manager in a synthetic fiber plant had a special passion for anything new and spent a great deal of money for a wide variety of automatic control systems. Yet there continued to be fluctuations in product quality even after these automatic systems were installed. When it was finally decided to do a process analysis, the production people ran into difficulties. Because the automatic control systems were interconnected into a single network, a change in one cause factor immediately prompted other cause factors to change as well.

Only after all the control systems were shut down was it possible to seek out causes and judge how much they influenced the product's quality indices. It was finally found that one of the few processes the plant manager had not put under automatic control had the greatest effect on the product's quality indices. Once this particular process was controlled, fluctuations in product quality were significantly reduced and the whole production process was stabilized. Further process analysis revealed another factor that was affecting quality, and once this was controlled the fluctuation was so slight that it could be attributed to sampling and measurement errors. In the end, it was found that none of the expensive automatic control systems the plant manager had installed was needed.

The statistical approach should be taken in deciding on the tolerable margin for error in making adjustments. Paying excessive attention to such minor factors as sampling and measurement errors can cause you to overlook more critical causes. Likewise, inordinate attention to random fluctuation can cause you to over-adjust. The control chart alone is not sufficient to detect casual causes related to fluctuations in product quality. I would refer you here to the studies that a number of other scholars and I have done on adapting the control chart to process adjustments, as well as to the excellent approach to making economically sound process adjustments devised by Genichi Taguchi.*

Even after appropriate process adjustments are made, equipment breakdowns, changes in material quality, and other unexpected factors may cause product quality to fluctuate beyond the established tolerance. These kinds of quality fluctuations will appear on the control chart as skewing, as your values will tend to be over or under the control limit lines or to cluster to one side or the other.

In its most narrow sense, the CA of the PDCA circle is interpreted as control in that it involves detecting abnormalities (through checking), seeking out their causes, and taking measures to eliminate these causes (action). Obviously this is not the same as making adjustments within preset limits. Yet people often confuse control and adjustment, failing to use the control chart correctly and thereby negating its effectiveness.

In the temperature control example cited at the beginning of this section, it was a simple process to make the necessary adjustments. But when the temperature depends on a complex combination of factors such as furnace size and fuel type, it can be helpful to have a control chart tracking these different factors so that problems can be readily pinpointed.

To repeat, the process of keeping these various factors within control limit boundaries is adjustment, while the process of identifying the causes of abnormalities and adopting measures to eliminate them is control.

12.3.2 Selecting Control Items

I have already discussed control items in Section 2.3.3, but I would like here to discuss how to select control items.

Control items are those items against which work results are checked to find the causes of irregularities so that they can be corrected and controlled. In terms of the PDCA cycle, these are the criteria against which you check (C) the output (D) so that you can act (A) and adjust. As noted above, adjustment and control are two different things, and furnace temperature would be a factor subject to adjustment rather than a control item.

Some people talk about check points for seeking out causes and control points for ascertaining results. The terminology used has not been standardized. Although I agree that check points are necessary, I consider them adjustable items that should be clarified in the planning stage and in technical and work standard manuals — they are not the same as control items. Of course, when control is defined as encompassing the whole PDCA circle, check points can be thought of as those control items that must be included in the planning stage,

---

* Taguchi's *Introduction to Quality Engineering: Designing Quality into Products and Processes,* was translated and published by the Asian Productivity Organization in 1986.

and in this broad interpretation, they would be equivalent to control items. Having made a distinction between adjustment and control, however, I prefer to limit control items to their narrow definition. Keeping check points distinct from control items should help workers to avoid the confusion of adjustment and control. Thus:

Check point: an item, either fixed or adjustable, that should be considered in the planning stage. For example, what kind of machine or raw material should be used (fixed items) or what kind of work conditions, temperature settings, and pressure settings will be required (adjustable items)

Control item: An item in the work process that is checked when there is an abnormality to find out the cause and to correct the problem

As you can see, check points and control items fulfill different functions. The word "point" has a narrower meaning than "item", and can refer to a point in time and a point in space.

Since the term "characteristics" has already been identified with quality characteristics, it would probably be less confusing to talk about control item indices and check point indices.

You should also keep in mind that control items are not target items, nor are control characteristics target values. As I made clear in my disucssion of policy control, setting up target values and telling everyone to do his best to attain these values is not what TQC is all about. True policy control involves diagnosing and analyzing current conditions, analyzing the gap between current conditions and target values, devising effective strategies to close this gap, and implementing these strategies.

In process control, too, target values and control items differ. Target values are what you set as the process goal, and only after you have planned a process to achieve this goal do you use control items to check on whether this process is working as it should. In this context, the target value can be considered an effect, the measures taken to achieve this effect its cause, and the control item the means of checking the cause against its effect.

Above all else, it should be obvious that control items are not what you use to check the final results of a process. Your final results may be that you have not achieved the expected sales target, but no amount of checking at this last stage is going to correct this. What needs to be checked is your policy for achieving the sales figure, and if this policy is not functioning as it should, it should be revised at an early stage so that the intended goal can be attained. In other words, control items are those items that will help you trace the causes for the effects you are trying to achieve in a work process, and lets you divide them into cause-related items and effect-related items. Since effect-related items indicate target values, it is clear that the control items are cause-related.

Sometimes the thing to be controlled is called the control point and the item used to control this the control item. For example, if you keep yourself fit by keeping track of your blood pressure, your health is your control point and your blood pressure is the control item. This kind of differentiation can be useful, but it can also be very confusing, and I would prefer to confine my discussion to control items alone.

In process control, indices for inspection characteristics are recorded on a control chart as control characteristics, but these are no help in devising work processes that will correct any irregularities that are discovered because they necessarily come at the final stage of a production process. What you need to do is to set control items for each step in the production process so that you can judge results in a progressive system that allows for revisions and corrections to be made in time to alter the final outcome. Recording the characteristic values of these control items on a control chart will help you detect abnormalities, trace their causes and take corrective action.

12.3.3 Process Control Standards

You need to have answers to the 5-Ws and the 1-H in process control, too.

1. Why is control necessary?
2. What is to be controlled?
3. Where in the process (at what step or stage) will this control take place?
4. When will control be instituted (at what point will measurements be made)?
5. Who (which division) will be responsible for this control, who will decide that there are irregularities, and who will take action to rememdy them?
6. How will this action be taken (the standards for determining abnormalities and the standards for implementing corrective action)?

12.3.3.1 Process Control Standards Manual

In preparing a process control standards manual, you should be careful of the following points.

1. The list of quality assurance activities mentioned in Chapter 4 and the quality chart discussed in Chapter 11 should be expanded to cover production stages in greater detail. An example of a quality assurance activities list has already been given in Figure 4.3.
2. The quality assurance activities list and the quality chart should indicate the items whose quality must be guaranteed in the production process and the standards by which they are to be judged. You should also draw up a quality assurance chart (also sometimes called a list of process assurance items) that will indicate the relationship between the quality assurance items established at the quality design stage and the quality assurance items in the production stage.

   While the design division will provide the manufacturing division with the blueprints for a new product, the quality characteristics for each part and their relationship to finished product quality is often obscure. As a result the people in production may arbitrarily make changes to facilitate production. The quality assurance chart is thus a tool to convey the design division's quality characteristic requirements to the manufacturing division. It can be made even more meaningful by including comments on the kinds of customer complaints that previous failures to assure certain quality characteristics have generated.

Both the quality assurance chart and the QC process chart to be discussed later are drawn up in the process of carrying out quality assurance activities. Do not forget to include analyses (quality and process analyses) of past defectives, examples of how important quality problems were solved, and examples of improvements made in processes through QC circle activities and other means. Factors related to the control technology discussed in Section 10.2.4 are as important here as those concerned with the particular technology being used by a plant. All of this kind of information can provide invaluable tools for preventing the recurrence of control problems.

3. In using the control chart to check for process abnormalities, it is important that the standards for determining whether something is a problem or not are very clear. These standards will necessarily vary for different workers at different levels in the production process. Thus the shop floor worker and foreman will be primarily concerned with small irregularities, while the people in management positions should be looking out for major, repeatedly occurring problems. Such is not, however, to imply that floor workers should ignore major problems. Anyone who becomes aware of a major problem should report it as soon as possible, no matter what his position. Yet if such problems are left unattended, it means management is not doing its job.

    I have found many factories where the control chart is nothing more than a textbook list of all possible irregularities. Very often there is no indication of the varying significance of these irregularities under different circumstances, even though there will be considerable variance depending on what the control motivation is. For example, the loss of a finger would not normally have that much of an effect on your lifelihood, but it could destroy your career if you were a concert pianist.

4. No one should attempt to correct a process problem on his own unless he knows through experience how it should be corrected. Major irregularities should always be immediately reported using a process irregularity report form.

    Some factories require separate process irregularity studies and process irregularity reports. Whatever the type of form you use, the person filling it out should always file it through channels and keep a copy for himself. If a form requires some kind of response, a time limit should be set of, say, 10 days, for the response.

    This process irregularity report form should include the following items:

Name of characteristic	Date and time irregularity occurred
	Nature of irregularity
Who checked it	When checked
	Method used in checking
	Results of check
Measures taken	Completed or not completed

5. When a process irregularity occurs, the first thing that has to be done is to trace its cause. This is a part of process analysis. As long as the problem is not a major one, the cause can very often be traced by going through the quality characteristics chart. In this process it is important to remember that any action that is taken needs to be checked later to confirm that it was effective.

A record should be kept of all actions taken, sometimes called an action chart, since this is how you institutionalize your company's expertise. This record should include information on:

Number of control chart used	Control standard	Number of irregularities
Factors determined to be causes	Numbers and how taken care of Numbers of those not taken care of yet, their causes, and why not taken care of yet	
Causes unknown	Number, what done, and by whom Whether or not a process irregularity report was filed	

12.3.3.2 The QC Process Chart

A process chart also showing control methods is called a quality control process chart. Figure 3.2 is an example of such a quality control process chart. In preparing a quality control process chart, keep the following points in mind.

1. Control items should cover items that are quality-related, production volume-related, and cost-related.
2. It is helpful to explain sampling and measuring methods and to indicate their margins for error. Note that excessively large margins for error can keep you from achieving your control purposes.
3. Explain how data should be organized and what kind of control tools should be used (e.g., control charts, process capability charts, histograms, and graphs).
4. Control methods (standards by which to judge irregularities, how action should be taken, and so on) should be specified in the process control standards manual, but it can be useful to include brief summaries of these methods and to refer people to these entries by number in the process control standards manual.

12.3.3.3 List of Job-specific Control Items

The quality control process chart lists control items in the same order as the process steps indicated on the process chart. Management should also prepare separate job-specific control item lists to facilitate daily control activities. Examples of such lists are shown in Figures 12.8 and 12.9. Following should be noted in this regard.

1. Simply initialing an item on the list is not quality control checking. Quality control means adhering to established standards in performing your job. Naturally, this means everyone must know his responsibilities and limits of authority, but that is not in itself quality control. Neither are texts and other information sources in and of themselves control resources. Control means checking to see that work is being performed according to agreed-upon standards and taking action when reforms are required.

2. It is important to establish priorities so that you will know where quality control should be applied when you do not have time to do everything.

3. Job-specific control items should be listed for three positions: yourself, your immediate superior, and your immediate subordinate. You will be responsible for supplying your superior with control information relevant to his control items and the person below you should be supplying you with information on his control items. Control items should interrelate. Proper control is not possible if the person below you is not paying any attention to factors that affect you and your superior dealing with minor control items. Neither is it meaningful to have your superior dealing with minor control items and the person below you with broader control items.

4. Records should be kept of all actions taken. Reviewing actions taken to see whether they were effective or not helps in deciding whether or not and how they should be made the new standards. Records also help when it comes time to assign this work to someone else.

5. Job-specific control item charts should be drawn up not just for daily control items but for control items related to important quality problems, policy control, and cross-functional management as well.

6. Having drawn up control item charts, you should go back and check them to make sure that your own responsibilities are clear and that the control items for the people immediately above and below you, as well as those for different divisions, interrelate in a meaningful way. Any points that remain unclear should be cleared up.

7. The job-specific control item chart is particularly useful when there are changes in personnel assignments. With the chart in hand, your successor will know what he should be controlling. Of course, people should not hesitate to change the control items and to institute other changes learned from experience.

12.3.4 Implementing Control

In undertaking process control following process control standards, keep the following additional points in mind.

1. If the process is stable and products are meeting specifications, control

Job	Targets	Control items	Impor-tance	Control documents		Frequency	Control method	
				Document	Author		When	How
Assuring quality of materials	Preventing contamination	Rate of error in checking materials	A	Error rate control chart	Person responsible for materials	Weekly	When exceeds limits	Study inspection method
Stabilizing product quality	Reducing start-up defectives	Process time	A	Process table	Line-one supervisor	Every other week	When one day or more than standard	Thorough review of measures in policy committee

Figure 12.8 List of Control Items (Partial sample for manufacturing section)

Job	Targets			Control items	Impor-tance	Control documents		Fre-quency	Control method	
	Quality	Volume	Cost			Document	Author		When	How
Reduce costs			Manu-facturing costs	Unit cost	A	Control table on unit costs	Cost control chief	Once a week	When exceed limits	Report to plant manager on cause
				Electrical power costs	B	Electrical power use graph	Power control chief	Once a month	When 1,000 kwh or more over standard value	Convene power committee to study causes and take action

Figure 12.9 List of Control Items (Partial sample for manufacturing division)

does not have to be zealously performed. Rather, your control energies should be directed at unstable processes, such as when a new production process is just being introduced (see Section 11.9) or when changes have been made involving new materials and equipment. In such priorty cases the number of control items should be increased and control procedures should be performed more frequently than usual.

2. Tracing the cause of a problem and correcting it should be done as quickly as possible once a problem is discovered. This is why training in process analysis is so important. Corrective measures should be thorough and should ensure that the same problem will not crop up again. Technical, work, and process control standards should be immediately revised to incorporate such measures as prove effective.

3. With the change from mass production of only a few products to small-lot production of many different products and the frequency with which new models and completely new products are being introduced, it is more important than ever that control be as thorough and mistake-free as possible. Institutionalized experience in the preparation of technical, work, and process control standards can make all the difference here, as pointed out in Chapter 11.

12.3.5 Checking the Effectiveness of Your Control System

Following questions should be kept in mind while checking the effectiveness of control system.

1. Has every effort been made to maintain measurement precision, and are measurements being made as quickly as possible?

2. Do control charts exist where these are most needed? Have the appropriate control items been selected? Is there any possibility that the control charts are not being interpreted correctly? Have appropriate specification and control boundaries been set?

3. Is there any confusion between means and end? Seeking out causes is not the same thing as taking corrective action. Have the procedures for taking corrective action been standardized and are they being cross-checked?

4. Is the information provided by the control charts and other control tools being applied most effectively?

5. Is inspection being conducted as an independent process? Has it been planned properly and are inspection procedures being checked frequently?

6. Is every effort being made to ensure inspection accuracy?

7. Are products being handled properly after inspection?

8. Have standards been established for production planning? How are production costs and lot sizes decided upon? Are the results of production planning being checked to confirm that things are progressing as planned? Has quality control been incorporated into production planning? Have product types been organized in an orderly fashion? Have procedures been established for making changes in production plans?

9. Are the procedures for changing inventory standards reasonable and effective? Do you know what is to be done in the event of excessive inventory? How are inventory reports handled?

10. What are the procedures for purchasing raw materials? Have the manufacturing division's needs been correctly transmitted to the purchasing division?

11. Are efforts being made to stablize processes (such as by having raw materials on hand and installing automatic control for production processes)?

12.4 Quality Assurance in the Manufacturing Process

The process control activities discussed thus far are an important part of quality assurance activities, but there is even more to carrying out quality assurance.

12.4.1 Methods of Transmitting Quality

It is important that quality remain consistent throughout each of the quality assurance steps — planning, design, production, sales, and services. Failure to do so often results in trouble.

The quality assurance chart and quality control process chart discussed in Section 12.3.3 are highly effective tools for transmitting quality. Figures 12.10 and 12.11 show examples of quality transmission routes. The important thing is to make sure that the same level of quality is maintained from one step to the next. Even if each section and division is fulfilling its own quality assurance needs, problems will occur if they fail to transmit these needs to the successive sections or divisions.

12.4.2 Control by Process Category

Certain production processes will be more important than others. The manufacture of an automobile's steering mechanism, for example, will require extra care because of the product liability risk. Such special-care processes should be differentiated from other production processes and controlled more strictly. There is a limit to the energy that can be spent on control, so every effort should be made to concentrate on the most important areas.

In controlling important process categories, special care should be taken with the following points.

1. The process should be clearly designated as an important process and the people working on it should be well aware of its importance. Procedures should be orderly and systematic, with every care taken that no impurities creep in and no parts are damaged.

2. Workers responsible for critical work stations should be specially trained, and only those who meet certain requirements should be allowed to work at such stations. The same stringent requirements should hold for outside suppliers, and subsubcontracting should be prohibited.

3. The foreman in charge of an important work process area should have the authority to stop the production line whenever he feels it necessary. The

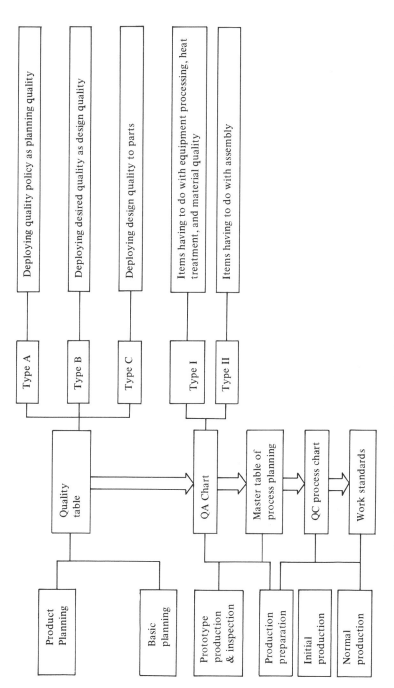

Figure 12.10 Communication Channels for Quality Concerns (Sample 1)

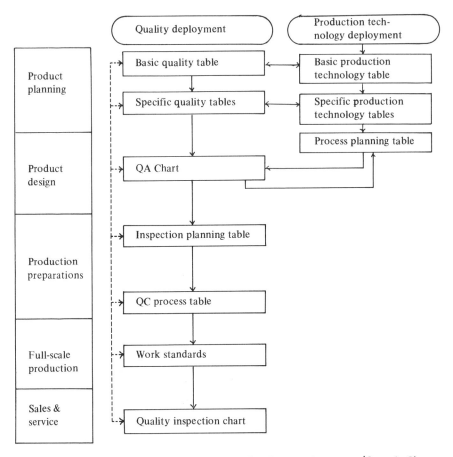

Figure 12.11 Communication Channels for Quality Concerns (Sample 2)

people involved in production technology and equipment safety and maintenance should get to the trouble spot as soon as possible when there is an emergency line stoppage and cooperate in finding the cause of the problem and correcting it.

4. There should be more control items than usual for critical processes, and control procedures should be more frequently carried out. Control boundaries should also be more stringent than normal. Information on problems and how they were handled should be speedily recorded in a special record book kept separately from those for other less critical processes.

12.4.3 Interim Inspections

As already noted in Section 12.2.3, periodic interim inspections should be made, automatically if possible, during the production process. Preferably, these interim inspections should be done by the person handling the production process on the assumption that he is the most knowledgable about the product at that particular stage. Busy carrying out the production process itself, however, a worker may fail to make the necessary interim inspections or may accidentally get uninspected items mixed in with inspected items. A system of patrolling inspectors can help to prevent such eventualities.

12.4.4 Product Liability Prevention in the Production Process

The importance of not producing defective products that lay you open to a liability suit has already been discussed in Chapter 5. Here I would like to focus on what can be done for product liability prevention within the production process.

1. Work procedures, methodologies, equipment, and tools should be made as foolproof as possible.
2. Raw materials should be checked to ensure that they have not been contaminated, and parts and components checked to confirm that they have been properly finished. Everyone should be fully aware of the consequences of a mistake here.
3. Quality stability items should be included in any revision of work standards and filed accordingly.
4. Purchase records should be maintained.
5. Records should be kept on special materials and parts and the reasons for their use.
6. Suppliers should be instructed in product liability prevention.
7. Limits of responsibility should be specified in contracts with suppliers.
8. Suppliers should be investigated to confirm that they have the necessary equipment, testing methods, and process control.

Careful control is needed whenever changes are instituted in the production process, and foolproofing is especially important in product liability prevention.

12.4.4.1 Controlling Changes and Alterations

While improvements in production processes are to be commended, the changes they necessitate in processes, equipment, and work procedures can often lead to new and unexpected problems. It is important to have a stringent control system to oversee such changes and prevent product safety problems before they arise.

Although the need for continual improvement mandates the use of new materials, new machinery, and new techniques as they become available, you have to exercise utmost control with special attention to the problems such changes engender, not only when the changes are made but even afterward to ensure that no problems develop.

QC circle activities directed at making improvements are important and often very effective, but sometimes problems can arise because improvements based on QC circle findings are instituted without first running a thorough check of the technology involved. Some companies do not even have any procedures for reviewing QC circle recommendations and revising standards accordingly. It is management's responsibility to see that QC circle improvements are carried over to all divisions and sections in a system of horizontal deployment to prevent problems before they occur.

12.4.4.2 Foolproofing

It is basic to quality assurance that (1) each individual performs his work correctly and that (2) everyone works together to make improvements. Emphasizing either of these to the detriment of the other will lead to trouble.

Thanks to TQC and company-wide quality control, Japanese product quality is among the best in the world. But there are limits to what can be done. We are all human, and no matter how good our intentions, are bound to make mistakes from time to time — a fact that tends to be overlooked in Japanese-style TQC with its assumption that man is basically good-intentioned.

Foolproofing means preventing careless mistakes and designing fail-safe systems that can be readily understood by the novice. Everyone knows the importance of preventing mistakes in production processes, but there has been relatively little study of how this can be done.

In the context of product safety, the product is viewed as a system consisting of many diverse elements. Assuring the safety of this system involves eliminating all potential dangers inherent in each of its individual elements and in their interaction.

A bad system is subject to system error because it still contains defective elements. A good system is subject only to human error. Human errors can occur in the designing stage as well as in the production process. For example, one company kept having fire problems with its balers. Upon closer examination, it was found that the hot exhaust pipes ran through the hay storage bin. Checklists on potential danger points can be useful in preventing such careless design error.

I do not know of any systematic study of foolproofing, but it can be roughly broken down into foolproofing systems and foolproofing triggers.
Foolproofing systems

1. Warning system: A buzzer or some other warning device indicates a problem.
2. Stopping system: The work process automatically stops whenever an irregularity arises.

Foolproofing triggers

1. Measurement aberration detection: A system that is activated by irregularities in the product's dimensions and form.
2. Irregular number detection: A system that is activated when something has not been performing the specified number of times.
3. Skipped step detection: A system activated when a procedural step is skipped.

Careless mistakes in the workplace are hard to avoid: a part with no obvious handedness may be attached backwards, steel parts may be assembled before they have been electroplated, only four places may be oiled when five should have been, and so on. The experienced worker can be just as prone to such careless mistakes as the novice. Simply telling workers to be more careful is not going to prevent mistakes, and a foolproofing system is needed that can automatically prevent errors from being made. To refer back to the above examples, a machine tool can be designed so that the component will not fit if it is accidentally put in backwards, parts that have not yet been electroplated can be automatically dropped from the line, or a meter can be affixed to the oil injection unit so that it is impossible to proceed on to the next step unless all five locations have been oiled.

Foolproof systems designed by engineering experts tend to be overly complex and better results are usually obtained by the people in the QC circle who know what problems tend to occur and how they might be prevented. Some plants even put up commemorative plaques marking foolproofing systems that have been devised by QC circles. Other companies publish foolproofing case studies which they distribute in-house and to their affiliates.

Foolproofing can be applied in the preparation of documents and other paperwork just as well as on the shop floor, and some companies are already doing this.

12.5 Improving Processes

So far I have concentrated on systems to maintain processes already in place. Now I would like to take a look at how to go about improving processes for better product quality and lower production costs.

12.5.1 Making Process Improvements

Much of this has already been discussed in Chapter 10 where I talked about methods of improving processes and their procedures, but it is worth reviewing the subject here.

Making improvements begins with seeking out problems. This means you will need to collect and analyze data on process capability indices and control characteristics, and process investigations and process analyses can be useful here.

12.5.2 Implementing Process Improvements

An overall improvement of production processes is just as necessary as the individual improvements made by QC circles within their respective work stations. Naturally, much more can be expected of the overall process improvement. As noted earlier in the discussion of the analysis of important quality problems, it is necessary to view the process as a whole, and forming a project team to diagnose the process is a good way to start.

One of the most effective approaches is to undertake a major experiment using actual factory equipment and materials under normal production conditions. But since this approach can temporarily lead to defective products and lower yield, the experts trained in such analytical tools as experimental planning cannot conduct these experiments òn their own responsibility. It is the plant manager who must take charge of the experiment, oversee its implementation, and devise solutions to the temporary disruptions that may occur.

I once happened to visit a plant where the technical staff had just successfully completed a small-scale experiment and were debating whether the experiment should be attempted on a larger scale using actual factory equipment. Lacking the proper authority, they could not arrive at a decision. Finally, I had them call in the plant manager and explain the situation to him. Once he understood the possibilities, the plant manager told the technical staff to go ahead and that he would take the responsibility for any problems that might occur. In this particular case, the resulting improvement in production processes proved to be even more effective than originally expected, but there was no guarantee, and it was up to the plant manager to make the final decision on whether or not to go ahead.

Undertaking a major project such as process improvement requires clear-cut policy guidance and support from management. Only with this kind of support is it possible for divisional and sectional responsibilities to be assigned and experiments to be implemented. Once results have been obtained they should be double-checked, institutionalized, and deployed throughout the company in an organized system.

12.6 Quality Control in the Purchasing Division

About two-thirds of a product's production costs are attributable to materials and parts costs. Impure materials and defective parts generate additional costs for the manufacturer, even if their costs are absorbed by the supplier. Processes are disrupted and deliveries delayed, and even if deliveries are not delayed extra costs can be incurred in the effort to meet delivery deadlines. Further costs may result from customer complaints and returned products.

It should thus be obvious that the purchasing division is just as important as — if not more important than — the manufacturing division for company-wide total quality control. Yet the purchasing division is often little more than a clerical office responsible only for placing orders and making payments. The purchasing division has a quality control responsibility that extends well beyond such duties, and it should play a greater role in quality assurance.

In speaking of the purchasing division, I refer to everyone within the company who oversees the purchasing of raw materials and parts and even outsourcing. Of course, the exact nature of this kind of division will vary from company to company. Some companies have two divisions, a purchasing division and a purchasing management division. For the purposes of this text, however, it is enough to simply refer to them as the purchasing division.

The purchasing division's quality control activities overlap the responsibilities of other divisions such as the quality assurance division, production control division, and inspection division. Even so it is the purchasing division that bears the primary responsibility for these activities. In many cases, not only raw materials and parts but their transport and packaging are subcontracted out, and even labour may be subcontracted out in the construction industry. All of these activities require quality control by the purchasing division.

12.6.1 The Purchasing Division's Role

The purchasing division's activities can be divided into (1) those related to assuring product quality and (2) those directly concerned with its divisional responsibilities. These activities involve:

1. Assuring product quality: selecting suppliers and subcontractors, arranging for quality assurance agreements with these suppliers and subcontractors stipulating quality requirements, quantity requirements, schedule requirements, and cost requirements, maintaining contact with suppliers and contractors, relaying instructions and providing assistance, and conducting inspections when substitute materials and parts are to be used.
2. Divisional responsibilities: Inspecting materials and parts received, supervising delivery deadlines, maintaining inventories, and processing orders and payments.

The PDCA circle should be turning for all of these activities. The effective implementation of quality control by the purchasing division ensures smooth operations and is an important part of TQC.

A relationship of trust and cooperation between buyer and seller is the basis of the concept of mutual benefit and corporate social responsibility which underlies all quality control activities, especially within the purchasing division.

12.6.2 Basic Purchasing and Outsourcing Policy

If the right materials and parts are to be purchased at the right price and delivered at the right time, there must be a well-defined purchasing and outsourcing policy. Such a policy provides the guidelines for making decisions and conducting quality control.

Taking unfair advantage of outside suppliers, going to them only when you cannot meet your own production schedules, or demanding unreasonably low prices that could cause them to go bankrupt does not make for long-term stable relations. Neither should suppliers be allowed to ignore the need for quality assurance, the need to reduce costs, and the need to stay abreast of developments technologically. A basic purchasing and outsourcing policy should aim at developing a close, cooperative relationship with suppliers. Important points to keep in mind are:

1. Quality should always come first. Both the manufacturer and its suppliers should make the end-user's concerns and needs their own.
2. Delivery dates should be strictly adhered to. Not having materials and parts when and where they are needed can needlessly interrupt production.

3. Improving quality and reducing costs should be the primary aims of any material and parts substitutions. All substitutes should be carefully inspected and information on their quality, design, and production methods conveyed to all divisions concerned.
4. Do not make speculative purchases.
5. Supplier initiative should be respected at all times. Innovative improvements should be encouraged for high-quality materials and parts at reasonable prices.
6. The manufacturer should be sincerely concerned for the supplier's welfare and should provide assistance and cooperation where appropriate.

Decisions as to which parts to outsource and which to manufacture in-house should be made carefully. I know of one company that decided to outsource all those parts requiring highly sophisticated technology, retaining for itself the less-sophisticated and easier-to-manufacture simple parts and components. When market demands changed and the company realized that it did not have the technology to keep up, it stopped outsourcing and scrambled to make its own hightech products. Yet the lack of equipment and knowhow led to numerous defectives.

The purchasing division workers who come into contact with outside suppliers should always keep in mind that they are representing the company. They should always be polite and should make an effort not to reflect badly on the company's good name. Contract relations with subcontractors should always be based on the company's basic purchasing and outsourcing policy, and must never be subjective or arbitrary. It helps here to have selection criteria agreed to by all divisions concerned and clearly spelled for all to see and follow.

12.6.3 Selecting Suppliers

Suppliers should be selected not simply for their production and quality assurance capabilities but also for proximity and delivery convenience and a number of other considerations as listed below. They:

1. Should understand and be willing to cooperate in carrying out your company's management policy.
2. Should have a stable business record and good reputation.
3. Should maintain high technical standards and be responsive to new developments.
4. Should be able to guarantee confidentiality.
5. Should be conscientious about fulfilling contractual obligations.

Suppliers that you already work with should be periodically evaluated by these standards as well, and you should maintain records on the decisions that were made after such evaluations.

12.6.4 Evaluating Suppliers

In addition to quality (defective rate, customer complaints, quality evaluation points), price (discount rates, effectiveness of value assurance activities in monetary terms), and delivery reliability, suppliers should be evaluated in terms of management, company finances, working conditions, and future prospects.

You should also look to see whether quality control activities are being carried out systematically, how good the supplier's design and manufacturing capabilities are, and whether it is making positive efforts to develop new products. And because you have a vested interest in the supplier's quality once you have decided to purchase from a given company, you should go beyond evaluation to cooperate with the supplier's efforts to make improvements, such as by participating in quality control audits and helping to solve important quality problems.

12.6.5 Purchasing and Outsourcing Contracts and Quality Assurance Agreements

Given that the supplier is an independent company, it will be necessary to draw up a contract with terms that you can both agree on. The contract should among others cover the following.

1. Items to be covered in the contract

   Quality: Purchasing specifications, inspection standards, length of warranty, follow-up services, packaging and transport methods, handling of defectives, and special requirements.

   Quantity and delivery: Order volumes, lot sizes, delivery times, and delivery places.

   Prices and methods of payment.

   Other items: What is to be done when any of the above conditions is to be changed, procedures for resolving problems that may occur, compensation for defective materials or parts (how product liability issues resulting from problems with the supplier's materials and parts are to be resolved), confidentiality, information exchange, bonus-penalty systems, penalities for breach of contract, procedures for altering the terms of the contract, materials, and the provision of equipment and measuring devices.

2. Items to be covered in a quality assurance agreement

   Redundant inspections should be avoided when you know a supplier is conscientiously carrying out its own quality assurance activities. If possible, materials and parts should be accepted on the strength of the supplier's own quality evaluation. Both manufacturer and supplier should cooperate closely to reduce the number of defectives, resolve complaints at the earliest opportunity, and lower costs. The quality assurance agreement should therefore cover:

   Quality assurance responsibilities.

   Items to be implemented for quality assurance.

   Standards, specifications, and provisions for making changes.

   Inspections to be made cooperatively.

   The handling of defectives.

   Documents showing how quality assurance is being carried out.

Evaluations of quality records.

Quality control diagnoses.

The duration for which the agreement is binding and provisions for its alteration or renewal.

12.6.6 Quality Control Guidance

The manufacturer should provide guidance on quality control at the request of the supplier. Such guidance should never be forced on the subcontractor.

The benefits of quality control activities performed by the supplier should be accrued in large part to the supplier, and not be completely absorbed by the manufacturer. This should be done even when the manufacturer played a supportive or guiding role in making the improvements. Encouraging the supplier to work positively for quality assurance this way can be a major factor in raising quality assurance standards.

Follow the advice given in Chapter 7 when instructing outside suppliers in quality control.

12.6.7 Improving Purchasing Operations

Improving purchasing operations can be divided into (1) improving the quality of purchased materials and parts and (2) improving the way in which the purchasing division performs its divisional responsibilities. The first area has already been covered in the discussion of process analysis and I will not go into further detail here. The second area includes eliminating delayed deliveries and lowering inventory costs. Statistical analysis can be a useful tool in both areas.

It is common to blame the supplier for delayed deliveries, but careful analysis often reveals that the manufacturer is actually at fault. Sometimes conflicting or impossible delivery schedules are set up that completely ignore the supplier's production and processing capabilities. In the case of outsourcing, the manufacturer may be late in providing the necessary materials.

Quality control should always be based on hard data, and this is just as true for purchasing. Both manufacturer and supplier should maintain clear records. The purchasing division is the interface between your company and its outside suppliers, and it is imperative that it be well versed in quality control methodology and problem-solving.

13 | Quality Control in the Office

13.1 Quality Control in Non-manufacturing Divisions

13.1.1 Quality Control in Administrative and Clerical Divisions

Every company has non-manufacturing divisions: planning, personnel, general affairs, accounting, purchasing, and sales to name just a few. In a manufacturing company such staff divisions are typically considered completely separate from the manufacturing-related line divisions that are actually producing the company's products. And, of course, there are numerous businesses such as retailing and services that are wholly made up of such divisions.

Contrary to expectations, the kind of quality control that applies to office work is not really any different in principle than the kind of quality control applied in manufacturing. Everything I have said about quality control so far is equally valid for quality control in office work. In this chapter I will elaborate on those quality concerns that are especially important in office work.

13.1.2 The Role of Non-manufacturing Divisions

In retail and service companies, white-collar workers make up nearly 100% of the corporate structure. Even in a manufacturing company, the non-manufacturing divisions usually have most of the management people and are closer to the levers of corporate power. It is thus all the more important that these staff divisions function effectively and efficiently. And as already pointed out time and again, quality control is one of the best ways to ensure this.

Quality control in the non-manufacturing divisions is just one part of TQC, just as quality control on the line can only be effectively implemented when it is everyone's concern, not just of the people in the manufacturing divisions. With a good quality control programme, white-collar workers develop a better understanding of the crucial role they play in product quality assurance. Both line and staff have to be involved and closely cooperating in TQC.

While there is a growing awareness of the importance of quality control in non-manufacturing divisions, this still lags far behind the level of quality control being implemented in manufacturing divisions. Companies in the retail and service sector have been slow to catch up to their manufacturing counterparts when it comes to meaningful and effective quality control.

13.1.3 Problems in Implementing Quality Control in Non-manufacturing Divisions

One of the reasons quality control tends to be overlooked and defectives often go unnoticed in the staff divisions is that their "products" are so intangible. We seldom perform inspections on our market surveys, services, accounting, and other staff output, yet there are a lot more defective products – defective in the sense of not meeting the user's requirements – here than you would expect. This is all the more reason that quality control is so important here.

Yet the non-manufacturing divisions fall behind when it comes to quality control. Some reasons for this are:

1. No one really understands what quality control is supposed to be. It is assumed that quality control is limited to production technology.
2. The people in staff divisions do not realize how important they are to product quality assurance.
3. Few people understand what quality control is in the context of office operations. There is not enough awareness that the next process is the customer and the customer needs to be satisfied, even with paperwork.
4. The emphasis is on individual performance, and it is not considered important that work be structured so that anyone can perform the same job.
5. Effective quality control requires a firm grasp on reality, but people in staff divisions seldom make an effort to seek out the hard facts about their own work.
6. There is insufficient understanding that quality control is prevention, and time is spent instead on correcting problems after they occur.

The same quality control concepts and methodology that are used in quality control for industrial products can be applied equally effectively to non-manufacturing operations. Too many white-collar workers rationalize their lack of effort in this direction by claiming that their work is different from manufacturing. Yet quality control has been effectively applied in many non-manufacturing divisions and companies.

13.1.4 Introducing Quality Control in Non-manufacturing Divisions

One of the most common and probably best ways to introduce quality control into non-manufacturing divisions and companies is through the QC circle. The QC circle is an especially effective tool for getting staff employees involved. By encouraging workers to seek out and solve problems close at hand, the QC circle provides an easily understood focus of activity and its effectiveness becomes obvious to one and all within a very short time.

Keep in mind, however, that the QC circle provides a stepping stone to introducing TQC, and is by no means sufficient in and of itself. Granted the QC circle is highly effective in encouraging teamwork on problem-solving and is thus a major part of TQC, it does not encompass the whole company, every division, and every level of authority from worker through top management. The difficulty in expanding from the QC circle to TQC is that TQC is all too often introduced as only a vague concept without any specific guidance from the company president about what he hopes to achieve through TQC. Because workers cannot really understand what TQC is supposed to be about, they cling to their QC circle activities on the assumption that it is enough to concentrate on their own immediate quality control concerns.

Management, particularly top management, plays a vital role in TQC, and top management needs to be more aware of this. A company is likely to have many of its white-collar workers in sales, accounting, or administration, for example, and mistakes by any one of these people can have dire consequences for the company as whole. Even though their numbers may be small, the fact that they are central to the company's operations means that they are central to the company's survival.

Management − especially top management − participation is thus essential for TQC. TQC cannot possibly succeed without the wholehearted participation of the company president and other top executives. Management cannot sit back and expect to reap the benefits of a TQC programme in which they are not actively involved, because there will be no benefits without their full participation.

QC circles are an effective way to start because they involve line workers in making improvements at their own work sites and show fairly quick results. Yet you cannot stop there. Nor can you assume that these QC circle activities will fuse together into TQC. There must be a clear statement of purpose and a clear commitment from top management. The emphasis on quality will quickly turn sour if management appears to think that such QC activities are beneath them. Only when everybody throughout the company is making a coordinated, concerted effort for efficient quality will you have TQC.

13.2 Office Work and Quality

13.2.1 What is Office Work?

People think they know what office work is, but they find it very difficult to give a specific definition. The basic elements of office work are preparing and filling out forms and documents, conducting various surveys and studies, planning, making liaison with suppliers and customers, number-crunching, organizing, and performing other internal and external communications functions. Whatever the division's name − general affairs, personnel, purchasing, or what − the basic elements are the same. As such, these operations correspond to the manufacturing divisions' cutting, grinding, moulding, welding, painting, and so on. Whatever is being manufactured, even in construction and shipbuilding, the physical activities are simply combinations and repetitions of the same basic elements. The same is true in office work. Every division, no matter what its name, is performing the same compilation, organization, and other functions in combination and repetition. In this sense, there is no difference between the manufacture of tangible products and the intangible output of the office.

Because office work consists of information collecting, processing (categorizing, analyzing, and evaluating), filing, reviewing, and transmitting, office work can be defined as information exchange for the purpose of achieving corporate goals.

To take this one step further, the staff divisions produce information. For example, customer service division's responsibility is to supply the personnel, product, financial, and other information that the user (customer) needs, and the benefits that the user derives from this information is the measure of the information's quality.

13.2.2 Office Work Quality

The person who uses a product is the final judge of its quality, and a good product is one that meets the user's requirements. Quality control teaches that the next process is your customer, and this is a most important axiom. But in adhering to this rule, don't forget that there is an end-user at the end of all these processes. Likewise, there are users for the office's output as well, and every effort should be made to provide the kind of product the user needs on time and at the lowest possible cost. Good output meets the user's needs and quality operations ensure that there is good output.

This principle holds true for both manufacturing and non-manufacturing output, whether the product is tangible or intangible. Yet non-manufacturing divisions tend to forget that they are creating products that someone else will be using, and they all-too-readily assume that their work is an end in itself.

I once visited one hard-working planning and research division that spent a great deal of time and effort collecting information, organizing it, and preparing and publishing an in-house monthly research report. The people in this division complained, however, that they had very little feedback on their reports from the rest of the company. Upon questioning them, I found that they had never tried to find out what kinds of information the rest of the company needed. Instead, they had arbitrarily decided what they thought everyone else would want to know instead of going around to each division to find out what kind of information would be most useful. This is equivalent to manufacturing a product without researching the market first, and it is little wonder that the market (their readers) ignored the product. You can't expect the product to sell under such circumstances. The correct approach would be to conduct a careful study of the market, to find out exactly what people want to know, and then and only then to collect and compile the information.

13.2.3 Two Degrees of Quality Responsibility

Quality control is by no means limited to industrial product quality control, and it can be just as effectively applied to the plans drawn up by a planning division and the various financial documents prepared by an accounting division. In banks, hotels, and other service-sector enterprises, too, the services that they sell are prime candidates for quality control.

In manufacturing, construction, and other sectors that produce tangible products, staff divisions have an added quality control responsibility in that they are responsible not only for their own divisional output but for the line divisions' output as well. The administrative divisions thus have two major quality concerns:

1. The quality of their company's manufactured products.
2. The quality of their own operational output.

It is important to remember that quality control in the administrative divisions is not limited to making staff operations more efficient. Figure 13.1 shows some of the quality control concerns that need to be addressed by administrative divisions. Some people in administration are willing to admit partial responsibility for line output as part of their "quality control activities in the broader sense," but this is nonsense. Administration's responsibility for product quality is not "in the broader sense." It is in the only sense.

13.2.3.1 Manufactured Product Quality

The staff divisions in a manufacturing company often assume that they have no responsibility for product quality because they are not directly linked to the company's production lines. Thus the sales division may work hard to sell the product but forget that it can play an important role in the product's quality control by relaying customer comments and complaints back to the manufacturing divisions.

A look at Figure 13.1's list of product control activities in which staff divisions should participate clearly shows that product quality control is as much their concern as it is of the production line. Company rules and regulations should be very clear on this point.

These quality control activities are fairly self-explanatory, but it may help to point out some other specific responsibilities and concerns.

The planning and research division's job is to identify those activities, products, and control systems that will be required in the future.

The personnel division should be just as concerned with what people are assigned to do as it is with the number of people the company requires to maintain product quality. As such, personnel is also responsible for quality control education and training.

The general affairs division must create the organizational framework for implementing quality control and establish the necessary rules and regulations to ensure that quality control is effectively carried out.

The accounting division provides the design people with cost analyses for new products still in the planning stage, identifies cost problems in the manufacturing

	Duties to Ensure Product Quality	Other Divisional Duties
Planning	Product planning, drafting long-term quality assurance plans, drafting long-term QC plans, new product planning, planning product phase-outs, drafting product line-up plans, forecasting required quality and volume	Profit control system, coordination in policy control system, drafting and checking long-term management plans, investment capital control, affiliate control
Personnel	Personnel placement, QC training and education	Employee welfare, health insurance, safety control, suggestion system, employee awards, life and other insurance, hiring, employee education, employee loyalty
General affairs	Specifications and standardization, documentation, delineating lines of authority and responsibility, organizing channels of communication for information on quality, and keeping people abreast of developments relating to product liability law	Coordination of rules and regulations, documentation, investor relations, secretarial services, public relations
Accounting	Planning and tracking costs, calculating quality costs	Budget control, financial management, financial planning, cost control, credit control, receivables collection, investments
Purchasing, materials and subcon-tacting	Selecting suppliers and sub-contractors, contracting with suppliers and subcontractors on quality standards, specifying quality requirements, deciding purchasing volume, setting delivery schedules, negotiating costs, evaluating and coordinating suppliers and subcontractors, assisting suppliers and sub-contractors, studying possible substitutes	Inspection of materials and parts received, schedule control, storage control, ordering, paying suppliers and subcontractors
Sales & service	Product planning, inventory control, drafting catalogues and product brochures, processing complaints, collecting and passing along information on quality	Sales plan, sales control, servicing, accepting complaints
Plant & facilities	Planning facilities and equipment, designing and maintaining plants, environmental considerations	Planning energy-savings, planning labour-savings, reducing maintenance and power costs, preventing pollution
Storage & transport	Packaging, storage and custody, transport, preventing deterioration	Storage control, reducing shipping costs

Note: For information on purchasing, materials, and subcontracting, see Section 12.6.

Figure 13.1 Staff Quality Control Functions

processes, and specifies the financial limits on quality control activities by comparison with the costs of, for example, processing customer complaints.

The sales division conducts research on consumer needs, provides information on the correct use of the company's products, and otherwise provides those kinds of backup services that are essential to marketing any kind of product. Product liability should be a major concern of this division.

Juran has stated that product quality is first and foremost a management issue, not a technological issue. This is easy to understand when you consider that the sales division, for example, is closest to the customer while the design, inspection, and related divisions are usually tucked away somewhere in the company's production facilities far away from the product's market, where they can only be as good as the feedback they get from sales and other front-line divisions.

It may be useful here to list the product liability prevention responsibilities of each of the principal staff divisions.

1. Planning and research division
   (1) Collecting and analyzing information on domestic and foreign laws related to product liability.
   (2) Studying how safe competitor's products are, both domestically and overseas.
   (3) Reviewing the company's own safety standards.
   (4) Conducting surveys and studies to learn customer opinions and needs.
   (5) Conducting surveys to gauge employee awareness of the company's responsibilities to society.
   (6) Studying domestic and foreign product liability prevention programmes.
   (7) Reporting to top management on product liability case law.
2. General affairs and legal divisions.
   (1) Studying domestic and international laws and case law.
   (2) Establishing corporate safety regulations and standards.
   (3) Preparing and filing evidential documentation.
   (4) Preparing crisis-management systems.
   (5) Submitting applications to the competent government agencies to acquire the necessary certification.
   (6) Checking on legal aspects of product quality (design, labelling, publicity, instruction manuals, warnings, etc.)
   (7) Making the necessary changes to meet legal requirements (design, product naming, product form, labelling, etc.)
   (8) Evaluating product quality from the legal standpoint (safety of contents, safety of container, packaging safety, etc.)
   (9) Acquiring product liability insurance.
   (10) Introducing product liability prevention programmes and publicizing product liability case law.
3. Purchasing division
   (1) Maintaining purchase records.

(2) Maintaining records on special parts and materials and the reason for their use and supervising purchases.

(3) Providing instruction to suppliers.

(4) Specifying limits of responsibility and preparing contracts for suppliers.

(5) Investigating and confirming that suppliers have the necessary installations and equipment, testing methods, and process control.

4. Inventory and transport divisions

(1) Checking on packaging safety, labelling, and other legal requirements.

(2) Checking that packaging is sufficient to prevent product quality deterioration during shipment or storage.

(3) Checking on extent of danger caused by inferior packaging, breakage, and label loss.

(4) Devising measures to prevent quality deterioration during storage and transport.

(5) Organizing and maintaining distribution records that include intermediary distributors and retailers.

(6) Establishing standards and procedures for product recalls.

5. Advertising and publicity divisions

(1) Checking on legal regulations concerning advertising and publicity.

(2) Checking on legal regulations concerning premiums and other sales promotion activities.

(3) Checking all advertising and publicity material for product liability problems.

(4) Checking on functional and service warranties.

6. Sales and customer service divisions

(1) Checking all sales documentation and other printed matter for incorrect labelling and misinformation.

(2) Checking instruction manuals for readability and ease of understanding.

(3) Checking on changes in product quality that occur with aging, the time limit on warranties, and disposal methods.

(4) Maintaining complete sales records, including data acquired from intermediate distributors and retailers.

(5) Checking publicity material explaining correct product use.

(6) Checking customer complaint processing systems, conducting employee education on complaint processing, and maintaining records of all customer complaints and how they were handled.

(7) Establishing standards for the disposal of discontinued and defective products.

(8) Establishing feedback systems for the collection of information on product use and trouble.

(9) Establishing and implementing sales training programmes.

(10) Establishing customer service standards and records, analyses, and feedback systems.

(11) Providing instruction to intermediate distributors and retailers.

Other areas that should be covered include: estimating potential losses from product liability trouble (accounting division), promoting product liability prevention education and preparing documentation on past product liability complaints and trouble (personnel division), and checking on legal aspects of product liability requirements and providing product liability prevention education and inspection programmes for suppliers and affiliates (purchasing division). As the above list clearly shows, product liability is a company-wide concern for both line and staff divisions.

13.2.3.2 Maintaining Quality in Divisional Operations

Quality control can also be applied to the following types of divisional activities.

Planning: Earnings control system and policy control system, drawing up and checking long-term operational plan, investment control, and control of affiliates.

Personnel: Social security, health insurance, safety control, labour-management relations, suggestion system, awards, insurance, hiring employee education, improving employee morale and cutting turnover.

General affairs: Corporate rules and regulations, document forms, stock-holder relations, secretarial work, publicity.

Accounting: Budgeting, capital procurement planning, asset management, calculating costs, credit control, recycling, investment.

Purchasing: Inspection systems, delivery control, inventory control, orders, and payments.

Sales: Marketing strategy, sales control, customer services, complaint processing.

Plant and facilities: Energy- and labour-conservation programmes, cutting maintenance costs, energy-economizing, pollution prevention.

Storage and transport: Inventory control, cutting delivery transport costs.

Effective and efficient forms and documentation are as important to quality control in staff divisions as technology is in the production process.

Of course, quality control will not be equally important for all staff division activities. Strategy is an equally important part of marketing, and past experience can contribute to effective advertising and publicity. This is especially true in television advertising and programming, where an off-beat seat-of-the-pants idea may be the season's hottest property. The media's receptivity to unusual (i.e., untried and untested) ideas make it difficult to apply quality control in this field. Still, quality control can be applied within the limited context of analyzing the reasons past commercials and programmes have succeeded, deciding what kinds of presentations will be best received, and producing predictable success.

Remember that quality control is basically a diagnostic system to discover problems in work procedures and output so that they can be resolved using conventional technology and control techniques. Going ahead with the treatment without making a thorough diagnosis can only lead to trouble.

At the same time, this does not mean that quality control has to be applied to absolutely everything. Over-zealousness can actually obstruct the very product quality assurance that is, after all, the whole purpose of quality control. Only when quality control achieves quality assurance does it make sense to expand it to other areas, but even then care should be taken to ensure that you never do quality control for quality control's sake.

13.3 Control in Staff Divisions

Whenever we embark on an activity, no matter what it is, we begin first with a plan that states our ends and our means, go on to carry out the plan, review the results, and revise the original plan if it proved inadequate. This is the basic quality control cycle of planning, doing, checking, and acting. There is no reason to change this quality control cycle for staff divisions.

Control, as Juran says, encompasses the process of drawing up a plan and all the activities that go into carrying out this plan. Quality control, then, is the application of this kind of control to product quality. Thus, quality control or management is the establishing of a plan for product quality and encompasses all of the steps required in implementing this plan. In other words, quality control is planning and implementing the most economical method of manufacturing a product that will be maximally useful and meet the consumer's requirements.

It should hardly need to be pointed out that the PDCA circle must actually begin with checking, that is checking on current conditions, to establish a foundation on which to base your plans for improvement. The famous Deming circle (Figure 13.2) can be applied to all corporate activities throughout a company.

In manufacturing, this circle is applied in four steps: (1) designing a product, (2) manufacturing the product, (3) inspecting and selling the product, and (4)

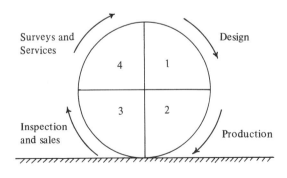

An emphasis on quality,
a sense of quality-responsibility

Figure 13.2 The Deming Circle

surveying consumer reactions to the product so that you can revise the product as necessary to meet consumer requirements. While the first three steps can be carried out completely within the corporation, the final fourth step must be carried out outside of the company. Furthermore, sales, surveys, and services come under the primary jurisdiction of staff divisions.

This holds true even for service and sales industries that do not manufacture tangible products. In such industries, the equivalent of manufacturing takes place simultaneously with sales, and generally no quality inspection is performed. Neither are these services as carefully "designed" as their industrial product counterparts.

13.3.1 Control and Diagnosis

Control means going back to the planning stage to make very basic changes, not simply repairing defective products as you come across them. Health care is a good analogy. Taking care of yourself means making sure you do not get sick, not simply curing yourself when you do. Control is prevention.

Control is correcting the cause, not treating the effect. This is done by carefully studying the effect, tracing its causes, and eliminating the causes of mistakes. This requires getting a firm grasp of the nature of a defect and diagnosing it to find its cause or causes. It is impossible to treat the problem effectively until after this diagnosis has been made, and you need to know every-thing there is to know about a defect to make your diagnosis.

For example, let us look at the case of one of your company's suppliers who is habitually late with parts deliveries. The purchasing division warns the supplier repeatedly, but to no avail. When you finally look into the situation, you find that something is holding up the delivery of raw materials from your company to the supplier — the cause of the problem lies within your company, not with the supplier. Further investigation reveals that the people responsible for sending the raw materials to the supplier always wait until they fill a whole truck because they have been told that that is more economical. The actual cause then, in this particular situation, is that the purchasing division has not made it clear to the materials people that scheduling has priority and that late shipments can generate far bigger costs than half-empty trucks.

13.3.2 Control Based on Facts

Quality control is control based on factual evidence. The statistical method provides a useful tool in performing quality control diagnosis. Without statistics, you do not have any facts to base your decisions on. But data alone do not give you a clear picture of the facts. You need to know how to interpret the data, just as a doctor needs to be trained before he can make any sense out of an electrocardiogram or electroencephalogram. By using statistical tools to organize your data, you can spot defects and diagnose their causes. This approach is called statistical quality control, SQC for short, and can be effectively applied in both line and staff activities.

13.3.3 Defining Your Activities

For quality assurance in staff activities, just as with product quality for line products, you start by defining the specific activities needed to achieve your ends. This is done by answering the 5-Ws and 1-H.

Why do you need to do this?
What are you going to do it to?
Where will you do this?
When must you perform the activities?
Who is responsible?
How will you carry out these tasks?

Failing to answer any one of these questions can prevent you from fulfilling your duties effectively.

One of the principal reasons that quality control has not taken hold in the staff divisions is that the divisions' duties have not been clearly delineated. Even if they are well-defined, they have not necessarily been incorporated into official corporate policy rules and regulations.

It is wishful thinking to assume that quality control education will ensure that staff divisions practise quality control. Each division's quality control responsibilities must be clearly spelled out, and this aspect of organizational planning is the job of top management.

13.3.4 Approaches to Problem Solving

There are two possible approaches to seeking out and solving problems: the analytical approach and the design approach.

The analytical approach starts with the defect or problem and traces it back to its cause. It is a back-tracking approach that can be highly effective when you have an effect to work with, but it does not work when you are trying to forecast possible problems that may crop up with a completely new activity. The conventional seven QC tools are analytical tools to be used when you are trying to make improvements.

The design approach is a systematic attempt to define what has to be done to achieve a certain goal. This is the approach to use in launching any kind of new endeavour. A sequential approach in contrast to the back-tracking approach of analysis uses functional deployment to achieve its objectives. Functional deployment is one of the best ways of clarifying what staff activities will be needed to introduce and promote TQC effectively. And the tools for functional deployment are the new seven tools of quality control to find out where current activities fall short and what new activities are required.

13.3.5 Controlling Quality Control

Once you have defined the necessary quality control tasks, you need to decide on how you will keep track of these tasks to ensure that they are being performed correctly and effectively and to change them when necessary. In terms of the Deming circle, once you start doing, you need to know how to check and act. Here too, the 5-Ws and 1-H apply.

Why do you need control?
What are the control items?
Who is responsible?
When must control be carried out?
Where is control required?
How will control be performed?

Meaningful control demands answers to all of these questions. The tendency is to concentrate on defining the control items only, but effective control covers a much broader area and can only be executed after you have answered all of these questions. This is the process of standardizing control activities, and your control items are your control standards.

I have already explained the significance of control standards for manufacturing processes in Section 12.3.3, and the same basic concepts apply to staff processes, with a few caveats given below.

1. Control is not the kind of mindless adherence to standards that consists of simply rubber-stamping documents that pass over your desk. Checking and acting are the heart of control — checking to see that work is being performed to standards and that the standards are meaningful and acting as appropriate to revise the work or the standards when they are not.

2. The numerical values that are assigned to control items are quality indices not target values. They are the indices needed to check on whether the level of quality required to attain the target values is being maintained. And when quality is not up to par, these indices help to define the kind of action that should be taken.

For example, a sales office can set itself the goal of doubling sales, but it is unlikely they will achieve this goal without indicators to mark their progress. Making your target values your control items may tell you when you have fallen short, but it does not show you how to achieve your ends. The control item must provide a guide for implementation. If you know that a certain product did not sell well because of insufficient publicity, you can make the publicity your control item, checking it against the monthly sales figures to see whether it is having the desired impact. If the correlation can be confirmed, all you need to control is the publicity and you will get your sales.

13.4 Total Quality Control Activities

TQC is more than QC that everyone takes part in. QC circles have, of course, become an integral part of many staff divisions and can prove highly effective in making improvements in regular divisional activities. This is to be commended, and should certainly be encouraged. Yet QC circles alone do not make total quality control. Effective as they are for tackling sporadic problems, they do not address hidden, chronic issues. In this sense, QC circles are insufficient to radically improve divisional performance.

Neither does TQC mean everyone pursuing quality control on his own. Rather, as the term total implies, it is everyone working together to achieve shared quality control goals.

Sales, service, and other non-manufacturing companies have been showing increased interest in TQC recently, but their efforts to introduce the concept have unfortunately yet to go much beyond instituting QC circles.

13.4.1 Quality, Management, and Quality Control

In Chapter 1, I used the illustration of three overlapping circles shown in Figure 13.3 to explain the nature of TQC. There I was talking about TQC for the manufacturing and construction industry, but the same concept can be applied in non-manufacturing industries for quality control of their many services and other "products."

Rather than repeating the entire thesis, I will therefore limit myself to touching on just the highlights for non-manufacturing.

There are two aspects of TQC: activities to ensure manufactured product quality and activities to enhance corporate management.

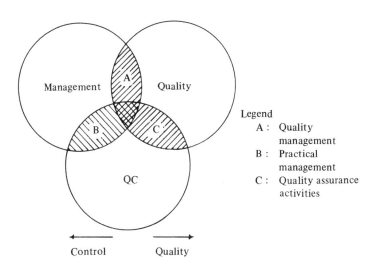

Figure 13.3 The Two Directions in Quality Control

Quality assurance for manufactured products is the starting point of all quality control, but it can also be applied to non-manufacturing divisions and companies as quality assurance for general clerical and administrative activities. The emergence of new financial services as money markets move toward deregulation is one manifestation of how quality control can be applied for new product development (the most important aspect of which is quality assurance).

Activities that directly benefit corporate management, called practical management activities, encompass all activities related to cross-functional management and corporate regulations aimed at standardization, policy control and quality assurance being the only exceptions.

Maintaining high product quality is increasingly important to corporate management, and true quality management is directed more at improving product quality than at increasing profits.

Finally, though not directly related to these activities, are activities to improve quality control methodologies.

13.4.2 Quality Management

Today just about every company has long-term or at least medium-term management policies and plans. New technical developments and changes in the labour market mandate long-term planning – especially now that the pace of change seems to have picked up. Yet all too often, these plans are far from practical, instead being wish-lists of idealistic goals with little or no consideration of how this goal is to be achieved.

It is the planning division that is responsible for devising practical long-term management plans and following them up to see that they are fulfilled. Because this division has little contact with quality control, it is likely to create idealistic plans without no thought to the company's current conditions or possible changes in the business climate. Here too, the control circle needs to be applied starting with checking. Quality control's statistical tools can be very helpful in gauging current conditions and forecasting changes, yet the people in planning do not even know that such useful tools exist. The more important the division to the company's future, the more it needs quality control.

A manufacturing company should have separate plans for each product it manufactures to cover all those clerical, administrative, sales, and service-related activities that are peripheral to the actual product itself. The planning division's primary concerns, however, tend to be profits and investment, and it is the rare company that has a separate division just to devise and implement plans. As a result, the planning function often falls to the specific operating division, where they do not have the personnel or expertise to do much planning in any but, maybe, the sales division. In theory, this planning should cover finding what the market requirements are and planning how to meet them with maximum efficiency, but this is usually relegated to the design department and everyone else forgets about it.

13.4.3 Policy Control

In keeping with the company's long-term management policy, the priority concerns for each year should be stated so that every effort can be applied to meeting these concerns within the year. This is policy control, and important part of TQC in any company.

Policy control is essential to effective corporate management, and yet there are many cases in which it is not even acknowledged until TQC is introduced into the company. Policy control is most effective when the QC approach is applied to analyzing current circumstances, developing policies on the basis of the findings, and checking to ensure that policy control activities are fulfilling their purpose.

Because the concept is introduced with TQC, the tendency is to have the TQC headquarters take care of policy control, even though this, like long-term planning, should actually be done by the planning division. This problem is compounded when the lack of QC-awareness keeps the TQC headquarters from functioning effectively.

A system needs to be developed and the necessary tools made available to implement meaningful policy control. People in the design division realize this as a matter of course, but clerical and administrative people are seldom so well trained.

The planning division needs to recognize that policy control is the most important quality control activity it can perform, and it should consider itself the leader as far as TQC goes.

13.4.4 Cross-functional Management

Cross-functional management is an inter-divisional activity. Within the individual division it is a relatively simple task to ensure that orders given by the division head are carried out as intended. When different divisions have to work together, however, it is not so simple, since you must have cooperation among workers at the same level and there are no clear-cut vertical lines of authority. Thus it is necessary to have a system that will smooth the way for cross-functional cooperation and coordination.

An integral part of TQC, cross-functional management covers, in addition to product quality assurance activities, cost control and delivery control (production volume and scheduling). These are all areas in which staff divisions figure importantly, and all of these different control activities interact and are performed simultaneously rather than separately and sequentially. In setting up systems for these various control activities, you must define the role to be played by each division for quality, cost, and delivery control.

The administrative divisions perform dual roles, carrying out their own production activities, so to speak, and supporting the actual manufacturing lines. The personnel division is a good example. In addition to assigning people to management positions, arranging for employee training programmes, and deciding on salaries, one of the personnel division's most important tasks is that of planning personnel assignments throughout the company. Training workers is a time-consuming process — people cannot be quickly reprogrammed like a machine with just a few adjustments — which means plans for acquiring and training the right kind of people must be made well in advance of any move into a new field. In a country such as the United States it is relatively easy to lure trained specialists away from other companies, but the Japanese pattern of life-time employment means that there is little mid-career mobility and the company has to train its own people. Unfortunately, the personnel division does not always realize how important it is in the company's long-term planning.

If the company's staff divisions are to effectively support the manufacturing divisions, you have to have some system linking them together and promoting coordination among them. This is cross-functional management. Personnel management is one kind of cross-functional management because it involves coordination among all departments and is not solely a concern of the personnel division. Some other kinds of cross-functional management in which staff divisions play a major role are orders processing, sales processing, purchasing control, and information control.

There are two approaches to quality control: the project approach and the systems approach. The project approach concentrates on specific quality problems, seeking out priority problems, analyzing their causes, and correcting them. The systems approach involves establishing a system of communication linking divisions, carrying out activities within the framework of this system, and constantly improving the system through application of the PDCA circle. Cross-functional management takes the systems approach and is implemented the same as the quality assurance activities described in Chapter 4. Operating within such a system also serves to improve work procedures within the staff divisions.

13.5 Quality Control and Computerization

13.5.1 Office Automation and Quality Control

In essence, the staff divisions' job is information processing directed at achieving the company's goals. The trend today is to introduce computers into the workplace to speed up and rationalize this information processing. This is certainly commendable, but there are some people who assume that computerizing office work this way has nothing to do with quality control or can even eliminate the need for quality control.

Yet for truly effective office automation, there is a need first to clarify how information should be processed within the TQC context before you even think about computer networks.

Computer can compile and calculate data with incredible speed and accuracy, but if there is no quality control of the original data, you can end up with no way to tell the silk from the sow ears. It is the old GIGO (garbage in, garbage out) syndrome. One company discovered to its horror that minor input errors, including mistaken entries on the original vouchers, were responsible for 80% of the defective output. This kind of catastrophe shows how computerization can quickly compound problems rather than improve efficiency. When calculations were made by hand, the original careless error would have been quickly spotted and corrected. But the computer does not distinguish between a correct number and an incorrect one. It simply performs the programmed calculations and spews out valuable results and junk with equal authority. It makes no sense at all to computerize your office unless you have a system of quality control in place that will catch such careless errors before they go into the computer.

It is also important that everyone in the company understand why computers are being installed. Simply having the equipment does nothing for your efficiency if people do not use it. One office found that no one had time to look at, interpret, and apply the reams of data output from their computer. The machine was functioning, but to no avail. This kind of situation results when management has not specified what data are needed and how they should be applied. In other words, management has not defined the basic control items.

In many instances, it is more meaningful to have the data presented as graphs, histograms, and other visual forms. Computers can prepare such material readily, but it is up to the people using the computer to tell it what to do.

Just as you have to know what you are looking for in the data, there should be standards for collecting data so that figures can be meaningfully compared. Very often, this will entail analyzing different activities and setting common standards. You will also need some kind of criteria against which to judge the effectiveness of your computers and office system. Data on operating times and error frequency, for example, can provide valuable information on which to base improvements of the system.

Far from being unrelated or redundant, quality control is prerequisite to and a continuing part of computerizing your office.

13.5.2 Computer-aided Quality Control

This brings us to computer-aided quality control (CAQC) which can be as useful for staff as for line divisions. Because quality control takes a statistical approach to analyzing and interpreting data, computers are very useful in making the necessary calculations. Computers also help to automate and speed up all manner of information processing. For example, inspection ratings can be immediately calculated and the information fed back along the line. If the parts come from an outside supplier, orders can be automatically adjusted in consideration of what you know about the last shipment. The day's quality costs can be computed so that management can act on the information the next day. Losses incurred from repairing defective products become obvious when they can be calculated on the spot.

Computers can also be a strong ally in product liability prevention by providing a means of collecting and organizing quality records and making it possible to extract the information you need when you need it without a long time-consuming search through the archives.

Computer-aided quality control should not be limited to one process or one set of quality data but should be applied on a company-wide basis to create a corporate quality information network for collecting, interpreting, and transmitting information. This kind of computer network first becomes meaningful when it helps to speed up the PDCA circle. Just as your computer network should be applied to quality management and policy control, it should also be used in cross-functional management including quality assurance and cost control.

Great advances are being made in information processing technology, and computer applications in quality control are certain to become more widespread.

If quality control has not taken firm root in every division, however, no amount of computerization will improve things. You have to know what you want to do before you can programme the computer to do it.

13.5.3 Management Information Systems

People have known about the need for management information systems for a long time. And computerization has made it all the more evident that some kind of quality control system is needed for management information. The many problems that arise with office computers are caused not by the computers but by the way they are used.

Even though it is the company's planning division that should be responsible for instituting a management information system, planning people tend to be put off by the high-tech image of computers and telecommunications equipment. Because of this computerphobia, plus their general lack of management skills, they tend to pass the buck on this to the engineers in the computer division. Granted that the computer people have the ability to prepare individual financial forms and statements and to process management directives and information related to sales and production control, they cannot be expected to make sense out of the hodgepodge of available data unless there is some overall system of coordination.

For an effective management information system, the administrative divisions, particularly the planning division, must make an effort to institute firm quality control and promote computerization as a quality control aid. No programme of computerization can succeed otherwise.

The computer people's role in TQC in this management information system is:

1. To provide useful management information to the company's top management. Top management needs information that relates to specific control items. This should not be the raw data but should be presented in graphs and other visual forms that show what is happening. This enables top management to make the right decisions quickly.
2. To provide data analysis for annual and long-term management planning. This involves performing the checking and action steps of the PDCA circle, finding out why the goals were not achieved, interpreting the effects on the company of changes in the business climate, and so on. Several proposals should be presented along with their respective advantages and disadvantages so that top management has a choice to select from.
3. To provide progress reports on TQC and its effectivness. This information should keep top management and divisional heads informed of the progress being made in instituting TQC and how close the company has come to achieving its quality control objectives.
4. To provide reports on computer programming. This would include reports on how various programmes are being applied in the different divisions, what new programmes are being developed or revised and why, how employees are being trained and otherwise encouraged to apply computer programmes, how

the computer programmes are contributing to total quality control in such areas as quality assurance, cost control, production control, and new product and new technology development, and how the company's computer programmes compare with those being used by other companies.

14 | The Quality Control Audit

I have already pointed out that the PDCA circle of planning, doing, checking, and taking corrective action needs to be applied to the whole TQC system as well as to product quality control itself. The auditing I will be discussing in this chapter could just as well be called checking or inspecting, but because these terms tend to suggest that you are specifically looking for faults, many companies prefer to call the process a diagnosis (even though you would obviously take action to correct any problems that might be discovered) or audit.

In companies where TQC is only a vague concept with no specific guidelines as to how it should be implemented, you will find that problems are seldom corrected at their source. Because of the lack of a specific programme, the top management has no idea where TQC is failing, what, if anything, is being done to remedy these failures, whether quality control plans are being correctly implemented, or whether or not the original plans themselves are flawed.

Effective TQC requires competent management of the whole TQC programme. This is top management's responsibility. Of course, since TQC is carried out on a daily basis, there is an ongoing review of its progress and a constant effort to keep the whole process on its intended track. In referring to a TQC audit or diagnosis, however, I am speaking of diagnosing and judging TQC from a much broader perspective that encompasses every section and division.

An important aspect of this kind of diagnosis is to ferret out the hidden chronic problems rather than focus on the more obvious occasional problems. This means quality control audits should be made at regular intervals and the company's TQC programme reviewed and revised in line with the audit results.

14.1   The Product Quality Audit and Quality Control Audit

Quality assurance has numerous functions, many of which I have already discussed. If there is a plan as to how these functions are to be performed and if everything is carried out exactly according to this plan, theoretically the customer should be getting exactly the product quality he requires. Still, even after preshipment inspection, it is always possible that product quality will deteriorate in the time it takes the product to reach the customer. This is why it is so important to conduct a survey of products after they have reached the customer to check on whether they are still at the required quality levels. If product quality has fallen, it is because there is a flaw in one or more of the numerous quality assurance functions, and corrective action is required. This kind of checking and correcting is what the product quality audit is all about. It is, as explained in Chapter 10, a process of evaluating the degree to which a product's quality characteristics measure up.

It is equally important to evaluate the whole quality assurance system and check on its suitability. This is a quality assurance system audit or a quality control audit and involves an overall inspection of every aspect of quality control to check on how effectively it is being carried out. Quality control audits can be made from outside the company or from within. The Deming Prize inspection process discussed in Chapter 9 is one example of an external quality control audit. After a company has been implementing TQC for a while, it can ask to have a quality control audit made by members of the Deming Prize Committee. This audit is made using the Deming Prize checklist and is followed by a report including recommendations by the Deming Prize Committee members. This report can prove invaluable in improving your TQC programme.

14.2 The Need for a Quality Control Audit

The most important quality control audit is that conducted by the company president, but no audit will be effective unless its targets have been clearly defined.

14.2.1 The Purpose of a Quality Control Audit

Following are the major purposes of quality control audit.

1. Achieving company policy goals

   Product quality is not, of course, the sole concern of company policy, but many companies that have instituted company-wide total quality control programmes naturally include the quality control audit in their corporate policy. In many instances, the primary purpose behind the company president's quality control audit is to check on the progress that has been made in carrying out company policy. This check, however, should include not only an examination of the progress that is being made but also a review of company policy to ascertain whether it has set appropriate goals in the first place. It is not unheard of for a company president to discover in the process of a quality control audit that the original corporate policy is flawed and its goals inappropriate.

2. Achieving product quality goals

   Achieving product quality goals is, of course, the whole purpose of quality control. Unfortunately, in many cases quality policy is not clear. A company may claim that it is aiming for world-class quality without specifying what world-class quality means. All too often, the primary concern in quality control is resolving customer complaints about product quality, particularly where such complaints can lead to financial loss for the company. Quality should be judged by how closely the product meets the customer's needs and benefits the customer, and this should always be the standard against which the company president judges the quality policy goals and the progress being made.

3. Achieving quality functions

    Company presidents tend to look at results rather than processes. Yet making improvements and preventing the recurrence of problems is an ongoing process, and the system under which this process takes place should be regularly evaluated. The president should be looking into how work processes have been changed, how they have been simplified, and whether they are being performed effectively.

4. Educating the president and other top executives

    One of the major purposes of having the company president perform a quality control audit is to educate the president himself. I remember one situation in which the company's founder was finally getting ready to hand control over to his son. At the time, the son was already on the board of directors and headed the company's technical efforts. Even without being asked, I told him he should assume responsibility for quality control. At the time, he was very reluctant, but he later realized how performing regular quality control audits had given him invaluable insight into the company he would soon be heading. In effect, the quality control audits had provided him with instruction in the fine art of being a company president. Nothing else gives you so thorough a look at your company.

5. Understanding the president's responsibilities

    In many companies, no one really knows what the president's responsibilities are. Particularly when it comes to quality control, the president does very little because it is not clear what he should do. Defining control items can help to clarify the vital function the company president and his top management people must fulfill in total quality control.

14.2.2 The Effectiveness of the Quality Control Audit

The quality control audit is effective for the following functions.

1. Controlling the quality control process

    Diagnosing the quality control process often will help to reveal critical flaws in the original quality control plan. You are, in effect, diagnosing the groundwork on which quality control is based, and in this sense the quality control audit contributes to refining and improving your quality control programme.

2. Getting a handle on actual conditions

It is often said to be lonely at the top, but I believe this is simply because the person at the top has lost touch with how the company is really functioning. Depending solely on reports prepared by subordinates is not going to give the president an accurate picture of his own company. He must get out of the presidential suite and see for himself how his people are working. The facts and figures collected in the process of a quality control audit can help give the president a clear picture of his company's health. With current trends toward internationalization, it is no longer enough to have a firm grasp of conditions within the company. It is just as or maybe even more important to know how your company is responding to the rapidly changing external business climate.

3. Improving employee morale

The quality control audit provides an ideal opportunity for the president to meet and talk with QC circle members. Occasional inspection tours alone are not going to tell you how hard your employees are working. The quality control audit, on the other hand, provides an opportunity for employees to report directly to the president on their quality assurance endeavours and for the president to see the results for himself. The company president and other top management executives tend to be only distant figures for the average employee. Having a chance to talk directly with the president and show him what they are doing for the company can be a great boost to employee morale.

4. Self-diagnosis

The president's quality control audit is at the same time an audit of the president himself and the role he fulfills. Only the most complacent corporate head will fail to realize that most of the TQC problems he encounters in the process of performing the quality control audit can be traced directly back to his own failure to participate actively. Furthermore, the president is as responsible for the company's external reputation as he is for what is going on inside his own organization. He has a responsibility to society at large, and conducting quality control audits is one important means of fulfilling this responsibility.

14.3 Establishing a Quality Control Audit Policy

While the company president may have a keen interest in knowing how well corporate policy is being carried out, he is likely to concentrate solely on results rather than processes. He does not stop to consider why goals are not being achieved, where the problems are, whether measures have been taken to resolve these problems, and all the other concerns of implementing a quality control programme. A quality control audit that lacks this penetrating analysis is no quality control audit at all. At the same time, policy control alone is not the whole of company-wide total quality control.

Your policy for conducting a quality control audit should take the following points into consideration.

1. All aspects of TQC must be audited.
2. Interaction among different divisions as well as within individual divisions should be diagnosed.
3. The diagnosis should be as objective as possible.
4. Even though you need a systematic diagnosis programme, every effort should be made to avoid just going through the motions.

14.3.1 Auditing All Aspects of TQC

All quality assurance procedures should be subject to quality control: quality design, material purchasing, storage, designing, manufacturing equipment maintenance, standards, process analysis and control, inspection, defective product disposal, product shipment, and much more — including even management of the workers who carry out these procedures and the cost control that provides the economic foundation for total quality control.

In investigating the various quality assurance activities that are carried out within the company, you should be looking for inadequacies and misguided activities that can be corrected and redirected. For example, if the sales division is not collecting sufficient information to be applied to product quality design, measures should be instituted to correct this situation. Not a single aspect of the company's operations can be overlooked when it comes to product quality — not even its warehouses, power division, drainage ditches, or waste disposal areas.

Products are much more than the tangible products that the company manufactures. Research results are the laboratory's product, the effectiveness of the advertising department's advertisements are its product, and so on. Likewise, a product must be evaluated not only in terms of its physical characteristics but also its cost, its simplicity of production, the size of the run, yield, and more.

14.3.2 Auditing by Division and by Function

In addition to diagnosing the quality control activities taking place within divisions, the quality control audit must also look at the various cross-functional quality control activities related to quality assurance and cost. These aspects are usually included in a presidential quality control audit encompassing the whole company, but they are often overlooked in divisional quality control audits such as might be conducted by a factory manager within his own particular division.

Every effort should always be made in performing a quality control audit to maintain a broad-ranging perspective that includes the intricate relationships among divisions as well as the relationships within a single division.

The myopic diagnosis is the most useless. This kind of diagnosis focuses on extreme detail all the while ignoring more crucial issues. A poorly classified histogram of inspection data will be criticized, overlooking the more critical fact that inspection standards are not rational, or a control chart will be criticized for allowing too much leeway between acceptable and unacceptable quality levels when, in fact the primary cause of defective products is deterioration of raw materials during storage.

Some companies have recently established their own inspection offices and sections, a welcome trend since it signifies acceptance of the importance of regular inspections. Unfortunately, this can breed inspection for inspection's sake, leading to inordinate emphasis on form rather than content and resulting in a harried management wasting time trying to solve petty problems.

To avoid this narrowing of focus, it can help to form an inspection team made up of upper management people from each division. You might also want to include an outside specialist in quality control, with the understanding that this outside expert is only there in an advisory role. When it comes to quality audits by the company president and top management, the final evaluations must be made by the president and top management. Still, the outside specialist can provide valuable pointers. The president, who is likely to concentrate on how close the company is to attaining its policy objectives, can learn much from the outside specialist's broader and more quality control-oriented questions.

14.3.3 Maintaining Objectivity

As with just about any kind of inspection, the quality control audit should be made by someone other than the person in charge of actually carrying out quality control activities. Having a team of people from other sections and divisions criticize your own division's quality control activities can generate animosity among employees — all the more reason that an impartial outside expert should be included — and it is best if the team reports its findings to someone higher up who then issues the necessary directives and recommendations.

14.3.4 Avoiding Rote Auditing

One of the worst things you can do with quality control auditing is to charge off in blind pursuit of ideals and to create a lot of red tape and unnecessary documentation in complete disregard for how the company actually works. Everyone is trying to work toward quality control goals as speedily and effectively as possible, and the whole point of a quality control audit should be to check on whether the quality control system is conducive to this end. While this is not to deny the importance of having a systematic and organized audit programme, you should not get so wrapped up in the forms that you forget what they are for.

It is nearly impossible to create streamlined standards and regulations that will exactly fit the circumstances right from the start. There are bound to be redundancies and shortcomings at first, and regular checking provides the means for progressively eliminating such flaws.

14.4 Quality Control Audit Targets

Here I will limit myself to the items that should be subject to a quality control audit in a manufacturing plant. These items are:

1. Be sure to look at all production processes, particularly the way they interact.

2. In addition to the internal flow, there should be a careful inspection of the various routes extending outside the factory.
3. Finally, the finished product or products, production equipment, and overall production capacity should be inspected.

14.5 Planning a Quality Control Audit

14.5.1 Introducing the Quality Control Audit

The first quality control audit is not usually made until some time after TQC has been taking place within the company, but I recommend performing an audit at the very initial stages of introducing TQC into the company, even before a formal TQC promotion plan has been drawn up. Of course, no one within the company is going to have the experience required to this right off, which is why an outside expert should be requested to conduct this very first quality control audit. The company president and other top management people should certainly participate in the process, for they will find it very educational.

The initial quality control audit can help to clarify the specific problems that should be tackled through TQC, thereby providing a focal point on which to evolve a TQC promotion plan (including a programme for more effective control) to solve these issues. Lack of data will hamper this process somewhat, but problem points will soon emerge as TQC progresses. Starting with a quality control audit should help to clarify the directions that TQC should be taking in your company. Later audits will provide guidance in getting TQC back on the right track if it has gone off on a tangent. This kind of initial quality control audit is uncommon, but I believe it can be very useful and recommend it highly.

14.5.2 The Quality Control Audit as a Part of TQC

In general, the quality control audit:

1. Should be incorporated into the TQC programme.
2. Should be conducted at the end of each TQC year or as a part of a TQC promotion month.
3. Should be announced well ahead of time so that everyone knows when it will be done and how it will be organized.

Preparing for the quality control audit is the task of the TQC promotion headquarters, with the obvious stipulation that any plan it devises must be approved by the executive management conference. It is also up to the TQC headquarters to ensure that the recommendations and directives that come out of the quality control audit are acted upon.

In this process, the TQC headquarters must never forget that it exists to support quality control activities in every division and at every level in the company, not to issue commands or directives. A TQC headquarters bent on finding fault or exercising authority is going to be disliked and eventually ignored by everyone. The TQC headquarters must become a centre that everyone willingly comes to for advice and guidance.

14.6   Carrying Out the Quality Control Audit

All recipients of the Deming Application Prize implement quality control as a company-wide activity. In these companies, top management has made a conscious decision to implement TQC as a means of achieving management policy goals. The quality control audit team is made up of the president and his top executives and visits every division, section, and office of the company to check on the progress being made toward achieving quality control goals.

In the factory, it is the plant manager who conducts the quality control audit, and each division head does the same for his division.

Yet whatever the level, there are certain points to be careful of.

14.6.1 Audit Data

While the quality control audit should be carefully thought out and planned, this does not mean that everyone must prepare new charts and diagrams just for the occasion. Elaborate presentations are not bad in and of themselves, but the whole point of the QC audit is to get a picture of the company in its routine daily activities. As long as TQC is being implemented, there will already be a plentiful supply of materials, reports, and the other paraphernalia of quality control. Some company executives may discount these charts and diagrams as a waste of time, but they make it much easier to explain what has been done and what is planned in the shortest possible time.

The Deming Prize Committee has two auditing approaches, neither of which is complete in and of itself. Schedule A provides for a question-and-answer format in which the committee members are briefed on the company's quality control programme and then ask questions. This approach, however, gives only an incomplete picture of the company's success with quality control and tends to favour the glib. Schedule B supplements schedule A by looking at the quality control charts and diagrams that the company is actually using. No matter how pretty, no diagram means anything if it is not being used regularly for better quality control.

14.6.2 Reporting on Audit Findings and Recommendations

After a quality control audit has been completed, the auditing team usually retires to a conference room to deliberate on its findings and decide on its recommendations. When I am on such a team as the outside expert, I usually start by taping a large piece of paper onto the wall and jotting down my observations. Being less accustomed to the procedure, the other members of the team are usually rather quiet at first, but they soon start to speak up, adding new points to my list as they grow more confident of what is and what isn't important. This can be one of the best educational experiences top management will ever have in the intricacies of quality control.

Although the outside expert may provide guidance, it is the company president or some other top executive who should present the QC audit team's findings to the divisions concerned. Later, the outside expert can give a lecture on quality control if he is asked, but however you arrange the programme, you should remember the need for full participation by everyone. People who just sit passively and listen are wasting their own and everybody else's time. Plenty of time should be set aside for questions and answers to ensure that everyone thoroughly understands the audit team's comments and recommendations.

Finally, the audit team's findings should be compiled into a written report that can be passed on to the divisions that have been audited.

14.6.3 The Need for Top Executive Action

The auditing executive's job is by no means over when he relays his comments on the quality control audit to the company's various divisions. Many of the problems that he has discovered will be attributable to mistakes in top management's own policy control. It is top management's responsibility to recognize their own shortcomings and to act to correct them.

No progress can be made with TQC if the company president loses all interest in quality control (and thereby causes the quality control staff to also lose interest) whenever there is a slump in the economy or when he does not see immediate results in the company's quality control programmes.

14.7 Pitfalls in Conducting a Quality Control Audit

When a quality control audit does not seem to do any good, it is most often because one of the following half-dozen points has been overlooked. These are especially dangerous pitfalls that can undermine the whole purpose of the quality control audit, and you should be asking yourself these questions whenever there is trouble.

1. Does everyone understand the purpose of the audit?
2. Will the audit be conducted correctly? Could there be an over-emphasis on form and petty details?
3. Will audit findings be immediately incorporated into the company's quality control promotion plans?
4. Are the truly critical quality control problems being overlooked as a result of excessive concentration on surface problems?
5. Will the audit team be looking at the company's actual daily operations or at special presentations that do not reflect actual conditions?
6. Are you going into the audit without any preconceived notions about what you will find?

Given on the next page is a check list I have prepared to be used in introducing and promoting TQC. Filling out this check list once every six months or so can give a very accurate picture of the progress that is being made, not only at your own company but at your affiliates as well.

The TQC Checklist

I. **Scale of implementation.**
  1. Whole company.
  2. Only in certain factories.
  3. Participating divisions.
      (1) Manufacturing.
      (2) Technology.
      (3) Clerical & administrative.
      (4) Sales.
      (5) Customer service.
  4. Only QC circles.

II. **Method of implementation.**
  1. President's announcement of start of TQC.
      (1) Has not been made.
      (2) Was made last year.
      (3) Was made 2-3 years ago.
      (4) Was made 4-5 years ago.
      (5) Was made more than 5 years ago.
  2. TQC promotion division (office, section, centre) established.
  3. The purpose of introducing TQC.
      (1) Has been made clear.
      (2) Has not been made clear.
  4. There is a TQC promotion plan and all activities are in accordance with this plan.
      (1) Yes.
      (2) No.
  5. Top management performs regular QC audits, and the TQC promotion plan is revised according to audit findings.
      (1) Yes.
      (2) No.

III. **QC education.**
  1. Is being carried out on a planned basis.
  2. Only those who request it are sent to outside quality control workshops.
  3. Percentages having received QC training (either inside or outside the company).
  (1) Top executives (%).
  (2) Middle management (%).
  (3) Clerical & administrative staff (%).
  (4) QC circle leaders (%).

IV. **Policy control.**
  1. No policy has been defined.
  2. Policy is defined, but not managed.
  3. There is a long-term management plan according to which annual policy goals are set.
  4. Presidential policy has been made clear, middle management has

developed this policy, and it is being carried out.

5. Periodic checks are made to see how much progress has been made toward achieving policy goals, with the following year's policy goals established in line with the results of these checks.

6. There is clearly defined product quality policy.

V. Quality assurance.

1. There is source control for new product and new technology.

2. Critical quality problems have been recorded and are being analyzed.

3. There are charts and diagrams of the whole quality assurance system and a list of the activities required at each step for organized quality assurance activities.

4. There is a quality information network.

5. Quality assurance is limited to reducing the number of defective products on the production line.

VI. QC circle activities.

1. QC circle activities.
    (1) Are being carried out.
    (2) Were implemented one year ago.
    (3) Have been in force for 2-3 years.
    (4) Have been in force for 4-5 years.
    (5) Have been in force for more than 5 years.
    (6) Are not being carried out.

2. QC circle activities cover.
    (1) Only part of the factory.
    (2) The whole factory.
    (3) The administrative, sales, and customer service divisions.

3. Registration with QC Circle headquarters.
    (1) All have been registered.
    (2) Some have been registered (%).

4. Participation in regional meets.
    (1) Participate.
    (2) Have presented reports.
    (3) Have received award(s).

5. Effectiveness.
    (1) As expected.
    (2) Inadequate.
    (3) Extremely disappointing.

VII. Control

1. Daily activities and policy objectives are controlled using lists of control items.

2. There is cross-functional management for
    (1) New product development control.
    (2) Quality assurance.
    (3) Cost control.
    (4) Production volume control.

3. Production line control.
    (1) QC process charts and tables.
    (2) Work standards.

VIII. Effectiveness.
    1. TQC has proved highly effective.
        (1) The nonconformance rate has been reduced.
        (2) Sales have gone up.
        (3) Profits have increased.
    2. TQC has been only partially effective.
    3. TQC has had very little effect.

15 | Quality Control Past and Future

Quality control is not something complete and whole but rather something that is constantly changing and evolving, taking on new forms to adapt to changing needs and times. Companies have been introducing and implementing quality control for only around 50 years, and there is still considerable room for improvement. Moreover, quality control is always amenable to reform, and its inherent capacity for change and development is probably one of quality control's strongest appeals.

I have been fortunate enough to have had ample opportunity to participate in and study quality control right from its initial introduction into postwar Japan, and have assisted many companies in introducing and promoting quality control. In this final chapter, I would therefore like to review the history of quality control in Japan as I have seen it and to discuss some of its future possibilities.

15.1 Early Beginnings

At the beginning of this century, a variety of methods for improving production efficiency were developed based on the time-motion studies of Frederick W. Taylor (1856-1915) and Frank B Gilberth (1868-1924) and the methodology of Harold B. Maynard (1902 –). In the 1920s, Walter A. Shewhart (1891-1967) of Bell Telephone Laboratories published a series of writings on the application of statistics for industrial product quality assurance. His famous work entitled *Economic Control of Quality of Manufactured Products,* published in 1931, introduced the control chart as an effective tool for manufacturing process control, and this marked the beginning of quality control. Not long afterward, in 1935, the British statistician E.S. Pearson published his work titled *The Application of Statistical Method of Industrial Standardization and Quality*

Control in which he introduced another type of control chart that later became a part of British industrial standards.

Quality control became a wartime focus of attention in the United States in response to the need for rapid production of reliable military supplies. Workshops were held throughout the country to familiarize workers with the Z1-1, Z1-2 (1941), and Z1-3 (1943) war-time control chart standards and their applications. In 1946, the regional quality control groups that grew out of these workshops were consolidated into the American Society for Quality Control (ASQC), and it was not long before similar groups were being formed on an international scale. A committee on the application of statistical methods in industrial technology was created within the Institute for Scientific Information (ISI) in 1953. In 1956, the European Organization for Quality Control (EOQC) was established, counting among its members today more than 20 countries including several Eastern European countries. The EOQC holds a meeting in one of its member countries every year.

A major international quality control organization today is the International Academy for Quality (IAQ) originally made up of 21 individuals involved in quality control: seven from Japan, seven from the United States, and seven from Europe. In 1969, the world's first international conference on quality control, at which the IAQ was born, was held in Tokyo under the joint sponsorship of the Union of Japanese Scientists and Engineers (JUSE), ASQC, and EOQC. The conference was called for by quality control specialists around the world who were eager to know how Japanese products had attained such high quality levels in so short a time after Japan had been devastated by war. Since then, the IAQ has held international conferences once every three years, rotating the conference's location among the United States, Europe, and Japan. The first IAQ conference was held in Washington, D.C. in 1972.

15.2 Quality Control Comes to Japan

A Japanese translation of Pearson's *The Application of Statistical Method of Industrial Standardization and Quality Control* was available in prewar Japan, and a few Japanese statisticians did attempt to apply statistical quality control to the military industry that was developing, but it was not until after the war that quality control was fully adopted in Japan.

The intial step was taken in 1946 during the Occupation when W.G. Magil and H.M. Sarasohn of SCAP's Civilian Communications Section undertook to instruct the Japanese telecommunications industry in quality control. Two years later, JUSE set up a research committee of five members that was later to be known as the QC Research Group. Most of the authorities on quality control currently teaching in Japan's leading universities are former members of this group.

Both JUSE and the Japanese Standards Association began offering basic courses in quality control in 1949, the same year that the Japan Industrial Standards (JIS) were established. Another basic course in quality control, currently sponsored by the Central Japan Quality Control Association, was first offered in 1952 by the Nagoya-based Central Japan Industries Association.

The famed Deming came to Japan at the behest of SCAP in 1949 and again in 1950 as a consultant in statistical research. On his 1950 visit, Deming was invited by JUSE to hold an eight-day seminar on statistical quality control, and, for those of us in the QC Research Group, this was our first in-depth exposure to quality control. An authority on statistics and statistical research, Deming has published numerous authoritative works on sampling during his years as a U.S. government specialist and university professor, and his lectures on the subject have had a profound effect upon the development of quality control in Japan. For this and for his advisory service in Japanese governmental statistics, Deming was awarded the Order of the Sacred Treasure, second class, by the Japanese government.

Having published his 1950 lecture series as a book, Deming donated the royalties from this book to JUSE, which used the funds to create the Deming Prize in 1951 in commemoration of Deming's friendship and for the promotion of quality control in Japan. Today, JUSE provides the roughly Y 10 million required annually to maintain the Deming Prize. Awarded to individuals and groups that have made significant contributions to quality control research and to corporations that have excelled in applying quality control programmes, the Deming Prize is well known among students of quality control in Japan and overseas.

In 1954, JUSE invited Juran to conduct courses on quality control for top and middle management people. Juran is an international authority on quality control and has conducted lectures on the subject at universities and academic conferences around the world. His theories on management's role in quality control and how quality control should be applied have profoundly influenced the quality control movement in Japan, and Juran, too, has been awarded the Order of the Sacred Treasure, second class, by the government of Japan.

Both Deming and Juran visited Japan numerous times, and they have provided invaluable leadership and inspiration for Japanese quality control, Deming teaching us about the uses of statistical quality control and Juran elaborating on quality control implementation.

The quality control movement has generated many excellent publications. The monthly journal *Hinshitsu Kanri* (Statistical Quality Control), was first published by JUSE in March 1950. The Japanese Standards Association's periodical on standardization (first published in 1946) was renamed *Hyojunka to Hinshitsu Kanri* (Standardization and Quality Control) in 1964 and is published under this name even today. In April 1962, JUSE began publishing the monthly FQC (Quality Control for the Foreman), formerly known as *Gemba to QC,* and this publication spurred the formation of the small-group quality control circles that are now active in companies around the world. Founded in 1970, the Japan Quality Control Association also publishes a periodical called *Hinshitsu (Quality)*.

Even as it has promoted the diffusion of quality control, JUSE has worked to enhance its practice through such activities as the Quality Control Symposium that it has sponsored since 1964.

Feigenbaum, formerly in charge of quality control for General Electric, was the first to promote total-quality control, stating in his 1961 book Total Quality Control that materials control, process analysis, process control, and pre-shipment product inspections should be combined in an integrated system of quality control using quality cost as its criterion for evaluation. In Japan, where top management's participation in quality control, as suggested by Juran, and the QC circle composed of frontline workers were already well-established, total quality control was not a completely new concept. While Feigenbaum's contribution to TQC's development in Japan must be acknowledged, there are certain differences between his brand of TQC and the Japanese-style TQC currently being practised.

15.3 Recent Trends in Quality Control

While no survey has been made of the actual number of companies implementing TQC in Japan, the growing number of participants in quality control seminars and publications on quality control indicate a certain and rapid increase in their numbers. And even as they have been applying quality control to their operations, these companies have found that the rapidly changing business environment has mandated changes in the nature of quality control as well.

Because a thorough and detailed analysis of these changes and future trends in quality control would demand massive tomes and go well beyond the scope of this book, I will limit myself here to my own personal observations. To begin, I would like to go back to an article on theories of quality control that I wrote in 1954 for the journal *Hinshitsu Kanri* (Statistical Quality Control). In this article I discussed some of the distinguishing characteristics of Japanese industry at that time. These were:

1. Most Japanese industries were imported industries, very few having been developed on the basis of original Japanese research. Thus Japanese technicians were not creators or innovators. Unlike the innovator who bravely struggles to overcome many problems in attaining his clearly defined goal, the person who simply imports the fruit of the innovator's achievements is more concerned with processes than with goals.

2. The emphasis was on quantity rather than quality, more effort being expended on producing volume than on creating products elegantly suited for specific uses. This trend was especially pronounced during the war years and led to a lot of waste caused by a single-minded pursuit of production without regard to the purpose for which a product was supposedly being manufactured.

3. There was considerable imbalance among the different elements making up the manufacturing process. In particular, wide discrepancies in material quality often proved fatal for production.

Times have changed considerably since then. Still, I see little improvement in the substance of control education within industry. Granted there is more emphasis today on the kind of basic science education that was previously missing. But education in control technology and the philosophy at its root — that the goal of technology should be process, quality, and economy — remains perfunctory to this day.

Thirty-three years ago the concept of TQC did not yet exist, but even then I warned against what I saw as another major failing of Japanese industry, a tendency to place more importance on the individual's abilities than on how to organize individuals to work together toward a common goal. To quote myself: "Quality control is the most effective means of doing this, but once individuals have acquired the necessary statistical knowhow they tend to jump to the mistaken conclusion that that they have already achieved quality control." This tendency is still evident today, and the need to organize individual capabilities into a concerted effort to attain a given goal is not yet well understood.

In that article I noted two areas in which quality control practices were deficient:

1. While workers may have acquired a grasp of statistical methods, no one really understands how these methods should be applied in quality control activities.
2. No economic analyses are made.

Considerable progress has been made on the first point and it is no longer the problem it once was, but the second point still tends to remain a blind spot. While quality control has undeniably made enormous strides since the 1950s, it is clear that many of the problems remain.

I would like next to look at the development of quality control in Japan in terms of product quality, quality assurance, and practical administration.

15.3.1 Product Quality

Consumer needs and attitudes toward product quality have changed in a number of ways as stated below.

1. Diversification: New product applications and internationalization have generated considerable diversification in use characteristics. In particular, changing values have created problems in how exactly to quantify and measure highly subjective quality characteristics.
2. Increasing sophistication and complexity: New responses are required to meet higher quality requirements, product miniaturization, and the use of microelectronic products.
3. Greater durability: Products today are expected to be durable, such as condominiums built to last 100 years.
4. Lower cost of quality: There is increasing demand that quality cost less, particularly as calculated over the product's entire life cycle.
5. New interpretations of product liability: Product liability has gone beyond

the issue of individual injury to include the product's adverse impact on the environment and society. Soaring insurance and litigation fees have made product liability extremely costly.

6. New products: Research and development has been speeded up as new developments in technology quickly make products obsolete.

7. Broader conditions of use: A product is expected to function properly under the most adverse conditions, working just as well in the tropics as in the frigid Arctic, in the vacuum of space as well as on earth.

8. Conservation of energy and resources: There is increasing demand for non-polluting "clean" products, better production yield, highly reliable design and manufacture with very little likelihood of breakdowns, the elimination of unnecessary model changes as older models are upgraded, and standardization to eliminate waste.

9. Safety: Damage-proofing and easy disposal.

10. Improved maintenance and repair: It should be simple to detect problems and their causes, and some products even have self-diagnostic capabilities.

11. Ease of use and storage: Better quality is expected of instruction manuals and other documentation for a product.

12. Improved work quality and information quality: Control items (control standards) should be meaningful and appropriate to the planned level of product quality.

In all of these instances, the systematic application of the kind of quality engineering discussed in Section 9.1.3 can be useful.

15.3.2 Quality Assurance

Considerable progress has been made in quality assurance activities including detecting defective products through inspection, repairing defective products, seeking out the causes of nonconformance, taking preventive measures against the recurrence of defectives, applying horizontal deployment to predict possible causes for defectives, and preventing the occurrence of defectives.

Quality assurance has also become a more wide-spread concern ranging from complaint processing and inspection procedures to improving processes and maintaining design quality. It has spread in the opposite direction as well, being applied in product distribution, instruction manuals and publicity materials, maintenance and repair services, and disposal, including collection and recycling. Other areas that were once the sole concern of clerical and office staff have been incorporated into company-wide quality control activities. These include clarifying quality policies, quality management, quality assurance system management, and other forms of participation by top and middle management as well as the increasing participation of floor workers in QC circle activities directed at process and other improvements.

Today quality assurance activities encompass the following items.

1. Preventing defectives on a parts-per-million (ppm) scale: In response to

product liability requirements, applying ppm standards to key manufacturing and assembly processes involving vital parts directly related to product safety.

2. Assuring new product quality: Tackling the question of how to prevent defectives among new products using new technologies that are still in the design and development stages.

3. Maintaining design quality: Applying functional deployment and the seven QC tools to ensure new product design quality, applications that are just as important as analyzing defective processes to find their causes.

4. Collecting, transmitting, and using quality information: Creating a quality information network and the tools to keep it active.

5. Setting up and managing a quality assurance system: Clarifying what is to be done and how control is to be applied in each of the quality assurance steps (including the customer's use of the product) and making quality evaluations along the way (such as design reviews).

6. Systems for assuring top-quality products: Creating systems in which only quality products will be produced and in which divisions work together in close cooperation.

7. Preventing design and manufacturing mistakes: Foolproofing processes and systems.

8. Accurate and easy-to-understand labelling, instruction manuals, and publicity materials.

9. Maintaining and improving production processes: Improving processes, enhancing trouble detection capabilities, training workers, and encouraging QC circle activities.

10. Improving services related to quality assurance: Improving and maintaining high safety, maintenance, and repair standards.

11. Cutting down on delivery times while at the same time maintaining quality: Stabilizing new product quality as quickly as possible.

12. Keeping production costs to a minimum: Keeping material and equipment costs to a minimum even while maintaining maximum product quality.

13. Developing technologies for improved quality assurance: Automating inspection processes, shifting from off-line to automatic inspections during production processes, and applying advanced technologies in design and manufacture such as CAD and CAM.

14. Tailoring quality assurance activities to keep up with technological developments: Devising quality assurance for electronic, integrated, and other advanced products, as well as studying the way different quality characteristics impact upon each other.

15. Maintaining close ties with suppliers: Establishing policies and an organization that reflect the growing dependence upon outside suppliers.

16. Adopting international quality assurance programmes: Exports, imports, international contracts.

17. Maintaining high business quality standards: Gathering the required information and clarifying and applying control standards.

15.3.3 Practical Administration

The following points can be considered in looking at practical administration and the directions in which it is developing within the TQC context.

1. In day-to-day management, it is necessary to first define the various steps involved and the respective duties of each division and job responsibility. Next, the control standards for each of these must be clarified and applied as promptly and effectively as possible. The TQC ideal is to have well-defined responsibilities and controls for every employee within the organization in a personalized form of internalized quality control.

2. Policy management involves defining policies for each year, stipulating goals, creating, developing, and implementing measures to attain these goals, and applying the lessons learned from one year to the formation of policies for the next year. Many companies have successfully devised challenging policy objectives directed at solving particularly difficult quality issues.

3. Functional management and the shift it has engendered from individual division management to interdivisional management has contributed to the integration of the quality, cost, and production schedule control processes that used to be handled separately.

4. The trend is toward researching and developing the tools and methods for problem-detecting quality control as opposed to the problem-solving orientation of conventional quality control with its emphasis on analyzing and diagnosing problems. This new approach to quality control is certain to lead to improvements on all fronts, particularly in research and development and sales.

5. TQC is spreading to include the whole corporate group, not just the manufacturer and its materials and parts suppliers but also all other companies with which it maintains any kind of affiliation.

15.4 Problems with TQC in Japan

Japanese cars, cameras, electrical appliances, and many more products are acclaimed overseas for their superior quality, quality that is acknowledged to stem from the Japanese company's dedication to total quality control. Much of this success we owe to Deming. The Deming Prize has made Deming a household name in Japan, but in his home country, the United States, he was for a long time only acknowledged among his academic peers, not coming into prominence in industrial sectors until around 1979. It is ironic that this recognition came only after Japanese-style TQC had been widely promoted and publicized in the United States. Some 30 years after the establishment of the Deming Prize in Japan, I feel that we Japanese have at last been able to repay him in small part for the great service he has done us.

Still, although TQC has made astonishing advances in Japan, that is not to say that all attempts to introduce and promote TQC have been successful. The tendency is to proclaim the successes while hiding the failures. Yet it stands to reason that the more companies that attempt to adopt TQC concepts, the more possibilities there are for failure and disappointment. While Deming Prize recipients are to be commended, not every company has prize-winning quality.

Having been involved in TQC since the very first, I have long asked myself why some companies have more trouble than others – why some fall flat on their faces while others reap a rich harvest of TQC results. While I have already discussed this to some extent in Section 9.4, it is worthwhile to review the main pitfalls here.

1. TQC is mistakenly assumed to be limited to QC circle activities, and companies that have instituted QC circles think they have attained TQC.
2. Having instituted QC circles, some companies are stuck because no one knows how to expand to a full TQC programme.
3. Some companies assume that TQC is limited to QC circle activities in the factory and policy control in the staff divisions.
4. All divisions throughout the company may be participating, but each division is concentrating solely on improving its own particular operations with no regard to the interdivisional relations.
5. Policy control is being applied only to increase sales and profits and is unrelated to improving product quality and the corporate culture.
6. All too often, cross-functional management is the last thing to be introduced and a quality assurance system exists in name only. There are no feedback channels or other programmes crucial to the checking and action parts of the PDCA circle, and practical quality control applications are generally lacking. What quality assurance systems are being applied are not being constantly upgraded and improved.
7. There is no clear-cut programme for implementing TQC. Quality is not stressed as a major corporate concern, resulting in a lack of quality consciousness among employees that tends to undermine QC circle activities and attempts at policy control. Overly concerned with increasing sales and thereby profits, management fails to apply policy control to anything else. This can hardly be called quality management. QC circles are also often misunderstood to be nothing more than forums for implementing improvements, and they are rated solely on how many improvements they make and how much money they save the company. The more important purposes of the QC circle – to create alert and active workers who take pride in what they do and who have a thorough understanding of their jobs – are ignored.
8. There are also problems in how TQC concepts are taught. For example,
   (1) Though a person may take part in a TQC course of study, he doesn't know how to apply what he has learned. TQC needs to be taught on a highly individualized basis in a one-on-one relationship for it to be effectively implemented later.
   (2) The primary purpose of TQC should be to improve the corporate culture overall, but in many cases it is directed primarily at a short-

term goal such as winning the prestigious Deming Prize.

(3) TQC instructors are left to develop their own ways of teaching and giving advice, and no attempt is made to standardize instruction methods. In other words, there is no quality control.

(4) TQC is not something that can be imposed from outside but must be a concentrated effort within the company. For many companies, however, this leads to unnecessary confusion and wasted effort.

(5) One of the reasons Japanese-style TQC has succeeded is the fact that it has been primarily promoted by the companies themselves, and university professors and professional QC consultants have not been involved in devising solutions to problems. This is as it should be, since no amount of TQC knowhow will work unless it is being applied by the people who are closest to the work. Unfortunately, many companies fail to take up where their consultants leave off, and their TQC ends up being nothing more than a series of lectures on the subject by prominent experts.

If this text helps in some small way to correct these kinds of problems, it will have been well worth the effort of putting together.

15.5 Outlook for the Future

Japanese-style TQC has been highly praised overseas, and every year there are more and more visitors to Japan who come specifically to study TQC. This has led to a growing number of foreign companies that are introducing QC circles and other TQC elements into their operations.

Yet as I have pointed out, Japanese-style TQC – company-wide quality control – is still far from perfect. If Japanese manufacturers are to continue to be the quality-leaders in their fields, TQC must be improved. Some of the tasks that lie ahead for company-wide quality control are:

1. Approaches need to be devised to solving the problems outlined in the last section, including systematizing the methodology for introducing and promoting TQC within the company. Policy control and cross-functional management are peculiar to Japanese-style TQC, and there is a need to clarify the purpose of these activities and to devise efficient methods of putting them into action.

2. New products and new technologies are being developed with amazing rapidity and costs are being drastically reduced at the same time. Diversification of needs has put new demands on product quality in terms of time and costs, and a whole new system of quality assurance is needed to respond to this effectively. Computer systems must be developed for more efficient and speedy quality information transmission and integrated control of quality, costs, and scheduling.

3. As noted earlier, manufacturers are now liable for their products' social and environmental impact. There is thus a need to develop products with

self-diagnostic capabilities, meaning the ability to guarantee their own quality assurance, if increasingly stringent product safety and maintenance demands are to be met.

4. By extension, further developments are to be hoped for in quality engineering, including new and better methods of labelling, measuring, and evaluating products, and in research and development of computer-aided quality control.

5. Studies need to be made of how quality control can be applied more systematically to those intangible activities that have tended to be exempted from quality control altogether. These include services, sales, research, and new product and new technology development (including the development of computer systems). Because these kinds of activities have been difficult to organize and integrate, companies have been slow to apply quality control principles to them, but the need is there.

6. In general, TQC tends to be limited to simple listings of separate quality control steps and processes and little attempt has been made to coordinate these listings into a systematic whole. While everyone is busy pinpointing the many different things that need to be done, devising effective methodologies, and instituting management systems, few have yet attempted to tackle the problem of how all of this should be put together. In this context, little progress has been made since the 1950s.

7. There is a similar need to collate the basic quality control theories and principles into some kind of systematic whole.

These and other problems need to be worked on, not only in Japan but worldwide, if TQC is to fulfill its potential for enabling all people everywhere to lead more rewarding lives producing better-quality products for themselves and their global neighbours.

INDEX

Accounting division, quality
  control in, 7
  applications of, 257
  and responsibilities for product
    quality, 253, 254, 255
Action stage of control circle,
  9, 10, 12
Activities in quality control,
  129-152
  balance between theory and
    practice in, 146-147
  cost considerations in, 138-142
  Deming Application Prize for,
    150-152
  failure to clarify scope of, 146
  implementation problems in,
    145-150
  industrial production and
    statistical tools in, 142-145
  in office work, 261-265
  for quality assurance, 132
  in quality control system,
    130-137
  ritualized and meaningless,
    problems in, 147
  in staff divisions. See Division
    activities in quality control

Actual value of product, 190-191
Adjustments in process control,
  229-230
Administration of quality
  assurance system, 73
Administrative divisions, quality
  control in, 249
  education and training for, 117
  responsibilities in, 252-258
Administrative management,
  practical, 19-20, 28, 35-41,
  262-263, 288
Administrative planning, compared
  to policy management, 35-38
Advertising division, product
  liability prevention
  responsibilities of, 256
After-sales service of product,
  quality assurance in, 75
American National Standards
  on quality assurance, 70
  on quality control, 14
American Society for Quality
  Control, 282
Analysis of quality. See Quality
  analysis

Analytical approach to problem
solving, 55, 260
Appeal of quality product, 6
Appraisal costs of manufacturer,
139
Assurance of quality. *See* Quality
assurance
Attitudes
of consumers toward product
quality, recent trends
concerning, 285-286
toward implementation of
quality control, problems in,
145, 147
Audit of quality control, 30, 76,
269-280
checklist in, 277-280
comprehensive nature of, 273
data collection in, 276
by divisions and functions,
273-274
effectiveness of, 271-272
establishment of policies on,
272-274
executive responsibilities in, 277
implementation of, 276-277
introduction of, 275
need for, 270-272
objectivity in, 274
planning of, 275
problems in, 274, 277-280
and product quality, 75, 269-270
purpose of, 270-271
and quality assurance system,
270
report on, 276-277
role of, 275
targets in, 274-275
Automation
in manufacturing, process
capability studies on, 227
of office procedures, 23
and quality control, 265-266
process control in, 229

Baby formula, product liability
case concerning, 87
Benefit: cost ratio on products,
140-141
Blueprint reviews, 198, 200
Broadcasts, in-house, disseminating
quality control information, 122
Budgeting, in policy management,
102
Bulletin boards, disseminating
quality control information, 122

Capability studies on production
processes, 218-224
Causes affecting product
characteristics, 207, 208-215
cause-and-effect diagrams on,
155, 213-214, 215
sample of, 156
correction of, 259
latent, in chemical
manufacturing processes,
208-211
optimum standards for, 214-216
selection of principal
causes, 211-213
Characteristic values of product,
4-5, 6, 167-168
measurements of, in
manufacturing process, 228
primary factors affecting, 208
process analysis of, 207, 208-215
and product structure, 195
quality analysis of, 193-198
substitute, 193, 196, 197
Checklist
on expected value of product,
188
on policy management, 106
on quality control audit, 278-280
on screening procedure for
Deming Prize, 151, 152
Check points, 59, 230-231
in process control, 230-231

Chemical manufacturing processes, latent causes in, 208-211
Chronic defects, 32-33
Circles
  PDCA circle. *See* PDCA circle
  quality control. *See* Quality control circles
Clerical division, quality control in, 249
  education and training for, 117
Clerical procedures in quality control, planning of, 49-50
Collection of data. *See* Data, collection of
Committees
  on product liability prevention, 92
  on quality assurance, 80
  on quality control, 52-53
Communication of quality information
  creation of network for, 33-34
  in process design, 226
  in quality assurance, 81-82
Competitiveness of product, cost: benefit ratio on, 140-141
Complaints of consumers
  and inspection standards, 71
  as measure of product quality, 167
  nature of, 163
  in new markets, 162
  processing of, 75, 163-165
  rate of, compared to product price, 163, 164
  surveys on, 162-165
Computers, and quality control, 265-268
  in computer-aided quality control, 76, 266-267
  in management information system, 267-268
  in office automation, 265-266
Configuration of product, 200
Conformance quality, 8-9, 131

Consciousness of quality among employees, techniques increasing, 121-128
Consumer Product Safety Act of 1972, 84
Consumer Product Safety Commission, 84
Consumer relations department, 93-94
Consumers
  complaints of. *See* Complaints of consumers
  cost in use of product, 139-141
    compared to benefits, 140-141
  injuries from defective products, 83-84
  legislation in protection of, 84
  quality requirements of, 15-16
    collection and analysis of data on, 76
    compared to manufacturer's quality requirements, 166-167
    as measure of product quality, 166-167, 168
    recent trends concerning, 285-286
  surveys of
    on complaints, 162-165
    in market quality survey, 162
Contests on quality control, 122
Contracts with suppliers, 247
Control, 9-12
  of costs, 108-109, 110, 176, 178
  cycle of, 9-12
  definition of, 9
  in development and design stages, 172-173, 187-192, 200-203
  effective, stages of, 10
  importance of, 13
  initial flow control, 201-203
  policy control, 103-106, 263-264
  process control, 229-239, 240, 241-242

role of manager in, 11-12
in staff divisions, 258-261
  defining activities in, 260
  and diagnosis, 259
  factual basis of, 259
  and problem solving
    approaches, 260
  of quality control, 260-261
Control charts, 41, 58, 59, 60
  in chemical manufacturing, 211
  definition of, 220
  for manufacturing section
    chief, 60
  in process adjustments, 230
  in process capability studies,
    218-220, 223
  in process control, 233
  in quality control analysis, 155
Control circle, PDCA. See PDCA
  circle
Control items, 41, 59
  chart of. See Control charts
  compared to check points,
    230-231
  daily, 57
  in development and design
    stages, 192
  job-specific, 41
    in process control, 234-235
    sample of, 42
  for manufacturing, list of, 236
  planning of, 57-61
  in policy management, 57, 102
  in process control, 230-232,
    234-235
    examples of, 236
  in quality control flow sheet,
    58, 59
  terminology for, 58
Control points, 231
Control standards, 131
  compared to quality standards,
    131
  in staff processes, 261
Control systems, policy, 130-106

example of, 104, 105
in non-manufacturing divisions,
  263-264
Coordination problems in quality
  control, 63-64
Cost of product, 4, 5, 138-142
  compared to benefits, 140-141
  and consumer complaint rate,
    163, 164
  control of
    in cross-functional manage-
      ment, 38, 39, 108-109, 110
    in development and design
      stages, 176, 178
    quality control in, 109, 110
  decisions on, in development
    of new product, 184, 186
  and design quality, 8, 138
  and liability issues, 86
  manufacturer's costs in, 138-139
  and profits, 21
  social costs in, 141
  user's costs in, 139-141
Cost of quality control analysis,
  158, 159
Criteria in quality control, planning
  of, 61-64
Critical path method, 187
Cross-functional management,
  39-40, 107-110
  cost-control in, 38, 39,
    108-109, 110
  important points in, 107-108
  in non-manufacturing divisions,
    264-265
  promotion of, 108
  in quality assurance, 76-77, 80
Current price method, in estimation
  of expected product value, 190

Daily control items, 57
Data
  categorized, in quality control
    analysis, 158
  collection of

in market quality surveys,
161-162
in quality assurance, 76
in quality control analysis,
153, 161-162
in quality control audit, 276
in quality design, regulations
on, 187
past, in quality control analysis,
158, 159-160
for quality design, 186-187
statistical. *See* Statistical analysis
stratification of, in quality
control analysis, 155
Day-to-day management, 288
policy management in, 97-98
Defective products
in chronic and occasional defects,
32-33
consumer complaints on, 71, 75.
See also Complaints of
consumers
consumer costs of, 83-84
in design defects, liability for,
88
distribution of quality loss in,
141-142
functional and non-functional
defects in, 166
labelling defects in, liability for,
88-89
liability for, 83-96. *See also*
Liability for products
management-caused, 33, 43, 124,
125
management responsibilities in,
31-33
in negligence, liability for, 88
prevention of, 67, 68
manufacturer's costs in, 139
process analysis of, 195
quality control circle activities
concerning, 124-125
recall of, 75
recording and analysis of, 74

regulations on, 226
repair of, 71
worker-caused, 33, 43, 124-125
liability for, 88
in zero defects movement, 124
Delivery schedules, management of,
in total quality control, 22
Deming, W.E., 13, 14, 283, 288
Deming circle, 13, 17, 142, 258
Deming Prize, 150-152, 288
creation of, 283
recipients of, 17
screening procedure in,
151, 270, 276
checklist on, 151, 152
Deming Prize Committee, definition
of quality control, 14
Deployment of quality, 46-47,
54-61, 193
development of quality control
functions in, 55-57
planning of, 46-47, 54-61
quality tables on, 193, 194, 195,
196, 197
selection of method, 199
steps to quality control functions
in, 54-55
substitute characteristics in,
193, 196, 197
Design approach to problem solving,
55, 260
Design of production processes.
See Production processes,
design of
Design of products, 6, 7-8, 187-192
control of changes in, 200-201
control items for, 192
costs of quality in, 138
data used in, 186-187
liability for, 85, 88, 198, 200,
203-204
planning quality of, 182-183
quality assurance in, 73-74
quality control in, 171-204
and cost control, 176, 178

diagram of, 176, 177
review of, 198-200
  of blueprints, 198, 200
  of concept, 200
  of prototype, 200
  stages of, 200
steps in, 174-176
system for, 176
Development of new products,
  22-23, 171-204
actual value of product in,
  190-191
applied research in, 171, 172
basic research in, 171, 172
control activities in, 172-173
control items in, 192
cost control in, 176, 178
data used in, 186-187
design change control in, 200-201
design quality in, 182-183
design review in, 198-200
diagram of, 176, 177
evaluation of quality control in,
  174
expected value of product in,
  188-190, 191
initial flow control in, 201-203
inspiration and quality control
  circle in, 198
inventory of corporate resources
  in, 179, 183
  technology map of, 179, 180
liability considerations in,
  198, 200, 203-204
market assessment in, 179, 181
price decisions in, 184, 186
process analysis in, 193-198
progress control and evaluation
  during, 187-192
prototypes in, 200, 201-203
quality analysis in, 157, 193-198
quality control education on,
  112
quality deployment in, 193
quality planning in, 182-187

factors considered in,
  183-184, 185
quality policies in, 176-179,
  184-186
quality tables in, 193
  examples of, 194, 195
in research and development
  division, quality control in,
  171-174
standard quality decisions in,
  184-186
steps in, 174-176
system for, 176
and technology, 193-198
technology assessment in,
  179, 180, 181
types of research in, 172
Deviation of quality among
  products, statistical analysis of,
  144
Directors, in cross-functional
  management, 40
Dispersion in quality characteristics,
  143, 144
  statistical analysis of, 144
Displays disseminating quality
  control information, 122
Disposal of products, as quality
  concern, 5, 54, 55
Dissemination of quality control
  information, 121-122
Distinctiveness of quality product, 6
Distribution of quality loss,
  in defective products, 141-142
Division activities in quality control,
  38, 134, 136, 253-261
  applications of, 257-258
  audit of, 273-274
  control standards in, 261
  cross-functional management of,
    107-110, 264-265
  defining activities in, 260
  in diagnosis of problems, 259
  factual basis of, 259
  failure to clarify scope of, 146

interdivisional, 38, 39, 134,
168-169
intradivisional, 38, 39
in non-manufacturing divisions,
249-268
organization chart of, 61
problem solving approaches in,
260
in product liability prevention,
255-257
in purchasing division, 244-248
in research division, 171-174
Division heads, in promotion of
quality control, 41-44
Documents
in policy control system, 104
in process control, 233-234
on quality control standards and
regulations, 61-64
Draft of policies, 104
Durability of quality product, 5

Ease of product use, and product
quality, 5
Economic factors, in quality
evaluation, 5, 184, 185
Education on quality control,
111-119
of administrative and clerical
workers, 117
in chemical manufacturing, 210
in development of new products,
112
dissemination of information in,
121-122
establishing programme of, 119
evaluation of, 118
of foremen, 117
"gold in the mind" approach to,
114
hours of, 115
importance of, 111-112
increasing quality consciousness
of employees, 121-128
of line workers, 116-117

in maintenance of quality, 112
of middle management, 111-112,
114-115
planning for, 49
quality control circle activities in,
123-128
of quality control staff, 115-116,
118
of research and development
staff, 117-118
subjects included in, 115
of suppliers, 248
of top management, 112-114
in work procedures, 228-229
Effectiveness
of process control system,
evaluation of, 237-239
of quality control audit,
271-272
of total quality control, 2
Efficiency qualities of products, 6, 7
Employee training
on quality control. See Education
on quality control
on work procedures, 210,
228-229
Engineering
industrial, in quality assurance, 19
quality, 134-137
diagram of, 135
responsibilities in, 136-137
reliability, 24, 145
in quality assurance, 94-95
Environmental concerns in product
quality, 2, 3, 16, 210, 211
in disposal of products, 5, 54, 55
Equipment in manufacturing,
automated, process capability
studies on, 227
Europe
product liability in, 86-87, 90
no-fault, 90
quality control in, 1, 17
history of, 282

European Organization for Quality
Control, 282
Evaluation of quality. *See* Quality
analysis
Exhibits disseminating quality
control information, 122
Expectations in quality control,
problems in, 148
Expected value of product, estimation
of, 188-190, 191
Expressed warranty, liability for, 89

Factual basis of quality control, 259
Failure costs of manufacturer, 139
Failure mode, effects and
criticality analysis, 195
Fault tree analysis, 195
Feedback on quality assurance, 80
Feigenbaun, Armand V., 1, 16, 17,
284
on factors affecting product
quality, 208
on manufacturer's costs, 139
on organization planning, 33,
50-51
on quality control system, 134
on responsibilities for total
quality control, 34
Flow sheet
in process studies, 217
quality control, example of, 58
Foolproofing systems, for quality
assurance in manufacturing,
242-243
Foremen, quality control
education of, 117
Functional factors in quality
evaluation, 184, 185
Functional management, 288
Functions of quality control, 54-61
daily, 57
development of, 55-57
steps to, 54-55
Future of total quality control,
290-291

General affairs division
applications of quality control
in, 257
product liability prevention
responsibilities of, 255
responsibilities for product
quality, 253, 254
Gilberth, Frank B., 281
Goal setting, in policy management,
98-99
Goals of industrial production, 3-4
Gregg, V,P., 183
Guaranteed quality, 224-225
compared to standard quality,
224
inspection margin in, 224
warranty of, 89

Histograms, in quality control
analysis, 155
History of quality control, 281-284
Horizontal activities in quality
control, 38
Hosho, use of term in Japanese
language, 68-69
Human factors
in quality evaluation, 184, 185
in total quality control, 23-24

Implementation
of process control, 235-237
of process improvements,
243-244
of quality control
in non-manufacturing divisions,
250
problems and solutions in,
145-150
of quality control audit,
276-277
Implementation Chart, 104
Implementation Results Report,
104
Implied warranty, liability for, 89
Improvements

in product quality
  quality analysis in, 157
  quality control education on,
    112
in production processes, 243-244
in purchasing operations, 248
Index of process capability, 221-222
Industrial engineering, in quality
  assurance, 19
Industrial product quality, 4-7
  definition of, 4
Industrial production
  goals of, 3-4
  and statistical tools, 142-145
Information system
  computerized, quality control
    in, 267-268
  in quality assurance, 81-82
Initial flow control, 201-203
Injuries of consumers, from
  defective products, 83-84
Inspection
  of products, 16, 67, 68
    defects found in, 226
    definitions of, 70
    on functional and non-
      functional features,
      166, 167
    and inappropriate handling
      after inspection, 166
    manufacturer and consumer
      quality requirements in,
      166-167
    poor procedures in, 166
  in quality assurance, 67-68,
    70, 240-241
  standards on, 71, 224, 225-226
  in quality control audit,
    30, 269-280
Inspiration, in technology
  development, 198
Instruction manuals, quality
  control of, 75
Insurance for product liability, 85

Integrated control of product
  quality, 1, 17
Intended use characteristics of
  products, 193
Interdivisional activities
  in quality assurance, 76-77
  in quality control, 38, 39, 134
    analysis of problems in,
      168-169
International Academy for Quality,
  282
Intradivisional activities in quality
  control, 38, 39
Introduction of quality control
  in non-manufacturing divisions,
    250-251
  planning of, 47-50
  priorities in, 47, 50
  problems and solutions in,
    145-150
  promotion plan in, 50, 65
  purpose of, 47
  and quality control audit, 275
  steps in, 148, 149
Inventory of corporate resources,
  179, 183
  technology map of, 179, 180
Inventory division, product
  liability prevention
  responsibilities of, 256
Irregularity reports, in process
  control, 233-234

Japan, 1-2
  consumer injuries in, 84
  divisional activities in quality
    control in, 136
  flow sheets for process studies in,
    217
  future of total quality control in,
    290-291
  history of quality control in,
    282-284
  lifetime employment in, 264

organization of quality control in, 136
problems with total quality control in, 288-290
product liability in, 87
  legal considerations in, 90
  preventive policies on, 92
quality assurance in, 68-69
quality control circle activities in, 124, 126, 127
recent trends of quality control in, 284-288
style of total quality control in, 15, 17
traditional dependence on imported technology in, 183
Japan Consumer Information Center, 84
Japan Industrial Standards, 282
  Award for Outstanding Performance, 150
  on inspections, 70
  on process capability, 220, 221
  on product quality, 6
  on quality assurance, 69
  on quality control, 14
  on quality control charts, 220
Japan Quality Control Award, 150, 151
Japanese Society for Quality Control, 134
Japanese Standards Association, 282, 283
Job-specific control items, 41
  in process control, 234-235
  sample of, 42
Judgment of quality, 142-143
  measurements in, 142, 166-167
  in office work, 252
  standards for, 71
Juran, Joseph M., 7, 283, 284
  on control, 9, 258
  on control circle, 10, 127
  on failure of quality control programmes, 45

on management responsibilities, 43, 255
on new product development, 179
on quality assurance, 70
on quality control, 14

Kanemi Soko, product liability case against, 87

Labelling of products
  liability for, 75, 85, 88-89
  quality assurance in, 75
Latent causes in chemical manufacturing, 208-211
Lectures
  in dissemination of quality control information, 122
  in quality control education, 113
Legal division, product liability prevention responsibilities of, 255
Liability for products, 2, 22, 71, 72, 83-96
  commercial losses in, 90-91
  in consumer injuries, 83-84
  and consumer relations, 93-94
  in Europe, 86-87, 90
    no-fault, 90
  evaluation of, in development and design stage, 198, 200, 203-204
  in Japan, 87, 90, 92
  for labels and instruction manuals, 75, 85, 88-89
  legal considerations in, 87-90
  management role in, 91-92
  in negligence, 88-89
  policies on, 90-91, 92-93
  prevention of, 90, 92, 240, 241-243
    in changes and alterations of production processes, 241-242

division responsibilities in,
255-257
foolproofing systems in,
242-243
quality assurance activities in,
240, 241-243
in special-care processes, 240
product liability prevention
committee on, 92
responsibility for, 84-87, 255-257
settlement value in cases
concerning, 85
and social costs of product, 141
in tort laws, 89-90
in total quality control, 22,
91-94
in United States, 85-86, 204
warranty period in, 85-86, 89
yearly number of cases
concerning, 83-84, 85
Lifetime employment system in
Japan, 264
Line workers, quality control
education of, 116-117

Magil, W.G., 282
Maintenance of product, in after-sales
service, quality assurance in, 75
Maintenance of quality
activities in, 130-131
in divisional activities, 257-258
management in, 11
quality analysis in, 157
quality control education on,
112
Management, 19-25, 27-44, 251
apathy of, concerning total
quality control, 145
in control circle, 11-12, 29-30
in control planning, 40-41
in cross-functional management.
See Cross-functional management
day-to-day, 288
policy management in, 97-98

defects caused by, 33, 124,
125
in determination of priority
quality problems, 30-33
in functional management, 288
increasing quality consciousness
of employees, 122-123
in inspections and audits, 30
in management by objective, 38
middle management in,
41-44, 145
quality control education of,
114-115
obstructive managerial types in,
27-28
in organizational planning, 33-35
in policy management, 30,
35-38, 97-106, 288
in practical administrative
management, 19-20, 28,
35-41, 262-263
recent trends concerning, 288
problems in, 29
product liability responsibilities
of, 91-92
promotional activities of,
28-29, 34
in quality assurance, 28
in quality management, 20-21
in non-manufacturing
divisions, 263
responsibilities for product
quality, 30-35
top, quality control education
of, 112-114
Management information systems,
computerized, quality control
of, 267-268
Manufacturers
liability for product, 84
quality costs of, 139
quality requirements of,
compared to consumer
quality requirements, 166-167

Manufacturing processes. *See*
  Production processes
Manufacturing section chief,
  control item chart for, 60
Map of company technology, in
  new product analysis, 179, 180
Market factors, in quality evaluation,
  184, 185
Market for new product
  assessment of, 179, 181
  complaint surveys in, 162
Market quality surveys, 161-162
  consumer survey in, 162
  purpose of, 161
Market value method, in estimation
  of expected product value, 190
Marketing division, 6-7
  quality assurance
    responsibilities of, 6-7, 77
Materials
  in chemical manufacturing,
    affecting product quality, 209
  purchasing of, quality control in,
    244-248
Maynard, Harold B., 281
Measurements
  in chemical manufacturing,
    affecting product quality,
    210-211
  of conformance to standards, 131
  of quality, 142
    in analysis of quality control,
      166-167
    consumer complaints in, 167
    inspections in, 166-167
  of use characteristics and
    substitute characteristics, 228
Middle management
  failure to recognize role in
    quality control, 145
  quality control education of,
    114-115
  quality control promotion by,
    41-44

Mobilization planning, in policy
  management, 100-102
Morinaga Company, product
  liability case against, 87
Motivation for implementation of
  quality control, 145-146

National Electronic Injury
  Surveillance System, 84
Negligence, product liability in,
  88-89
New markets
  assessment of, 179, 181
  complaint surveys in, 162
New products, development of.
  See Development of new
  products
Newsletters disseminating quality
  control information, 121
Nippon Kayaku chemicals company,
  total quality control in, 17
Non-manufacturing divisions,
  quality control in, 249-268

Obstructive managerial types,
  in total quality control, 27-28
Occasional defects, 32-33
Office work, 249-268
  in administrative and clerical
    divisions, 249
  applications of quality control
    in, 257-258
  automation of, 23
    and quality control, 265-266
  computer-aided quality control
    in, 266-267
  computerization of, 265-268
  cross-functional management of,
    264-265
  definition of, 251-252
  implementation of quality
    control in, 250
  information system in, 267-268
  introduction of quality control
    in, 250-251

judgment of quality in, 252
policy control in, 263-264
in product liability prevention,
    255-257
quality assurance in, 262
quality management in, 263
responsibilities in, 252-258
    for manufactured product
        quality, 253-257
    of staff divisions, 253, 254,
        258-261
    total quality control activities in,
        261-265
Operation detail, 217
Operation sheet, 217
Operation quality, 7
Operations, total quality control
    improving, 23
Operations research, in quality
    assurance, 19
Organization of quality control, 136
    chart on, 61
    diagram of, 137
    planning of, 33-35, 49, 50-54
        establishing standards and
            regulations in, 52
        issues in, 50-51
        principles of, 51-52
        promotion centre in, 53-54
        quality control committee in,
            52-53
    and responsibilities for product
        liability, 92-93
    in United States and Japan,
        comparison of, 136
Originality of quality product, 6
Outsourcing policies, 245-246

Pamphlets disseminating quality
    control information, 121
Paperwork
    in policy control system, 104
    in process control, 233-234
    on quality control standards
        and regulations, 61-63

Pareto, Vilfredo, 32
Pareto diagram, 31, 32, 155, 212
Past data, as basis of quality control
    analysis, 158, 159-160
PDCA circle, 9-12, 154
    action in, 9, 10, 12
    checking in, 258
    control and adjustments in,
        229, 230
    in day-to-day management,
        97, 98
    management responsibilities in,
        11-12, 29-30, 40-41
    planning in, 9, 10, 11-12
    in policy management, 102-103
    in quality assurance, 80
    steps in, for effective control, 10
Pearson, E.S., 281, 282
Personnel division
    applications of quality control
        in, 257
    cross-functional management of,
        264-265
    responsibilities for product
        quality, 253, 254
PERT (programme evaluation and
    review technique), 187-188,
    189, 198
Physical appeal of quality product,
    6, 184, 185
Planning point method, in estimation
    of expected product value,
    188-190
Planning quality control, 45-65
    compared to policy management,
        36, 37
    control planning in, 56-58
    coordination problems in, 63-64
    of criteria and standards, 61-64
    defining product quality in,
        45-46
    and employee mobilization,
        100-102
    on introduction of quality
        control, 47-50, 65

management responsibilities in,
11-12, 40-41
on new products, 182-187
factors considered in,
183-184, 185
organizational, 33-35, 49, 50-54
paperwork in, 61-63
and policy management, 36, 37,
102
promotion plan in, 53-54, 65
chart on, 65
quality analysis in, 46-47
and quality control audit, 275
quality control committee in,
52-53
quality planning in, 45-47
and quality policies, 46
Planning stage of control circle,
9, 10, 11-12
Plant and facilities division
applications of quality control
in, 257
responsibilities for product
quality, 254
Policies
budgeting for implementation of,
102
categories of, 35
check items on, 106
control items in, 56, 102
on control systems, 103-106
example of, 104, 105
planning of, 102-103
in day-to-day management, 97-98
deployment chart on, 104
on development of new products,
176-179, 184-186
dissemination of, 121-122
documentation of, 104
draft of, 104
on employee mobilization, 100-102
goal setting in, 98-99
implementation chart on, 104
lack of, problems in, 146

on liability for products,
90-91, 92-93
management responsibilities in,
30, 35-38, 97-106, 288
chart of, 104
compared to administrative
planning, 36, 37
of middle management, 41
in non-manufacturing divisions,
263-264
planning of, 102
on price of new product,
184, 186
priorities in, 36-37, 99-100
on purchasing and outsourcing,
245-246
on quality assurance, 73
on quality control audit,
establishment of, 272-274
on quality planning, 46
requirements of, 35-36
on standard quality, 184-186
Posters disseminating quality
control information, 122
Post-production quality control, 74
Practical administrative management,
19-20, 28, 35-41, 262-263
recent trends concerning, 288
Presidential total quality control
audit, 30
Preventive policies
on defective products, 67, 68
manufacturer's costs in, 139
on liability for products. See
Liability for products,
prevention of
Price of product. See Cost of product
Priority quality problems,
management responsibilities
in, 31-33
Problem solving approaches, 55, 260
Problems in quality control
analysis of, 153-169
in Japan, 288-290

management responsibilities in,
30-33
and solutions, 145-150
Procedures in quality control,
planning of, 58-61
Processes in production. *See*
Production processes
Processing of complaints, 75,
163-165
Product(s)
defective. *See* Defective products
design of. *See* Design of products
inspection of. *See* Inspection, of
products
liability for. *See* Liability for
products
new, development of. *See*
Development of new products
quality of
audit of, 269-270
characteristics in evaluation
of, 4-5, 6
in conformance, 8-9
consumer needs and attitudes
toward, 285-286
definition of, 4, 6
in design, 6, 7-8
of industrial products, 4-7
integrated control of, 1
operational, 7
policies on, problems in lack
of, 146
recent trends concerning,
285-286
responsibilities of non-
manufacturing divisions for,
249-268
significance of, 4-9
social changes affecting, 2-3
Product liability committee, 92
Product Liability Reform Bill of
1986, 86
Product responsibility, 84
Production processes, 205-243
analysis of, 205-217

cause-and-effect diagram in,
213-214, 215
in design and development
stages, 193-198
importance of, 205-208
of latent causes in chemical
manufacturing, 208-211
on optimum standards for
causes, 214-216
on principal causes, 211-213
procedure of, 216-217
on relationship of causes and
effects, 207, 208-215
statistical approach to,
207-208
capability studies on, 218-224
assessment standards in, 222
charts on, 218-220, 223
definition of, 220-221
distribution of quality
characteristics in, 221, 223
numerical values in, 221-222
procedure of, 223-224
process capability factors in,
222-223
process capability index in,
221-222
in chemical manufacturing,
208-211
control of, 229-239, 240- 241,242
adjustments in, 229-230
check points in, 230-231
control charts in, 233
control items in, 230-232,
234-235, 236
effectiveness of, evaluation
of, 237-239
implementation of, 235-237
irregularity reports in,
233-234
quality assurance in, 232
quality control process chart
in, 234
in special-care categories, 239
standards on, 232-235

target values in, 231
costs of quality in, 138-139
design of, 217-229
  decisions on manufacturing
    methods in, 224-229
  flow sheets on, 217
  inspection standards in,
    224, 225, 226
  process capability studies on,
    218-224
  standard quality and guaranteed
    quality in, 224-225
  technical standards and work
    standards in, 226-229
improvements in, 243-244
inspections in, 224, 225, 226
  interim, in quality assurance,
    240-241
liability for defects in, 88, 240,
  241-243
  in changes and alterations of
    process control, 241-242
major quality control activities
  in, 206
quality assurance in, 74, 239-243
  in liability prevention,
    240, 241,243
in quality evaluation, 184, 185
role of non-manufacturing
  divisions in, 253-257
simplicity of, and product
  quality, 5
special-care categories in, 240
specifications on, 217
Production routine, 217
Production schedule, in cross-
  functional management, 38, 39
Productivity, in total quality
  control, 22
Profile method, in estimation of
  expected product value, 188, 191
Profits
  in quality management, 20
  in total quality control, 21

Programme evaluation and review
  technique (PERT), 187-188,
  189, 198
Progress control and evaluation,
  in development and design
  stages, 187-192
Project approach to quality control,
  133, 265
Promotion centre
  functions of, 53-54
  problems in, 147-148
Promotion of quality control
  and cross-functional
    management, 108
  by middle management, 41-44
  planning of, chart on, 65
  priority items in, 50
  problems and solutions in,
    145-150
  promotion centre in, 53-54,
    147,148
  steps in, 148, 149
Prototypes, in design and development of new products
  construction of, 201-203
  review of, 200
Publicity division, product
  liability prevention
  responsibilities of, 256
Purchasing division, quality control
  in, 244-248, 259
  activities in, 245
  applications of, 257
  in contracts and quality assurance
    agreements, 247-248
  in evaluation of suppliers,
    246-247
  improvements in, 248
  and product liability prevention
    responsibilities, 255-256
  in purchasing and outsourcing
    policies, 245-246
  in quality control guidance of
    suppliers, 248

and responsibilities for product
quality, 254
in selection of suppliers, 246

Quality analysis, 153-169
categorized data in, 158
characteristic values in, 167-168
comparison of approaches in,
158-159
complaint surveys in, 162-165
consumer quality requirements
in, 166-167, 168
cost of, 158, 159
in design and development
stages, 193-198
and diagnosis of problems, 166
experimental approach to, 158
importance of, 157-161
in inspection of products. See
Inspection, of products
market quality surveys in,
161-162
measurements in, 142, 166-167
methods of, 153-157
in office work, 252
past data in, 158, 159-160
in planning stage, 46-47
procedures in, 155-157
in quality assurance, 81
quality table in, 196
by quality troubleshooting
team, 168-169
regulations on, 168
standards in, 71
in technological problems,
160-161
tools in, 154-155
use of results, 160
Quality assurance, 6, 17, 19, 67-82
activities in, 71-72, 94, 95-96,
132
chart on, 79
administration of, 73
in alterations of production
processes, 241-242

audit of, 270
committee on, 80
cross-functional management in,
76-77, 80
definitions of, 68-70
diagram of, 77, 78, 80, 82
evaluation system in, 81
feedback on, 80
foolproofing systems in, 242-243
important functions in, 72-76
information system in, 81-82
inspection procedures in, 67-68,
70, 240-241
and liability for defective
products, 71, 72, 94-96, 240,
241-243
management in, 28
in manufacturing process, 238-243
in non-manufacturing divisions,
262
in process control standards, 232
in purchasing division, 247-248
quality transmission routes in,
238, 239-240
recent trends concerning,
286-287
in repair of defective products, 71
in sales division, 55-56, 57
significance of, 67-72
in special care processes, 239
standards in, 71, 73
supervision of, 75-76
system of, 61, 76-81
Quality Assurance Guidebook, 69
Quality consciousness of employees,
techniques increasing, 121-128
Quality control
definitions of, 13, 14-15
history of, 281-284
importance of, 13
recent trends in, 284-288
Quality control audit, 269-280
Quality control circles, 123-128,
148-149, 261-262
conduction of, 125-128

formation of, 125-128
in non-manufacturing divisions,
  250-251
problems in, 147
purpose of, 123-125
in technology development, 198
Quality control committee, 52-53
Quality control education. *See*
  Education on quality control
Quality control flow sheet, 58
Quality control process chart, 234
Quality control staff
  organization of, 136, 137
  quality control education of,
    115-116, 118
Quality control system, 58,
  130-137, 265
Quality deployment. *See*
  Deployment of quality
Quality engineering, 134-137
  diagram of, 135
  responsibilities in, 136-137
Quality evaluation system, in
  quality assurance, 81
Quality functions, 67-68
Quality information system, in
  quality assurance, 81-82
Quality management, 20-21
  in non-manufacturing divisions,
    263
Quality planning, 45-47
Quality policies. *See* Policies
Quality standards
  compared to control standards,
    131
  handbook on, 130
Quality tables, 193, 196
  examples of, 194, 195
  quality wanted in, 193, 196
  substitute characteristics in,
    193, 196, 197

Random-sample testing of product
  quality, 142-143

Reading material, in quality control
  education, 113-114
Recall of defective products, 75
Recent trends in quality control,
  284-288
Reform of standards in quality
  control, 11
Regulations
  on data collection for quality
    design, 187
  in policy control system, 104
  on quality analysis and
    diagnosis, 168
  on quality control
    coordination of, 63-64
    on defective products found
      in inspections, 226
    documentation of, 61-64
    planning of, 61-64
Reliability engineering, 24, 145
  in quality assurance, 94-95
Reliability of product, statistical
  analysis of, 144-145
Repairs
  in after-sales service of product,
    quality assurance in, 75
  of defective products, 71
Reports
  on irregulations, in process
    control, 233-234
  on quality control audit, 276-277
  in quality control education, 113
Research and development division
  applications of quality control
    in, 257
  in development of new products.
    See Development of new
    products
  product liability prevention
    responsibilities of, 255
  quality control education in,
    117-118
  responsibilities for product
    quality, 253, 254

Resources of corporation, inventory
of, 179, 183
technology map of, 179, 180
Responsibilities
for product liability, 84-87
for product quality, of
management, 30-35
Review of new product design,
198-200
Ritualized quality control activities,
problems in, 147

Safety of products, 2, 3, 5
design review on, 198, 200
evaluation of, in development
and design stage, 198, 200,
203-204
legislation concerning, 84
liability for, and cost of products,
86
Sales
market quality surveys on,
161-162
total quality control increasing,
21-22
Sales division
applications of quality control
in, 257
control standards in, 261
product liability prevention
responsibilities of, 256
quality assurance duties of, 55-57
responsibilities for product
quality, 253, 255
Sarasohn, H.M., 282
Scatter diagrams, in quality control
analysis, 155
Section chief
of manufacturing, control item
chart for, 60
in promotion of quality control,
41-44
Seminars disseminating quality
control information, 122
Service divisions

product liability prevention
responsibilities of, 256
responsibilities for product
quality, 254
Service of product, after-sales,
quality assurance in, 75
Shewhart, Walter A., 281
Shin-Estu Chemical, company-wide
quality control in, 17
Simplicity of manufacture, and
product quality, 5
Slogans disseminating quality
control information, 121
Social changes, and product
quality, 2-3
Social costs of product, 141
Source management, in total
quality control, 22
Special-care processes, quality
assurance in, 239
Specialists in quality control, 34
Staff
of quality control division
organization of, 136, 137
quality control education of,
115-116, 118
of research and development
division, quality control
education of, 117-118
of total quality control
promotion centre, 34
Staff divisions. See Division
activities in quality control
Standards
control standards, 131
compared to quality
standards, 131
in staff processes, 261
inspection standards, 71, 224,
225-226
and guaranteed quality, 224
in process design, 224, 225
226
optimum standards for causes,
decisions on, 214-216

process control standards, 232-235
  preparation of manual on,
    232-234
in quality assurance, 71, 73
on quality control
  coordination of, 63-64
  documentation of, 61-64
  planning of, 61-64
and standard quality, 8
  control standards compared
    to, 131
  decisions on, 130, 184-186
  guaranteed quality compared
    to, 224
  handbook on, 130
  in process design, 224-225
technical standards, in process
  design, 226-229
work standards, 216-217
  establishment of, 130
  handbook on, 130, 217, 227
  non-conformance to, 131
  in process design, 226-229
working to, 130-131
Statistical analysis, 18, 55, 111,
  142-145
applications of, 143-144
on dispersion of quality
  characteristics, 143, 144
in process analysis, 207, 208
of quality control problems, 154
on reliability of product, 144-145
role in total quality control, 18
in technology development, 195
Storage division
  applications of quality control
    in, 257
  product liability prevention
    responsibilities of, 256
  responsibilities for product
    quality, 254
Stratification of data, in quality
  control analysis, 155
Study groups, in quality control
  education, 113

Substitute characteristics, in quality
  deployment, 193, 196, 197
Supervision of quality assurance
  system, 75-76
Suppliers of materials, 244-248
  contracts and quality assurance
    agreements with, 247-248
  evaluation of, 246-247
  purchasing and outsourcing
    policies concerning, 245-246
  quality control guidance
    provided for, 248
  selection of, 246
Surveys
  on consumer complaints, 162-165
  market quality, 161-162
System of quality control, 58,
  130-137, 265
  activities in, 133
  Feigenbaum on, 134
  in project approach, 133
  in quality assurance, 61
  and quality engineering, 134-137
  standards in, 130-131

Tables on quality. See Quality tables
Taguchi, Genichi, 230
Target quality of product, 8
Target values in process control, 231
Taylor, Frederick W., 281
Team approach to quality control
  analysis, 168-169
Technical standards in process
  design, 226-229
Technological problems, quality
  control analysis of, 160-161
Technological qualities of products,
  6
Technology development, 22-23,
  193-198
  inspiration and quality control
    circle in, 198
  for new product, assessment of,
    179, 180, 181
  quality deployment in, 193

statistical approach in, 195
Technology map of company,
in new product analysis, 179, 180
Temporal factors, in quality
evaluation, 184, 185
Terminology in total quality control,
problems related to, 148-150
Tools
in manufacturing, process anlaysis
and capability studies of,
227, 228
in quality control, 154-155
Tort laws, liability in, 89-90
Total quality control, 15-18
areas included in, 2
as common goal for common
good, 18, 20
definitions of, 1-2, 16
participation of every division
and worker in, 17, 18
Training
on quality control. *See*
Education on quality control
on work procedures, 210,
228-229
Training Within Industries, 116
Transmission of quality, routes of,
238, 239-240
Transportation division
applications of quality control
in, 257
product liability prevention
responsibilities of, 256
responsibilities for product
quality, 254
Troubleshooting team in quality
control analysis, 168-169

Uniform Product Liability Law, 86
Union of Japanese Scientists and
Engineers, 118, 282, 283
United States
career mobility in, 264
consumer protection legislation
in, 84

history of quality control in, 1,
282
organization of quality control
in, 17, 136
product liability in, 85-86, 204
responsibilities for quality
control in, 34
Upstream control, in total quality
control, 22
User's costs, 139-141

Value of product
actual, 190-191
expected, estimation of,
188-190, 191
Vertical activities in quality
control, 38

Warning labels, liability for, 88-89
Warranty, liability for, 89
Work environment, affecting
product quality, 210
Work standards, 216-217
establishment of, 130
handbook on, 130, 217, 227
nonconformance to, 131
in process design, 226-229
Worker-caused defects, 33, 43,
124-125
liability for, 88
Worker training
on quality control. *See*
Education on quality control
on work procedures, 228-229
in chemical manufacturing,
210
Working to standards, 130-131
Workmanship defects, liability for,
88

Zero defects movement, 124